Praise for GUT!

Without a doubt, intuition is a decision-making tool that people should be using as much as they can. It has been part of my success, and the success of SHOP.CA. By following the advice in Sunil's book, you will be better able to use your own intuition in every situation, ensuring that you are as successful as possible in whatever you venture to do.

— Drew Green — Founder, CEO and Chairman of SHOP.CA

Intuition is an essential fuel for the success of business leaders and corporations. Sunil's book on intuition provides great insight as to the utility of intuition in business.

— Vinay Sharma, CEO, London Hydro

Sunil's book is an important addition to discussion about leadership and decision making. If decisions were only about the data then we would not need leaders.

— Kevin Higgins, Vice-President, Industrial Business Group — 3M Canada

It's taken me a lot of years, but I have learned not only to trust my intuition... but to recognize when it's speaking to me. Sunil's book GUT! will show you how it can speak to you.

— Ted Rubin — Social Marketing Strategist, Keynote Speaker, most followed CMO on Twitter, 2013 Forbes Top 50 Social Media Power Influencers

GUT!

What it is.

How to **TRUST** it.

How to use it.

Sunil Godse
Radical Solutions Group Inc.
www.gutincorporated.com

Copyright © 2014 by Radical Solutions Group Inc.

All rights reserved

Published by Radical Solutions Group Inc.

First Edition

No part of this book may be used or reproduced in any manner whatsoever without the prior written permission of the publisher or author, except in the case of brief quotations embodied in reviews.

This book contains trademarks belonging to the businesses being discussed. Those trademarks are included to identify those businesses and their brands, and not as trademarks of the author.

Every effort has been made to contact rights holders of copyrighted material. In the case of an inadvertent error or omission, please contact the publisher.

This book may be purchased for educational, business, or sales promotional use. Please contact the publisher or author for more information.

www.gutincorporated.com

ISBN 978-0-9920815-3-9
ISBN ePDF 978-0-9920815-4-6
ISBN ePUB 978-0-9920815-5-3

Cover design: adHOME Creative
Text design and typesetting: Daniel Crack, Kinetics Design, kdbooks.ca
Printed and bound in Canada

Always trust your intuition.

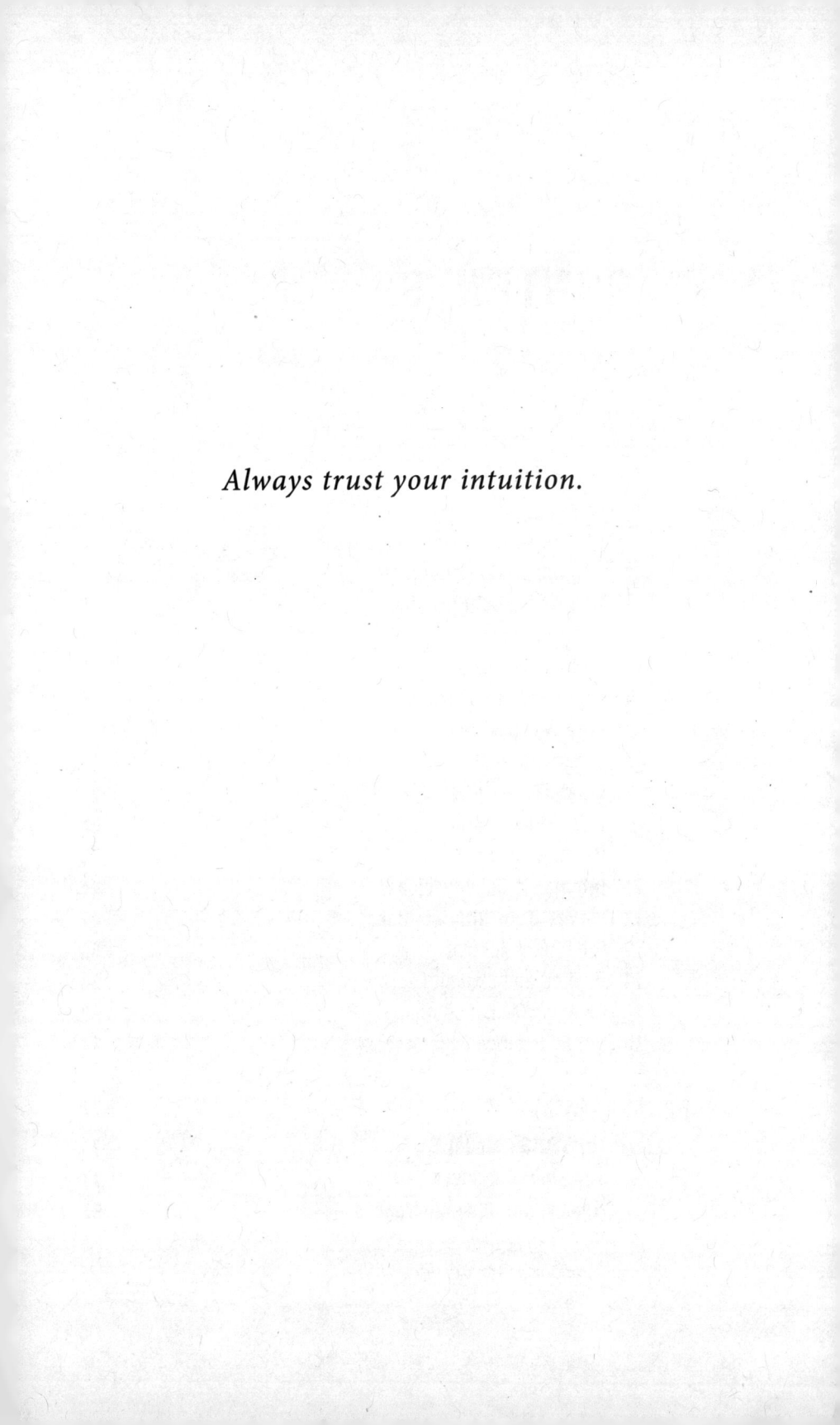

CONTENTS

Acknowledgements ix

PART 1 **WHAT IT IS** 1
   1 How Important is Intuition? 3
   2 Why Write About Intuition? 6
   3 The Interviewees 7
   4 Intuition Defined 8
   5 The Intuition Quadrant 9
   6 Creative Intuition 12
   7 Experiential Intuition 17
   8 Relational Intuition 22
   9 Situational Intuition 34
  10 Multiple Quadrants 39
  11 Intuition is Subconscious 44
  12 We Are Born With Intuition 47
  13 Intuition is Instant 50
  14 Implicit and Explicit Learning 54
  15 Common Misconceptions 62
  16 Not All Positive Experiences 64

PART 2 **HOW TO TRUST IT** 71
   1 The **TRUST** Model 73
   2 **T**une Into Ourselves 77
   3 **R**emove Intuitive Hindrances 83
      3.1 *Fearing Failure* 85
      3.2 *Being Overly Emotional* 91

		3.3 Having a Big Ego	97
		3.4 Being Overly Rational	100
	4	**U**nderstand Our Intuitive Drivers	103
		4.1 Values	103
		4.2 Purpose	106
		4.3 Personal Vision	113
	5	**S**ense the Internal Indicators	118
	6	**T**ake Notice of External Indicators	123
	7	Moving Beyond the **TRUST** Model	126

PART 3	**HOW TO USE IT**	127
1	Finding Our Intuitive Medium	129
2	Alignment of Intuitive Drivers	135
3	Shifting Intuition Quadrants	142
4	Revisiting the **TRUST** Model	149

PART 4	**GUT! INCORPORATED**	151
1	Does Corporate Intuition Exist?	153
2	What is Corporate Intuition?	155
3	The Corporate Intuition Quadrant	156
4	Corporate Strategic Intuition	158
5	Corporate Operational Intuition	163
6	Corporate Relational Intuition	167
7	Corporate Situational Intuition	173
8	Multiple Quadrants	178
9	Shifting Corporate Intuition Quadrants	183
10	The Corporate **TRUST** Model	191
11	**T**op Down Intuition	192
12	**R**emove Corporate Hindrances	198
	12.1 Fearing Failure	198
	12.2 Corporate Ego	203
	12.3 Being Overly Emotional	211
	12.4 Data-Heavy Decision-Making	216
13	**U**nderstand Core Intuitive Values	225
14	**S**elect Appropriate Resources	231
15	**T**ransform the Culture	237
16	Maximizing GUT! Incorporated	245

Acknowledgements

The success in completing this book came down to two things – belief and commitment.

Without the belief that this was an essential topic to inform others and make the time commitment from my interviewees, this book could not have been written.

Without the belief that writing this book was a result of my own personal intuition and the commitment to giving me the time and space to write the book from my beautiful wife and lovely daughters, this book could not have been written.

Without the belief in my ability to transform an intangible and very personal characteristic in a tangible way and a commitment to bring these incredible stories of intuition to you, despite the various sacrifices I made to my family and friends, this book could not have been written.

I thank all of those who believed in me and made me a commitment.

I thank you for believing in me by buying this book, and after reading it, making a commitment to yourself that you will follow your intuition all the time.

Trust your GUT!

SUNIL GODSE

GUT!

PART 1

What It Is

I research new ideas very thoroughly, asking a lot of people about their experiences and their thoughts. But on many occasions I have followed my intuition; you can't make decisions based on numbers and reports alone. It's important to have the courage to follow through on a project if you truly believe it's worth pursuing. We all have an intuitive sense of what's best – follow it! This approach has never let me down.

– Richard Branson

CHAPTER 1

How Important is Intuition?

We all have intuition.

Intuition has consistently been credited with helping people realize success in either their personal or professional lives, or both, playing a major role in life-changing circumstances. Those who experienced intuition "just knew" that the decision, feeling or action being taken was the right one to make.

For those who have made major contributions to our world, intuition has been a key element in their ability to make things happen. Consider the following quotes from those we may recognize:

- ✔ *"The intuitive mind is a sacred gift and the rational mind is a faithful servant. We have created a society that honors the servant and has forgotten the gift."* – **Albert Einstein**

- ✔ *"[H]ave the courage to follow your heart and intuition... Everything else is secondary."* – **Steve Jobs**

- ✔ *"Learn to let your intuition – gut instinct – tell you when the food, the relationship, the job isn't good for you (and conversely, when what you're doing is just right)."* – **Oprah Winfrey**

- ✔ Quincy Jones answers an interview question asked by Jian Ghomeshi of CBC Radio: *"I've got to ask you about Michael Jackson... You produced Thriller.... which of course became the biggest record in history. What was that alchemy about you, Michael – what created that magic? Intuitiveness."* – **Quincy Jones**

✔ *"You have to leave the city of your comfort and go into the wilderness of your intuition. What you'll discover will be wonderful. What you'll discover is yourself."* – **Alan Alda**

Although we can look to successful people to talk about intuition, we can listen to our own stories because we all have it. Some are able to access intuition better than others. If we are able to tap into intuition on an ongoing basis, then we should be able to take advantage of the many opportunities that lie in front of us. Consider the following snippets of experiences of how intuition played a role for a few of the interviewees:

✔ Intuition helped Duart Townsend, Defence Program Coordinator for the Royal Canadian Armed Forces, make a decision to delay a vehicle under his command for 15 minutes. Despite pleas from his colleagues, Duart did not relent. That 15 minute time frame saved his troops from being involved in a perilous situation in Afghanistan.

✔ With her son *"laying in the hospital with the side of his stomach open and his intestines out,"* Kelly-Sue McDiarmid's son's life would be fraught with developmental disabilities. Yet, Kelly-Sue's instant intuition had her throw away both a six-figure salary and a marriage to take care of him and another special needs child who arrived sometime later..

✔ Mario Francella had a 10% chance of living. After his family spent a tremendous amount of money for his care, his guilt over being a financial burden to his family took him to the streets of Toronto, where he was homeless. His intuition consolidated a number of experiences which, combined with his incredible work ethic, helped him escape homelessness to become one of the youngest chefs to consistently win culinary awards, and propelled him into several successful career paths.

While intuition generally contributes to our betterment, ignoring intuition often leads to problematic situations. Consider the experiences from the following interviewees:

- Bruce Croxon, Co-Founder of Round13 Capital and former Co-Founder of Lavalife, ignored his intuition when bringing on a resource. Going against the values that he upheld, this decision cost his company an extra two years of production time and $22 million over budget.

- Howard Payne ignored his intuition when faced with an employer who asked him to ignore his personal values and forsake income and other opportunities to feed his greed. Not only did Howard lose thousands of dollars in income opportunities, but it cost him six months of unemployment due to the emotional turbulence he suffered.

- Twee and Rob Brown, serial entrepreneurs, found a perfect partner to help them operate a business they were looking to start. After this partner's lack of business acumen and inflated ego began to show, Twee second-guessed her intuition to save the friendship, hoping for the best, but knowing otherwise. A few months later, with time and money wasted, the business relationship dissolved, as well as the friendship.

The importance of intuition cannot be understated. Success followed those who trusted their intuition, and those who did not trust their intuition will not make the same mistake again.

Whether doing formal interviews or casually talking about intuition on a social level, each and every person I have had the pleasure of talking to on this topic has shared a story on how important a role intuition played in their lives.

So, why write a book on intuition?

The answer lies in writing my first book, *Fail Fast. Succeed Faster.*

CHAPTER 2

Why Write About Intuition?

Fail Fast. Succeed Faster. was written to showcase stories of failure from executives and entrepreneurs who led companies in a number of industries and of varying sizes. The theme of the book is quite simple – by learning from the stories of failure in the book, others would be much better prepared for their own business hurdles, saving them time, money, and valuable resources.

A common thread among these interviewees was that they ignored their intuition, leading to a significant business challenge or failure.

This prompted me to investigate intuition further to find out what intuition is, how it can be trusted, and how people use it in a personal, professional, and corporate context. It was at this point that GUT! was born.

It is hoped that after reading this book, we are able to tap into intuition more effectively to help enhance our personal, professional, and corporate lives. Doing so will allow us to take advantage of the many opportunities that otherwise might not seem available.

CHAPTER 3

The Interviewees

Although the interviewees in *Fail Fast. Succeed Faster.* were entrepreneurs and business executives, for this book it was important to reach out to others from all different walks of life as intuition plays a role in every aspect of our lives. This led me to cast a wider net when choosing interviewees, including a military pilot, a former homeless person, a surgeon, an accountant, a single mother with special needs children, and others. All in all, I had the fortunate opportunity to interview over 100 people on their intuitive experiences.

Of the over 100 interviewees, the intuitive experiences of a select number of them are used in this book. An interviewee's story will appear in a particular book chapter because the related intuitive experience was an excellent representation of that particular chapter's topic.

Although one person's story may be used to illustrate a specific chapter, the intuitive story that is told may contain details that also represent topics in other chapters. In fact, many of the interviewees' stories had characteristics of intuition, as defined in this book, which spanned multiple chapters.

In addition to the individuals formally interviewed for this book, there are an increasing number of individuals who shared their intuitive stories with me after learning about this book.

Every single person I have talked to about intuition has shared an intuitive experience. It is clear that these experiences played a significant role in their lives.

So, what is intuition?

CHAPTER 4

Intuition Defined

We know that intuition is intangible. We cannot readily identify it using a combination of our senses, as we can with a box, a fire, or an animal sound. Yet, for those who have had intuitive experiences, there is "something" that happens to them, with each "something" being unique to each individual.

We also know that intuition is complex in how it functions, and how it is used is unique to each individual. The way our intuition works is unique to each of us; the combination of our environment, experiences, and choices made will never be the same as for others.

Given the intuitive stories shared by the interviewees, personal experiences, and increasing academic research on intuition, we can formulate a definition of intuition that encompasses the collection of experiences, thoughts, decisions, and actions from those who have shared their stories of intuition.

Intuition can be categorized into one of four types: creative, experiential, relational, or situational (Chapters 5 to 10). Intuition itself is subconscious (Chapter 11), exists at birth (Chapter 12), is instant in nature (Chapter 13), and is informed by both implicit and explicit learning (Chapter 14), where ongoing experiences help inform intuition. There will always be misconceptions (Chapter 15) and not all intuitive experiences will be positive (Chapter 16).

The next few chapters will expand on these characteristics.

CHAPTER 5

The Intuition Quadrant

Our intuition can be characterized by four main types: creative, experiential, relational, or situational. The relative strengths for each intuition type and how it changes over time will be specific to the ongoing decisions and actions we make.

Where our current intuitive strengths lie based on these types can be visually represented by an Intuition Quadrant (Figure 1).

Creative Relational	Experiential Relational
Creative Situational	Experiential Situational

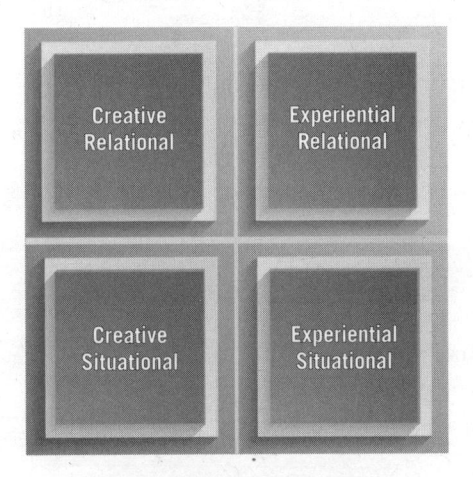

Figure 1 Intuition Quadrant

Based on a series of questions[1], we will be able to identify in which type of intuition we are stronger relative to the other types. The stronger we are in one particular intuition type, the higher up we traverse its related axis. Based on these strengths, we can then create a map of

---
1 www.gutincorporated.com/INzone

GUT! 9

our "Intuitive Zone of Influence", which stretches across the intuition quadrants.

For example, Figure 2 shows an individual who has an Intuitive Zone of Influence showing strength in both creative and relational intuition, whereas Figure 3 shows an individual who has an Intuitive Zone of Influence showing strength in experiential intuition.

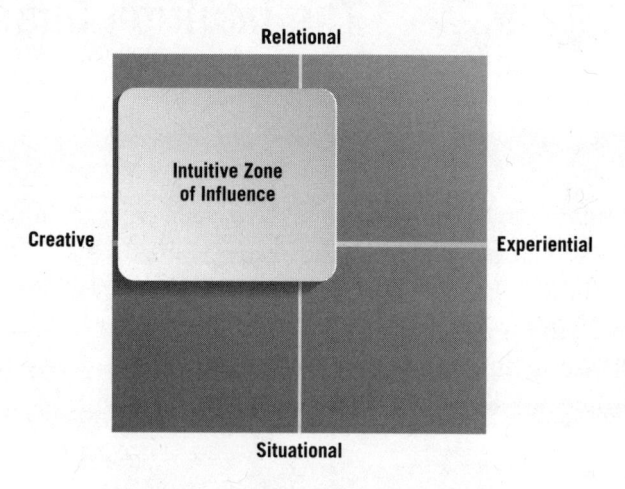

Figure 2 Intuitive Zone of Influence: Strong in Creative and Relational Intuition

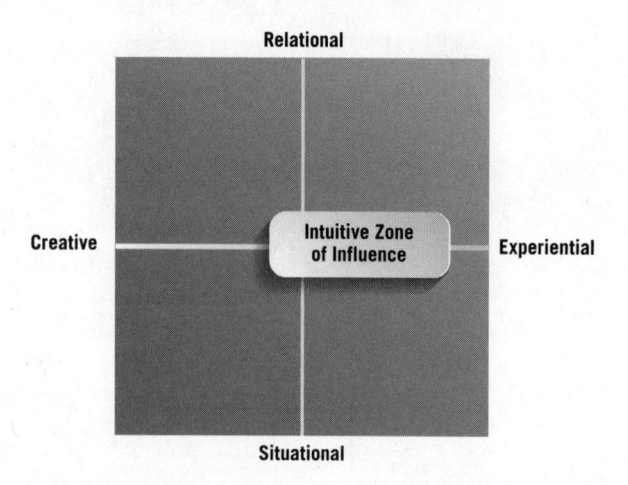

Figure 3 Intuitive Zone of Influence: Strong in Experiential Intuition

Another series of questions takes into account where we see ourselves in the future both personally and professionally, allowing a Desired Intuitive Zone of Influence to be mapped.

Identifying gaps between our Current and Desired Intuitive Zones of Influence gives us an indication of the intuitive areas we may need to gain strength in to sharpen our intuitive abilities as we progress. An example of this will be shown in Chapter 3 of Part 3, where an individual discovers that he or she needs to shift intuitive strengths.

The first quadrant, creative intuition, drives people to make decisions that may not make sense to others. Against the wisdom and advice of others, Terry Fallis acted on his creative intuition to self-publish his first Canadian book, *The Best Laid Plans*. This book became a bestseller and won a string of prestigious awards, transforming Terry's career.

CHAPTER 6

Creative Intuition

Creative intuition defies logic or conventional wisdom. Oftentimes there is little to no data or information that supports the intuition. Although seemingly risky in nature, creative intuition does not produce decisions that are irrational and subject to random thoughts. These decisions rely less on rational thought; instead, our experiences are crucial in informing the intuition.

Research shows that the areas in the brain responsible for intuition and rational thought are distinct from each other. In a functional Magnetic Resonance Image (fMRI) study conducted in 2004[2], researchers identified an area of the brain, labelled the X-System, that is thought to be responsible for intuition-based self-knowledge, or intuitive thoughts, and another area, labelled the C-System, where evidence-based self-knowledge, or rational thought, is processed (Figure 4).

This research study suggests that intuitive-based thinking has a neural pathway that is different than rational thought and relies on experiences. The study also shows that when using intuition, the majority of brain activity occurs in the X-System with some minor activity in the C-System, suggesting that rational thought and experiences do inform our intuitive thinking to some degree.

Those who make decisions based on creative intuition are often told that they make no sense and should not be carried out. Despite these differing opinions, intuition tells them that these decisions are the right ones to make and the related results prove others wrong, much like

---
2 Lieberman, Jarcho, and Satpute (2004) Evidence-Based and Intuition-Based Self-Knowledge: An fMRI Study. Journal of Personality and Social Psychology, 2004, Vol. 87, No. 4, 421–43 http://terryfallis.com/the-best-laid-plans

C-System Regions

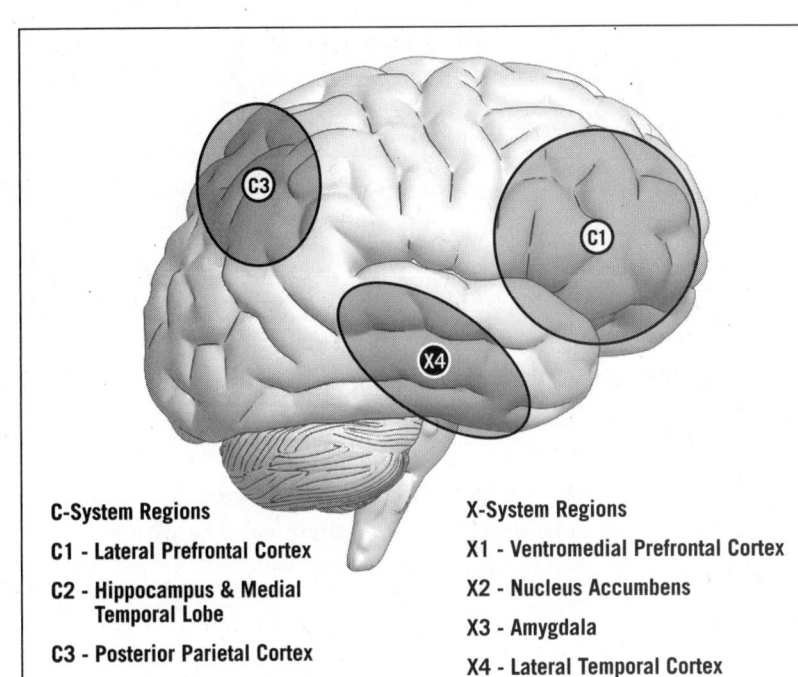

C1 - Lateral Prefrontal Cortex

C2 - Hippocampus & Medial Temporal Lobe

C3 - Posterior Parietal Cortex

X-System Regions

X1 - Ventromedial Prefrontal Cortex

X2 - Nucleus Accumbens

X3 - Amygdala

X4 - Lateral Temporal Cortex

Figure 4 Areas of Brain Activity Responsible for the X-System (Intuition Based Self-Knowledge) and the C-System (Evidence Based Self-Knowledge)

GUT! 13

the experience Terry Fallis had when self-publishing his first book, *The Best Laid Plans*[3].

GUT!

Terry Fallis is the author of four national bestsellers. His debut novel, *The Best Laid Plans*, won the 2008 Stephen Leacock Medal for Humour and was crowned the 2011 winner of CBC Canada Reads as the "essential Canadian novel of the decade." In January 2014, CBC aired a six-part television miniseries based on *The Best Laid Plans*, earning many positive reviews. It is also in development as a stage musical by Touchstone Theatre in Vancouver.

Terry wanted to write a satirical novel that used his experiences in politics as an outline for the content. However, the prevailing wisdom of the day told him that he should abandon this project quickly.

"I did a bit of research and looked around and a clear-headed logical analysis of the marketplace should have told me that my topic was all wrong. I mean, if you want to be published, why would you write a satirical novel about Canadian politics?

"I mean, everything, every indicator that you could imagine would suggest that this is not the thing to do. If you really want to get published, why not leap onto the latest bandwagon, which at that time would have been vampires, I think.

"And, if you're really going to take a thoughtful, logical approach to this with the aim of being published, you would have written a novel about vampires."

But Terry's intuition was telling him to ignore the logic and keep writing the political satire.

Once he finished the manuscript, he spent the next several months sending out plot synopsis, sample chapters, and query letters to agents and publishers to see if anyone was interested in his political satire.

"I diligently followed up and I didn't get a single rejection letter. I mean, what an impact I had on the traditional publishing world! I couldn't even make enough headway to get an automated rejection letter from any of them!"

---

3 http://terryfallis.com/the-best-laid-plans

One fine day, he received an email from a "potential" agent, with hopes held high.

"She emailed and said, 'You know, thanks for sending me this stuff. I've read it and it's pretty good and it's funny, but you've written a satirical novel of Canadian politics. What were you thinking??? I can't sell this in Canada let alone anywhere else, so all the best to you and thanks.' It was the one response I got after a year of trying."

Intuition hit Terry again as he began to release each chapter of *The Best Laid Plans* as a podcast, despite the prevailing wisdom of agents or publishing houses. As each chapter was completed, Terry noticed that he was getting positive comments from people all over the world and his listenership began to climb.

Terry had taken notice of a competition called the Stephen Leacock Medal for Humour, and his intuition led him to submit his book, not having any aspirations of winning. The submission requirement of 10 books cleaned out Terry's inventory.

He packaged up the books with the right postage and left the box on the reception desk in his office for the letter-carrier to pick up. After a short while, Terry began to doubt his intuition, but when he went to retrieve the box he discovered the letter-carrier had taken it five minutes earlier.

He was too late.

Having no real hope of winning, Terry followed up ritualistically on the Leacock Medal website to see how the rest of the submissions were doing. He recognized some famous authors whose books Terry had enjoyed reading. Seeing these names also gave Terry much more confidence that he was NOT going to win.

He was shocked when he discovered some months later that *The Best Laid Plans* had been shortlisted for the Leacock Medal. So, Terry and his wife drove to Orillia, Ontario, Canada, for the official announcement and then it happened ... he had won.

Terry was absolutely speechless. His wife kicked him under the table to let him know that he needed to make a speech and Terry ventured to the stage and took out a small square of paper with some "thank-yous" he never expected to read.

Terry's life as an author had just taken a severe turn. And it was all due to intuition.

"Without that podcast, I don't know whether I would have self-published and without self-publishing, I wouldn't have won the Leacock Medal. I wouldn't have signed with an agent. I wouldn't have signed with McClelland and Stewart. I wouldn't have won Canada Reads, wouldn't have had the TV series, wouldn't have the stage musical in development in Vancouver. Well, I mean, all of these things have happened miraculously as far as I'm concerned, I think because I decided to honour my intuition and write a satirical novel on Canadian politics."

GUT!

Since that time, Terry has written three other best-selling books and had started on his fifth book at the time of publishing this book.

Terry Fallis clearly used creative intuition to drive decisions that got him to write the book in the first place, have free podcasts available for everyone to access, and submit *The Best Laid Plans* for the Stephen Leacock Medal for Humour competition.

For Mario Francella, experiential intuition was a primary driver in overcoming homelessness and "being somebody".

CHAPTER 7

Experiential Intuition

Experiential intuition is primarily informed by ongoing personal and professional experiences. These types of intuitive decisions rely more on some element of logic and tend to be more rational in nature compared with creative intuition.

Although reliant primarily on experience, these intuitive decisions usually have an element of creative intuition, depending upon an individual's strength on the creative intuition axis, such as those made by Mario Francella.

GUT!

Mario Francella is the creator of THE DISCOVERY PROJECT, where he helps entrepreneurs with their self-discovery. Now successful in a number of business endeavours, Mario credits three specific experiences that informed his intuition and were instrumental in him overcoming being homeless.

Mario's parents came from Italy to Stouffville, Ontario, a very small town in Canada. With only $20 in his pocket, his father picked up a shovel, went door-to-door and helped people with their lawns or whatever landscaping needs they might have, seven days a week. He still owns the business, which has significantly grown since he started it 60 years ago.

The first experience that became instrumental in forming Mario's intuition was when the family used to get together every Sunday for a meal.

"Those Sunday surroundings with my brothers and my parents was my only childhood memory. I wanted to create that not just for my own family but I could create that for other families. The family came together surrounding food."

The next experience taught him the basics of making money.

"At 9 years old, it was the first and last time I asked my Dad for money. My friends were going on a camping trip and I asked him for $20. Back then, this was a lot of money. He flat out said no. I was kind of shocked and asked why. 'I never ask for anything. I work hard, I help Mom, I never disobey you guys. What if I go take out the garbage or cut the grass, or help Mom with laundry?' He said, 'Absolutely not. I am not going to teach you to be an employee.'"

Mario's father told him that he was going to give him $100. While Mario was relishing how great a negotiator he was, he went to grab the $100 bill and his father refused to let it go before giving him further instructions.

"We lived in a small town, Stouffville, very small population, all country, one corner store and the rest was strictly farmland and parks. In the dead of summer, my father told me to 'take the $100 and go to the corner store and buy every freezie or popular drink or anything that you and your friends enjoy.'"

Mario went to the store and after paying $97, emptied the store of its water, drinks, ice cream and freezies, most of which cost $0.10. His father instructed Mario to get the cooler, pack all of the treats in ice, take it out to the park and sell every item for $0.50 or $1.00.

Mario questioned why, but his father asked him to trust him.

Mario went to the park and began selling his wares.

"Now, I am marking it up $0.50 more than it costs, but people aren't going to get in their car and drive 10 minutes to the store. Pay an extra $0.50 and you have water. I ended up selling everything out and made about $250.00."

Mario returned home and excitedly went to tell his father.

"My father asked for his $100 back and told me never to ask him for money again. My father said 'I just taught you about supply and demand and you never have to worry about money again if you follow that structure.'"

Mario fell in love with business from that moment. He realized that being successful was about creating a product that people would need. It was also about being different and doing something with your life rather than sitting around and wasting it.

Two weeks after that incident, Mario's kidneys began to fail, and he found himself in excruciating pain and had extreme difficulty breathing. After emergency surgery, he overheard his mother and sister saying that the surgery did not go well. He had a 10 percent chance of living and spent the next few years in a terminal area of the hospital.

To support Mario's increasing medical bills, the family had to undergo tremendous financial strain, which left Mario feeling guilty. Mario moved out of his home, telling his mother he was visiting friends, and began living on the streets of Toronto because he wanted to do something with his life and not be a burden on his family.

He got interested in the squeegee business and noticed that people were not making much money, and what little money they made was often going towards alcohol or drugs, with some exceptions. From the business lessons Mario's father taught him, he knew that if he wanted to succeed in this business, he had to be different.

Mario would stand at the corner of Spadina Avenue and Lakeshore Boulevard in downtown Toronto, held up a sign he made that said "I'm not homeless. I am an entrepreneur. This is my squeegee business", wore a unique-looking tie, and began treating people stopped at red lights as customers.

"People would sometimes say 'No' and I would say, 'No problem. It looks like we can reschedule a time, here are my hours. As you can see the light has turned green and I have a line-up of customers behind you.'"

Hearing "no" did not deter Mario and he continued entertaining people.

"Some people would actually pull over and say, 'Good for you.' And some others asked if I was really homeless. I would say, 'No, I'm not homeless. I'm just home less.' They would give me $10 or $20 and I would be so thankful as I would have food for the next three days.

"I would look at my wrist to look at a watch that I did not have at the time and would tell a customer, 'I appreciate you being on time, can I *service the front window or the back?' I would tell them that I use "Pure 100% Lakeshore Water" and act like a salesman in a fun way. It would make people laugh. I would be seeing regulars. People would be finishing work, wave and would have a continuous amount of money for me. It was like I was able to build a clientele base."*

Mario realized that he could make people smile and enjoy the moment while making money at the same time by providing something of value, not just by walking up to a car looking depressed and asking for money.

The third experience Mario credits happened when he was staring at a black and white television set one evening at a friend's house.

"There was this cooking show with Julia Child, who came from nothing and started cooking for families and helping people. I was mesmerized. People were happy. I wanted to do that as I saw what she was doing."

Mario was enamoured with Julia Child giving people joy and coming together as a family. This is when Mario's intuition struck him.

The three experiences came together. Doing something that brought families together, making money by being different, and making people happy while providing value to them drove him to intuitively think about being a chef.

At the ripe age of 15, a high school dropout, no resume, no experience, no related skills, and unable to be employed legally, he showed up at the front steps of the top restaurant in Toronto at 6:30am to ask the owner for a job. He was told to get lost.

This did not stop Mario. This same routine happened every day, seven days a week for approximately two months, despite threats of calling the police and hearing the word "no" day in and day out.

Finally, the restaurant owner decided to hire Mario for free. Mario washed dishes and eventually got an opportunity to work the salad bar. With the staunch work ethic Mario had, he eventually worked his way up to being executive chef and began to win culinary awards at a young age. He transformed this experience into owning a catering company that became a huge success.

GUT!

As he continues in his entrepreneurial ventures, Mario's experiential intuition uses the three major experiences as a major backdrop for other decisions and choices. He also makes it a point to remind those who are homeless that there is a way out and uses his experiences on the streets to inspire others to discover their own strengths.

There are others whose decisions are primarily guided by relational intuition, where there is a strong sense of who they should keep company with personally or professionally. This type of intuition was essential for Carol and Andy Gates, who needed the right staff members in place to ensure that their restaurant operation was the best that it could be.

CHAPTER 8

Relational Intuition

Relational intuition is used when we are engaged in social interactions, normally where we are assessing an individual or a group. In particular, our intuition will guide us in answering the following:

- ✔ Is the person(s) being genuine or showing signs of deceit or hesitation
- ✔ Does the person(s) care about the conversation
- ✔ Is there a congruence between how people represent themselves and their actual actions
- ✔ Is there a fit between the individual being assessed and our own personal beliefs and values

In these situations, our intuition picks up certain cues from others to gain information about them. These cues are mainly visual in nature, such as facial expressions or body language, or auditory, such as tone and language.

Relational intuition is important when looking to build trust with another person or group of people. A 2005 research article[4] has shown that it takes approximately 14 seconds to gain the trust of an individual, and just as fast to lose this trust. Within this 14 second period, further research[5] has shown that there is a specific area of the brain that evaluates the beliefs, intentions, and emotions of others (Figure 5).

---

4 King-Casas et al. (2005) Getting to Know You: Reputation and Trust in a Two-Person Economic Exchange. Science; Apr 1, 2005; 78-83
5 Lee, K. H., & Siegle, G. J. (2009). Common and distinct brain networks underlying explicit emotional evaluation: a meta-analytic study. Social cognitive and affective neuroscience, nsp001.

Peak Brain
Activity

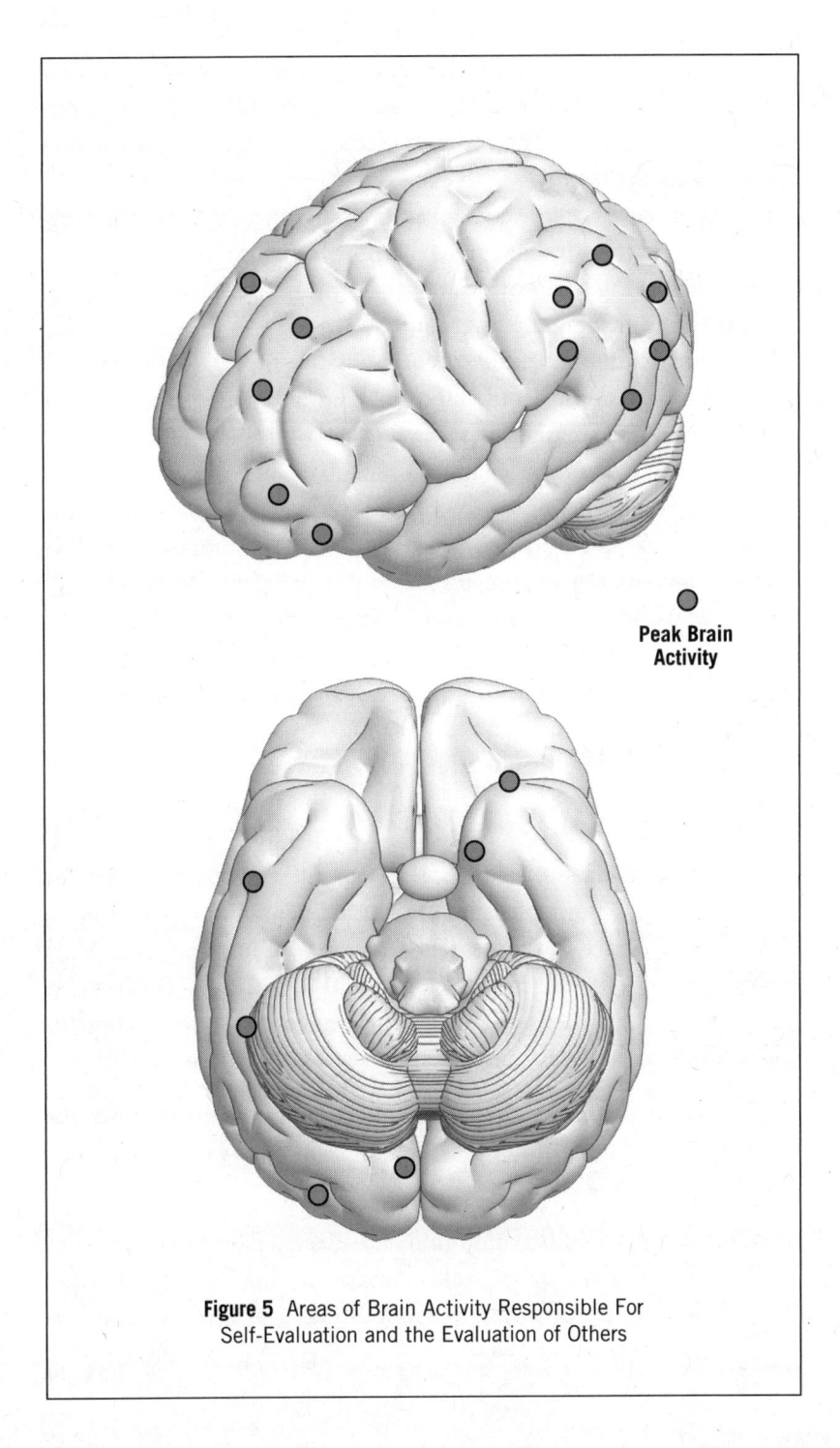

Figure 5 Areas of Brain Activity Responsible For
Self-Evaluation and the Evaluation of Others

Within that 14 second time frame, we observe and listen to cues from the other individual, building a portfolio of trusting characteristics. If an individual cannot be immediately trusted, more cues are needed to ensure that we are able to fully trust him or her.

If one or more of these cues gives us a sense that the person is being deceitful or unusually uncomfortable in a conversation or situation, relational intuition will provide an early warning signal to us that something may be amiss and that we should be cautious.

Relational intuition will always be evaluating others. If we have built initial trust with another individual, our intuition will be informed by positive cues based on the actions and words of others.

If negative cues begin to signal a potential concern with a trusting individual, we may let one or two go, or we may question the trusting relationship or even question the individual. Continued negative cues will amplify our relational intuition and signal us to break away, protecting us from possible precarious situations.

Carol and Andy Gates use this type of intuition to properly staff their restaurant with staff who will provide the ultimate customer experience and prevent those with less than ideal morals and values from scamming them, affecting their business financially.

GUT!

Andy and Carol Gates own GT's, a restaurant-style beach bar located in Port Stanley, Ontario. Because of their different intuitive abilities (to be discussed in Part 4), Carol's being in tune with the long term vision (strategic intuition) and Andy's being in tune with the day-to-day operations (operational intuition), they complement each other's strengths well when it comes to making decisions for the restaurant.

Carol: The two of us are great partners, both in life and business because I'm the planner and I'm always looking towards the future. But Andy naturally lives in the moment.

When asked about how intuition had affected their lives, they both are quick to talk about how Carol ended up meeting Andy at GT's after they had split, lining up intuition with destiny.

Carol: I was about 20 or 21 at the time and I had this feeling, this gut instinct that I wanted to work at the Crock and Block, which was a steakhouse on York Street at the time. I had been baking and working in the kitchen at Say Cheese, which was a really cool restaurant on Dundas Street, which no longer exists.

But I really wanted to get on the floor because, of course, you make more money getting tips. At Say Cheese, kitchen staff are much harder to come by than floor staff and so they really wanted me to stay in the kitchen. So I realized that the only way I was going to get on the floor was to move jobs.

I just had this absolute gut instinct that I should work at the Crock and Block. I put out my resume at a number of different places and at the end of that week, I had an interview at the Crock and Block and soon after, I was offered a job.

The Crock and Block had a little bar called GT's underneath it and it was the same owner that we eventually bought GT's from. I was a server and a supervisor for them for about three years. Eventually, I took a job at East Side Mario's as a kitchen manager, and that is where Andy and I met.

Carol and Andy's relationship had its ups and downs over the next few months. Three years after meeting Andy, Carol received a phone call from the former owner of GT's who was trying to woo Carol to Port Stanley, Ontario. This phone call would change her and Andy's life forever.

Carol: Mark, the owner at GT's, called and said, 'I've got this beach bar that I just opened last year and I really need you to come and help me manage this thing.' And I said, 'Well, I'm not going to leave a full-time, year-round position for a seasonal one. That's just crazy.' But Andy and I kept splitting up, but because we were working together I decided that the only way to really break up with Andy was to get away from him. So I took the job. It really worked out for me.

At the same time, Andy was looking for a new place to live, and his search for a roof over his head took him to Port Stanley.

Andy: I had a house with a friend of mine in London and we ended up in a situation where we had to sell the house. I really didn't know where I was going to go. My friend calls me and he says, 'I have this fabulous deal on a cottage in Port Stanley'. I can't turn this down as I get to live in this *fabulous cottage in Port Stanley. So, I take the cottage. And Carol hears through the grapevine that I got the cottage.*

Carol: *I'm not happy because I moved and took a job in Port Stanley to get away from Andy and then he moves to Port Stanley!*

Andy: *I managed to tactfully avoid her for the first two months or so. Finally my friends urged me to go to GT's on a Wednesday night when she was not supposed to be there. And she was. What are the odds? And it turns out it was the first night all year that she decided to actually stay and have drinks. And we have been together ever since.*

That coincidence which led to a lifetime of partnership suggests that intuition had aligned with a sense of destiny for Carol and Andy. Intuition also played a significant role in the offer to buy GT's.

Carol: *Zach was five months old when we discovered we were pregnant with Jonny. That spring, the previous owner decided to close down the London location because the Port Stanley location had been carrying it for a few years. At that point we just thought that we could be working six months a year. That's not bad when you have young kids and we could be home with the kids for six months and work for six months. We figured that would work out.*

Even though they worked in the industry, there was never an inkling that they would ever own a restaurant or bar. It was never discussed or dreamed about. Yet, when the offer came to buy GT's, Carol's intuition told her that it was absolutely the right thing to do. After a short discussion, Andy intuitively knew that they had the right attitude, skills and wherewithal to successfully run GT's. They decided to move ahead with the purchase.

Carol: *That Easter, we had Andy's brother over and Andy's brother said, 'You guys should buy the Port Stanley location.' I said, 'No, Mark would never sell it.' And so that Monday the usual office chit-chat begins and I tell the owner that Andy and I should buy the place, and he said, 'You guys couldn't afford it.'*

Carol gave the former owner various reasons why she could afford the purchase, and over the next two or three months, the former owner began to drop subtle hints that he might want to sell. All of a sudden, Carol's intuition hit her hard.

Carol: So one evening, I was in Port Stanley getting ready to open for that season and I'm probably about three months pregnant at that point and Andy was home with Zach, who was eight months old. And I'm driving home. It's like the light bulb goes off: he does want to sell the business. It was an absolute certainty. It was just absolute.

Carol wasted no time closing the intuitive thought.

Carol: And the next breath, the next thought was if he's selling, we're buying it. Actually, I just got goose bumps just telling you. I got home and I remember Andy and I were at our dining room table. He had Zach on his lap. And I said, 'I've got something really big to discuss with you.' For something that big, it was about a 10-minute conversation. 'Mark does want to sell it. I don't know if we can pull it off financially, but I think we should buy it.' From that moment on, it was details.

I don't think ownership is everybody's destiny, but we were asked about owning a restaurant a lot. We always said no, we're not doing that. It was never our dream, which is weird. It was never in our plan to someday open a restaurant, but now that we're here I don't think we could imagine anything else.

Andy and Carol have been able to rely on relational intuition to select the right staff to make the customer's experience the best that it can be.

Carol: Most restaurants have a fully trained staff. When you bring on one, two, three, or four new hires, you can then bring them along slowly. You give them the slower sections and you have them follow other people. We don't have that chance. We probably have about 35 floor staff and if we're lucky, half of them are returning staff. But even those returning staff have a new menu to learn.

Andy: They haven't served at GT's since September, and it's now May.

Carol: So they're rusty. You might have 15, or even more, brand new rookies. Here's your three training shifts and we'll do what we can to help you, but here's your full section. We don't have that opportunity to bring them along. It's very much sink or swim for the staff out there.

Andy and Carol also talk about how their intuition is used to help with staffing needs that are dependent on the weather for that particular day.

Andy: Every day you wake up and your intuition has to tell you how many staff given the weather.

Carol: On our busiest days, we would have 15 servers starting, unless it's a very special event. Most of our shifts are on a call-in basis for the servers, and sometimes the bartenders, depending on how many you have scheduled in the kitchen.

Andy: But you're always judging. 'Okay, I have 10 scheduled for today. Wow. It is absolutely beautiful. Should I get somebody else in? Is 10 enough?' Or the more difficult is when it's going to be a high of 22 degrees Celsius and cloudy today. If my goal for the day is to sell a thousand dollars, I think I'm probably only going to do 60 percent of that. Do I bring in 6 instead of 10? Where is my balance between good service and too much labour to do it? You are trying to keep good servers. It becomes frustrating if you just bring them all in every day and they know that, unless the weather's beautiful, they're going to stand around and not make money.

Andy and Carol use their relational intuition when looking to recruit talent. Bringing on the right type of personality and work ethic in their servers and bartenders is vital to their service-based business.

Andy: Every person potentially has our business on the line. For example, if you have a cook doing a lousy job, or not doing it properly and putting out bad food, it is damaging my reputation. I could have 12 great servers and if you get my 13th who is lousy, that's your only impression of the business.

Before a candidate gets a chance to be interviewed, Carol uses her relational intuition to pick up on various cues that provide information about the candidate's personality.

Carol: We will typically set up two full days of interviews and it's usually on a chilly day in April. So, I'm there in my hat and my mittens and these people who are coming up don't know who I am. They just think I'm the greeter or the hostess.

I watch how they walk up to the deck. Are they shuffling their feet? Are they meandering, or do they have a sense of purpose? That's a huge one for me. I want them to walk up with some energy and enthusiasm because if they're not going to walk into an interview with energy and enthusiasm, they're probably not going to bring it to their job. There was one where she's either drunk or hung-over. So that's a no. But the walking up, I find, has often been a good indicator to me if someone's going to bring energy and enthusiasm to the job.

Carol and Andy's relational intuition came to the rescue when they hired a resource that passed all the requirements in becoming a bartender, but began doing things that were illegal in nature.

Carol: *It was this person who was purposely out to con you. That's the one that got through. He was a secondary hire as we had to add more staff in June. He had a great interview.*

This person was offered employment, but soon after he started, Carol and Andy's intuition was telling them that something was wrong. Carol began to pay closer attention to him, looking for any intuitive indicators.

Andy: *You start comparing notes. At the end of your shift you cash out. You submit the money that's due. He cashed out and then he was ringing things in again. Well, one day Carol caught him.*

Carol: *He continued to ring in his own food and drinks under his number, which we would have caught.*

Andy: *At the end of the day, when he was done, his original receipt said that he owed $1,000. He submits that. The bookkeeper noticed that at the end of the day, he might have submitted $1,000, but it says he owed $1,029 because he rang in another $29.00.*

Carol: *I don't he think realized we were watching.*

Andy: *We let him go.*

Surprisingly, this same person returned to GT's as a customer.

Andy: *There was no point in being hostile. I said hello, chatted with him for a second and then his food goes out to the table, and he has a food complaint.*

Carol: He said he had gum in his wrap, which did not happen. I guarantee you that this did not happen in our kitchen. I talked to the kitchen staff and nobody had been chewing gum. This was a person who absolutely lied about that to try and get a free meal. We kicked him out and said get out. Get off our property.

Andy: I said here's your bill. Don't come back.

Carol: Yeah, hire slowly, fire quickly. And those are definitely words to live by.

Even when their relational intuition senses that a customer may be wrong, Andy and Carol balance acting on that intuition with what is good for the business.

Andy: The customer is not always right, but their perception is. Unless they are outright trying to scam you, if they believe they are correct, whether they are right or not, sometimes you have to promo or give it away. It's not worth proving your point to make them pay that $10 or whatever the case is because they're going to walk away, never come back, and make a point of doing it. Sometimes you need to take a negative and turn it into a positive, even when you know you are not wrong.

Carol: Right. Here's a good example. When we worked together at East Side Mario's, a customer ordered 20 wings and ate them. After she was done, and the server cleared her plate away, she complained and said, 'I ordered 20 wings but I only got 10. They were great, but I only got 10. Just charge me for 10.'

And the franchise owner looked at the check in the kitchen and it said 20 wings. It had been rung in correctly. He actually went to the garbage, plucked out the 20 bones, brought the 20 bones to the table and said, 'You're wrong. You ate 20. You're paying for 20.' She was irate and was never going to coming back.

Twenty years later, I remember that as an instance. Great, you got your eight bucks, but you lost a customer forever. I do believe that he was right. She got the 20 wings, she ate the 20 wings. But I don't think she should have been treated in such a way. He essentially accused her of lying and made her pay for it. I think she was just a customer that had made a mistake.

Andy: I admit I've gone to a table sometimes to deal with a complaint. You get talking to people and you realize they're looking at you and my intuition says they are telling me what they believe is the truth. Whether it's right or not, they are sitting there with their complaint and saying this is wrong. 'I'm unhappy. They did this.' And sometimes you go with it. Other times I know that this person is just trying to see what he can scam out of me and I have walked away from a table and said there is nothing I can do for you. Losing a customer who's trying to scam me? I haven't lost anything.

In addition to their focus on getting the right staff, their relational intuition is used when thinking about their customers' preferences for menu choices.

Andy: Everything we do is based on intuition. When you're looking at the menu and you come up with an idea, you're always trying to balance things. I have got a hundred items on my menu. In each category, you try and drop or replace the bottom one or two, and you're balancing that with what we think is right for the perfect customer at GT's.

One winter day, I was on the computer and spent hours and hours menu surfing. I went to different restaurants and pulled up their menus. I rarely take anything straight up, but I'll take the idea or even a name.

Carol: Texas fries.

Andy: Texas fries. I took that from somebody's menu and we renamed our steak sandwich this year, 'The man handler,' which is the name that somebody else had for a steak sandwich. And sales went up 50 percent!

Carol: Just from changing the name.

Andy: Just for the name change.

Carol: Steak hoagie to man handler.

Andy: Yeah. We went up 50 percent! Desserts have always been a black hole for us because people ask why we don't serve ice cream.

Well the problem is on a hot day and it's 35 degrees, it melts really quickly. Whether it's a pre-made frozen 'something' from the freezer, or somebody scoops it, you'd have to get that to the customer literally at that moment. On a busy day, I can't guarantee that somebody is standing there

GUT! 31

waiting to be handed their ice cream dessert to take it out. So, it sits for three, four, God forbid, five minutes in the kitchen, and then it's garbage. And who wants to go to the beach on a 30-degree day and eat a cheesecake or chocolate cake?

When searching for the ultimate dessert menu item, Andy's intuition hit him hard, with Carol's following closely after.

Andy: *I said to Carol, 'Have you ever heard of dessert nachos before?' She went, 'That's it.' And she said, 'I know how. I'm going to do it.'*

Carol: *That's going to be our dessert. It's going to be fantastic. I know exactly what they're going to be. Right away, it was like as soon as he said it, it was just, bam, that is going to be it.*

Andy: *We've done it the last two years and the first year we did it, we increased our dessert sales five times over.*

Carol: *It's just a floured tortilla that's sugared and then we put various toppings on it. So we have turtle and banana cream and berries, and sprinkles on it for the kids, which ironically is our most popular one. We have different sizes: single, share, and colossal. It's an awesome thing for people to be able to share at the beach.*

The colossal one is literally two and a half feet long, so as soon as one dessert goes out on the deck, everyone on the deck is like, 'What's that?' And then all of a sudden we get a run of dessert nachos because everybody wants to try it.

But it was absolute. As soon as he said it, it was just right. You have to listen to that intuition. There comes a point when you know that that's the thing. You have to make the decision and go with it.

Andy: *As a seasonal business, you have one shot at your menu. Once it's done and printed, that's it.*

GUT!

The ultimate success of GT's each and every season relies heavily on the intuitive decision-making of both Carol and Andy. Their relational intuition has played a critical part in hiring the right people and filtering out the bad apples and selecting the right menu choices to ensure that their customers have a fantastic experience.

With bad staff, you have a bad customer experience, and unhappy customers hurt both revenues and reputation. Relational intuition has to care for both of these concerns to ensure that GT's runs successfully each and every season.

Others, such as Duart Townsend, have their intuition triggered by a situation in which they find themselves. Duart's intuition played a vital role in curtailing a difficult flying situation, and a second situation that saved him and his crew from a disastrous military scenario.

CHAPTER 9

Situational Intuition

Situational intuition is triggered when there is an issue with a particular situation where our intuition picks up certain cues from the environment. Based on these cues, we might interpret the situation as being friendly, inviting or natural, or uncomfortable, dangerous or suspicious.

In some cases, these cues are quite overt as we are able to see, touch, hear, smell or feel things in the environment that will give us a good or bad feeling about the situation. In other cases, we may have a feeling about a situation that we cannot "put our finger on", yet we feel a sense of danger, for example. This is consistent with research[6] that has shown that an area of the brain focuses on environmental cues and their meanings (Figure 6).

Duart Townsend has had both types of situational intuitive experiences.

GUT!

Having served in the Canadian military for almost 30 years, Duart Townsend is currently a senior programme coordinator for air force-related projects within the Canadian Armed Forces defence programme. Immediately prior to that, he commanded and was responsible for the re-activation of a Royal Canadian Air Force heavy lift helicopter squadron operating Chinook helicopters.

---

6 Lee, K. H., & Siegle, G. J. (2009). Common and distinct brain networks underlying explicit emotional evaluation: a meta-analytic study. Social cognitive and affective neuroscience, nsp001.

34 GUT!

Peak Brain Activity

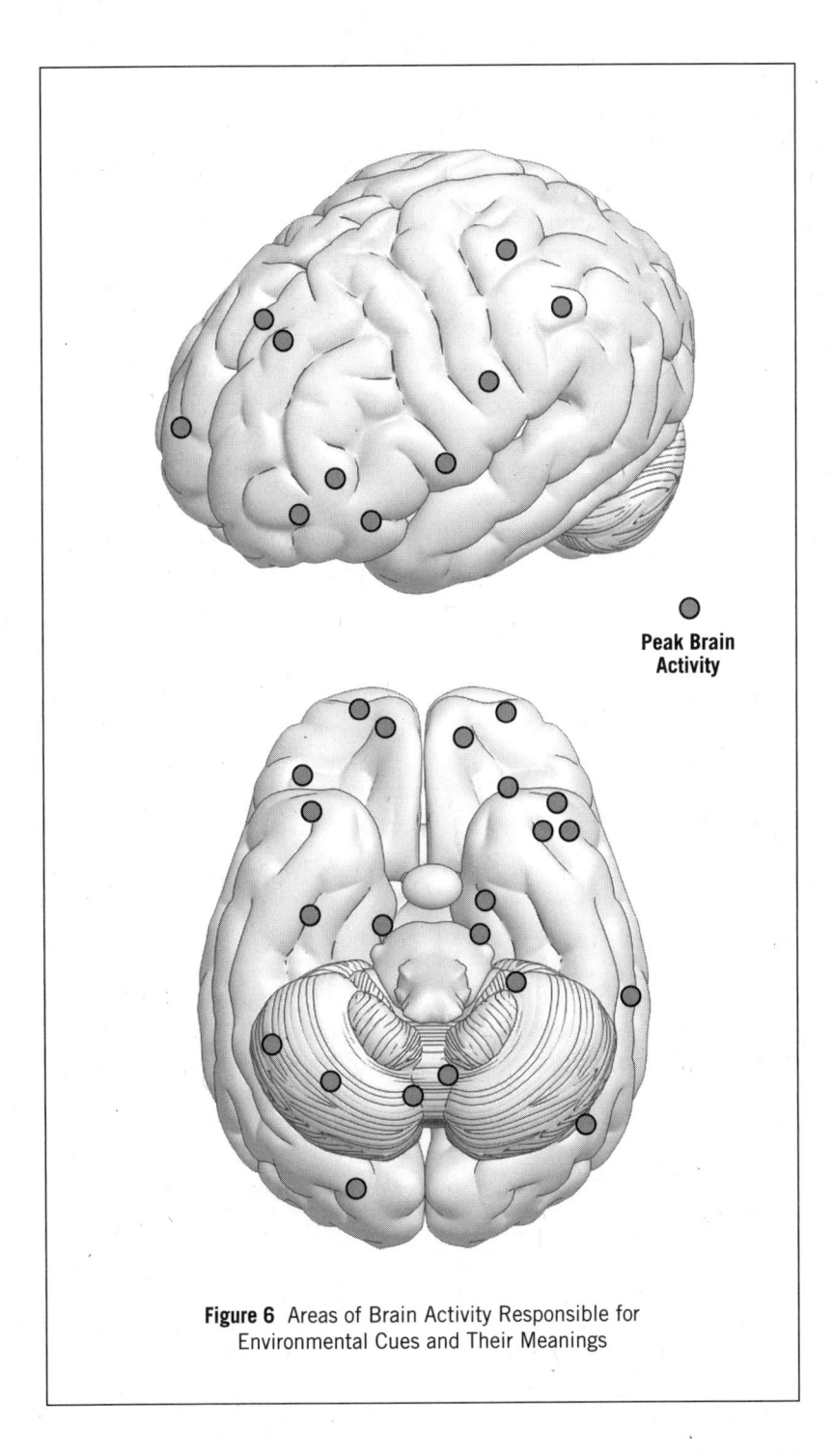

Figure 6 Areas of Brain Activity Responsible for Environmental Cues and Their Meanings

Duart began his operational career as a pilot after obtaining an undergraduate degree in physics and computer science at Royal Roads Military College. After completing pilot training, he entered into operations flying helicopters in support of the Army and Canadian special operations forces. He has had numerous operational tours on a variety of tactical helicopters and several staff tours that included major capital procurement and organizational restructure activities. Internationally, he was deployed to Afghanistan as a strategic advisor embedded in the Afghan government to assist in their national development program.

Duart's situational intuition was triggered while planning a flight back to the base of operations.

"A friend and I were looking to return to base on one particular mission and technically, with all the weather forecasts and weather conditions, we would have been entirely within our right or authorizations to fly. But for both of us, something was saying, 'You know what, do we really need to do that?' It was that hair on the back of your neck sort of rising up."

There was no immediate requirement for Duart and his colleague to return to base.

"I kind of looked over at him and said, 'What are you thinking' and he looked at me and said, 'I was just going to ask you the same thing.' And I said, 'Frankly, I'm thinking I don't feel like flying home tonight.' Neither of us, myself nor my colleague, were timid. We had certainly flown in our careers in some pretty crappy conditions so if something's telling us if we don't have to, maybe we shouldn't."

The intuitive decision was quick, but the logical supportive arguments took another 10 minutes to confirm the gut feeling.

"From the first time that we had everything available to us and we had to make a decision from when we were looking at each other like, 'Hmm, what's your gut feel?' that was like no more than a minute or two, followed by a 10 minute period of that deductive backup to, yeah, I don't think there's anything we can lose on this and we made the decision to put the craft down for the night and start it up the next morning."

As it turned out, this was absolutely the right decision.

"Later, other people who had been operating with the squadron locally said, 'Oh man, it's a good thing you guys didn't come up last night. It was just crap and the weather, nothing was lining up according to the forecast.' If we had actually come up, notwithstanding the acceptable weather according to the regulations, it turned out that the reality was, it would have been a lot crappier, even to the point where we may have ended up just actually putting it down in a field and trying to sort things out from there."

Duart and his colleague were grateful for following their intuition.

"You know that gut feeling, particularly if it's a potentially bad thing that could happen, you know, we kind of call it that spidey sense? We followed it along and there's nothing saying that our flight wouldn't be a success, but I certainly felt after talking to the other guys that it could have potentially caused a few more grey hairs! When things are under question, things can change on you in a heartbeat."

Duart's situational experience also played a crucial role when delaying his team by 15 minutes with no real reason apart from an intuitive sense to let another team go on ahead.

"For no other reason other than a gut feel, no logical reason at all, I ended up conducting a road move later than I would otherwise have done it. It was a delay for us departing the base. So, for no other reason than, 'Hey, let's push back our timing,' we actually traded with another unit that was departing from another installation. "Essentially we just basically swapped departure times out of this particular installation. That, I would say, was an intuitive sense. These other guys weren't pushing us to trade times because they wanted to get back early. It was nothing like that."

This decision to delay was an intuitive one for Duart, but it was not well understood by others.

"One of the guys in my group was actually interested in getting back to our home location and said, 'Really, what does it matter, 15 minutes is barely any time at all.' I was a major at the time and I was travelling with another major who said, 'Why not just go if we can do that now and then we'll get back earlier and get on with our stuff.' It wasn't a resistance but

GUT! 37

there was certainly an element of, 'Why push that 15 minutes, why don't we just go now?'"

This 15-minute delay turned out to be crucial for the safety of Duart's group.

"We actually ended up leaving and putting in time later, whereas this other unit actually ended up getting into, let's just say, trouble in terms of some difficulty along the way. We would have been following the same route if we had actually gone out first. And we probably would have been in less of a position to deal with the situation as capably, not because we're not trained to do it, but just because we didn't have as much of the capabilities as this other group that went out before us.

"We would probably not have fared as well as these other guys because they were heavier vehicles and better equipped and we were relatively light."

GUT!

In both of Duart's examples, his situational intuition helped him avoid difficult circumstances. The first experience could have resulted in a significant inconvenience, with he and his colleague isolated in a field far away from the home base. In the second experience, situational intuition was instrumental in avoiding a potentially dangerous situation abroad where Duart and his team were at risk.

Although some of us are strong in one particular type of intuition, others function highly in two or more quadrants, such as Kevin Fung.

CHAPTER 10

Multiple Quadrants

It is extremely rare for us to be strong in only one intuitive quadrant. Given that we will have amassed an incredible wealth of experience consciously and subconsciously, our experiences should inform all types of intuition.

Given the environment we find ourselves in as we age and the types of activities we enjoy, we will naturally develop an affinity for one particular type of intuition. We may also enjoy operating in an environment both personally and professionally that maximizes that one intuitive type. In this case, there is little incentive to become stronger in another type of intuition.

Those with similar strengths in two or more quadrants would have had experiences and education that would inform each of their strong intuition types. These individuals have an advantage in that they are freely able to make intuitive decisions across those intuition types in a particular situation.

In normal circumstances, it would be expected that as we age, we would gain strength in a number of the other quadrants, given the variety of situations we may find ourselves in and the related decisions and actions we take.

Kevin Fung was able to articulate intuitive experiences that spanned multiple intuition quadrants.

GUT!

Kevin Fung is a surgical oncologist for London Regional Cancer Centre located at London Health Sciences Centre in London, Ontario,

Canada. He is also an assistant professor in two departments at Western University in London, Ontario: the Department of Otolaryngology and the Department of Music Performance Studies.

One of Kevin's strengths lies in relational intuition, which is a necessary partner when forming a particular diagnosis.

"Intuition's a little bit like a gut feeling, like this person's going to have a terrible outcome, or perhaps there are some red flags that make me think that, well, maybe this person's expectations are too high, or possibly too low, or unrealistic or something. Just a gut feeling. It's something I can't really put a finger on. It's probably a constellation of things such as the way they look, the way they behave, certain words that they use when they speak. So, to me, there's a gut feeling that perhaps something is wrong, or we use it in a positive way, that something is right.

"So that's part of the art of medicine. I actually use that in my [diagnosis] and the way I interact with patients and communicate their treatment plans to them and their families. It's not like a textbook, you know – a patient comes with A, B, and C, this is your diagnosis and this is the plan, period. We really have to take into account lots of other things. So I think that intuition is used in medicine every single day and for us as diagnosticians as well as in medical doctors and surgeons."

Kevin's relational intuition becomes heightened when there is a mismatch between a patient's expectations and his, or when he senses that a patient is not being forward about what he or she wants. Kevin does his best to provide the right guidance and advice given the situation.

"Body language, I think, is one where, I know they are saying yes, but I can tell by their body language that they're saying no. So for instance, say a treatment plan could be option A or option B. Ultimately, they may end up choosing something that I have a feeling is not what they want and so I would use that intuition and say, 'You know what, even though you say you want to have the surgery, my gut says that maybe we should just sit on it. Let's just follow you. Let's observe and you come back in six months and we can re-evaluate your decision.'"

However, Kevin is quick to point out that this is specific to each case depending upon the severity of the medical problem.

"So that happens in very specific sorts of examples such as the management of thyroid nodules where observation is fine. It's safe. Certain other things like cancer that's growing out of your face, your neck, or throat, you know, there probably really isn't much choice at all."

In the end, however, despite Kevin's advice that is based on his intuition and medical training, the patient makes the ultimate decision.

"We are supposed to empower our patients with information. They make the decision, and they direct their care. We try our best and may say things like, 'Well, the chances of this working are about 10 percent. Do you still want me to do it?'

"And they'll say yes. But my intuition might say, you know, maybe I shouldn't have even given them the option, right? I'm only doing it because the patient wants me to.

"The opposite does happen. I know I can make you better and they say, 'No, I don't want it,' and walk out. And you can't do anything about it."

Kevin uses his relational intuition in his education with students, residents, and fellows. He provides a couple of examples.

"A visiting student wants to get into our program. They'll do an elective with us and try to impress us and I rely a ton on intuition. I know very quickly. I don't like you or you're a psychopath or I love you and I think you'd be a great fit for the program.

"They're well-dressed. They're punctual. They have good handwriting. I think it's intuition actually.

"And the same thing is with residents. I'm training them to do surgery. They actually do the surgery. I can probably say very safely within 60 seconds, I know right away that they're going to be okay, or not going to be okay because you can actually see visual feedback. It's a combination of, you know, are they doing it right, if it's their style. It's a little fuzzy, and I sort of put that to intuition.

"We have residency training programs. It's highly competitive. We've got 45 people applying for three positions, so it's cutthroat. And so we interview these candidates. Objectively we have the CV, publications, grants, references, awards and things like that. At the end of the day we're sitting around the table going on mainly gut feeling and intuition. Just my intuition tells me, this person wouldn't fit."

Kevin uses this relational intuition and applies it to his leadership roles.

"I have certain roles at the university and at the hospital where I chair committees and am a member of committees. We talk about things and again it's that human element. I use intuition quite a bit at these meetings when we're talking about strategies and goals and visions and things. I think that oftentimes I just go with my gut. If something seems wrong, I'll just say this doesn't seem right. If something seems right then I'll say, 'Well this doesn't seem wrong.'"

It is evident that Kevin's relational intuition is quite strong, but he also relies on his strong situational intuition, using it consistently when performing procedures where his skills as a surgeon are necessary to save the lives of patients.

"It's easy to read a surgical textbook, right? Step one, cut from here to here. Step two, you know. And then there are the rules – don't cut out this thing and don't cut out that thing. A lot of things we do are pre-programmed.

"I joke with my residents and say you should be able to have X-ray vision. You should be able to see through 10 layers of tissue and kind of know where things are.

"Intuition really has to do with moments in the operating room for things that I see, things that I feel. We can get tests, we can get scans, and things like that, but at the end of the day, this is a very kinesthetic service skill. You use your eyes and your ears and your hands and you just have that gut feel that perhaps, you know, you may want to do the operation in a slightly different way.

"The tumour feels mushy versus mobile versus stuck. There are certain kinesthetics or senses that may not manifest itself on a scan, X-ray, ultrasound, or MRI. It's an art really. It's a bit of an art form."

GUT!

It is clear that Kevin, like some of us, is strong in two intuitive types that he uses on a regular basis in patient interactions, in academic settings, and in the operating room. His intuitive decisions and medical training have an enormous impact on a patient's wellbeing, and in more extreme examples, life and death situations.

Kevin recognizes that using intuition in the medical arena is critical in many areas. Yet, it is not something tangible. Rather, as many of the interviewees have described, such as Brad Geddes, it is subconscious in nature.

CHAPTER 11

Intuition is Subconscious

Intuition is not objective in nature and cannot be pinpointed, as can touching a hot object, seeing a particular colour, or hearing a bell. Some individuals who were interviewed by researchers described intuition as being beyond consciousness[7], non-conscious[8] or subconscious[9].

Every one of the interviewees found it hard to describe how they felt during an intuitive experience. To them, intuition "just felt right". For Brad Geddes, "subconscious" is how he describes intuition.

GUT!

Brad is President of Zucora Inc, Canada's largest provider of home furnishing protection plans and customer care programs. Zucora was founded in 1979 and previously operated as Magi Seal Corporation until shortly after it was acquired by his family's holding company, Zeubear Investments Ltd.

"Well, I found it intriguing when you first raised the subject matter because, you know, my sense is intuition dwells in the subconscious so it's not something that's out there and open and fully explored or even thought about consciously.

"And so when you raised that, intuition, I don't even think about intuition, you know, and how does one qualify it, how does one quantify it. I mean, I don't know that you can necessarily identify it until you start to put your mind to it.

---
7 Sinclair, M., & Ashkanasy, N. M. (2005). Intuition: Myth or a decision-making tool? Management Learning, 36(3), 353-370.
8 Dane. E., & Pratt, M. (2007). Exploring intuition and its role in managerial decision making. Academy of Management Review 2007, Vol. 32, No. 1, 33–54.
9 Khatri, N., & Ng, H. A. (2000). The role of intuition in strategic decision making. Human Relations, 53(1), 57-86.

"So it really stimulated my thinking and where intuition played a role. And because it is buried so deep, I think, it's not present, you know, and at least from my perspective I haven't dwelt on it or focused on it as a tool or an instrument, and yet as I reflect on some of the experiences I've had, clearly intuition played a role.

"You don't think of it consciously I guess. This is the interesting part. I really find it fascinating."

Brad explains how he actually uses his intuition.

"As I reflected I thought, okay, when did intuition play a role? And it was usually, in most cases, encountering other people and at the beginning of a new relationship of some kind. Whether that's interviewing a candidate for a position and attempting to assess on first meeting that candidate, and whether or not they're right for the position and whether they have the right skills.

"The paper may say something, but it's that face-to-face (meeting). And I'll dwell on that for a second because that's something that I find I've been able to hone over the years. Lord knows I'm not perfect and I'm far from it and if I hit a 50 percent success rate I think I'm doing pretty good. But the rule we have in our organization is nobody gets hired unless I have a crack at them as the final step.

"So they go through the various teams and I never make the final decision. I give my feedback, but I want that opportunity to attempt to assess the individual, as best I can in a limitation of 15 or 20 minutes, of their character, what drives them, you know. I try to unearth some of that."

Brad talks about the personal connection he needs to have with the person being hired.

"Their qualifications could be exemplary and they could be a perfect match on paper for what the position is, but unless we have a personal connection, my flags go up because I know if I can't establish a personal connection with that person, then it's not going to be a good culture fit for us. Now it's not to say that I determine the culture; I don't. It's the rest of the organization that determines the culture, but I think I have a pretty good sense as to what drives other people in the company. So I find it's imperative for me and our company to at least have that opportunity to give my feedback."

There was an instance where there was a discrepancy between Brad and his team, despite Brad's intuition telling him not to bring on a certain employee.

"I think only on one occasion was the team against my feedback, which was negative, and said, 'No, we really think you're wrong about this one. We really think the person should be hired.' They were hired and they lasted two months, not to suggest that I was right, but, there was something about it I couldn't put my finger on."

There were two reasons why this individual did not work out.

"I think there was some pressure on the team to fill that role because we needed more resources in that particular capacity, so I think that kind of overrode the decision to get the job done, as opposed to get the job done right. And I think that may have obscured the decision making.

"And, no fault of the individual, I think that ultimately they, too, were in a similar role. They just wanted to get the job done and get hired and that was their motivation, not necessarily if it was the right job for them. And that's ultimately what happened. They came in, they were here for a month and a half, and went 'This just isn't for me.' And I respect that, you know, and I'm glad that we found it early because, unfortunately, whenever you hire an employee and they leave, it costs money. But, you'd rather have that happen sooner than later."

GUT!

Many of the interviewees concurred with Brad Geddes that although intuition is subconscious in nature, it plays a crucial part of our decision-making process.

Not only is intuition subconscious, but it starts forming well before we are aware of it. We are able to make decisions as soon as we are born. We may be too young to remember the decisions we made so early in life. Some of the interviewees found it hard to recollect early intuitive experiences, but for others, such as Michael Aniballi, the early intuitive experiences can be readily recollected.

CHAPTER 12

We Are Born With Intuition

We all are born with intuition.

At birth, our brain contains only slightly fewer neurons than an adult brain, which has over 100 billion neurons[10]. With each neuron firing a signal an average of 200 times per second, the brain is continually absorbing information at a dizzying pace.

Researchers[11] were able to find evidence that intuition existed in infants as young as two months in age, the earliest age at which testing can occur.

Although we have not had a significant amount of personal experience at such a young age, intuitive decisions can still be made because of the ongoing implicit learning taking place.

Despite the incredibly high number of events and experiences the brain absorbs, our intuition culls only those that are relevant to each one of us, even while distracted[12], which then inform our intention to make a decision or act.[13]

When interviewees were asked about their earliest intuitive moment, although it was difficult to pinpoint exactly when, many agreed that they experienced intuition early on in their lives. However, most found it much easier to remember a more recent, profound intuitive experience.

---

10 Blakemore, S & Choudhury, S. (2006) Development of the adolescent brain: implications for executive function and social cognition. Journal of Child Psychology and Psychiatry 47:3/4, pp 296–31
11 Hespos, S. & vanMarle, K. (2012) Physics for infants: characterizing the origins of knowledge about objects, substances, and number. Wiley Interdisciplinary Reviews: Cognitive Science; 3 (1): 19 DOI: 10.1002/WCS.157
12 Voss, J. L., & Paller, K. A. (2009). An electrophysiological signature of unconscious recognition memory. Nature neuroscience, 12(3), 349-355.
13 Schult, J. & Steffens, M. (2011) On the representation of intentions: Do personally relevant consequences determine activation? Memory and Cognition 39:1487–1495

Michael Aniballi vividly remembers an intuitive experience that occurred at an early age.

GUT!

Michael Aniballi was born in British Columbia and at the tender age of 4 moved to Ontario. His parents, twin brother, and older brother by one year, settled into a nice area just outside of Toronto and got ready for a new adventure, not the least of which was something called "school".

"With three boys so close in age, and moving to a new province, we didn't have any friends and school was starting almost immediately. Even though we had each other, at the time it seemed we were all so nervous we forgot about this little fact. Once we stepped outside of the house and started down the road to school we somehow knew we were all headed to different classes and would no longer be able to play and hang out together. For some strange reason I can barely fathom now, we began to separate as soon as we stepped onto the sidewalk outside our home ... it was every man for himself."

"At 4 years of age – this is back in the late Sixties – I can distinctly remember walking to school with my twin brother and intuitively thinking something's just not right here. At 4 years old, we shouldn't be walking to school by ourselves but again, this was the Sixties. It wasn't a long walk, and for the most part it was a very sheltered walk; but in my mind, I am thinking ... yeah ... there is something definitely wrong here.

"Now, I'm not old enough to know people get abducted, I'm not old enough to know that kids get attacked, or kids get beat up on the way to school. I'm in junior kindergarten. But there it was, a very, very distinct feeling. I can remember so clearly, something's not right, a showdown is on its way.

"We continued to walk like this for weeks, and sure enough on more than one occasion we were in fights on the way to school and at 4 years of age a fight is a traumatic thing, win or lose! It was then, for the first time I realized that, okay, this is why I didn't think this was a good idea."

GUT!

Michael's memory of this intuitive event is clear. When given time, a number of the interviewees have been able to talk about intuition at an early age. Many do not remember the age at which the intuitive experience happened, but do remember the event.

At an early age, although we are able to tap into our intuition, it may take a longer time to act on that intuition. As we gain more experiences, this time delay becomes smaller. Eventually, some of us are able to act almost instantly after an intuitive thought, like Don Johnson.

CHAPTER 13

Intuition is Instant

A key aspect to intuition is that it occurs in an instant in time, described as being quick[14][15], rapid[16] or without extended conscious deliberation[17] by researchers. Further research[18] has also shown that from a neurological perspective, decision-making and planning actually occur at the same time, vastly different than previous thinking[19] that action-planning followed decision-making in a serial fashion.

Although intuition is instant, there is a delay between experiencing intuition and being able to act on it. In fact, two research articles that looked at brain activity were able to show that there was a delay of seven seconds[20] and ten seconds[21] between an intention and an associated action (Figure 7).

Another research article[22] looked at both heart rate and skin conductance to show that intuition was triggered an average of seven seconds before an associated action.

This shows that we already know what decision or action we should be taking before we execute on it.

---

14 Williams, K. (2012), Business Intuition: The Mortar among the Bricks of Analysis. Journal of Management Policy and Practice vol. 13(5)
15 Khatri, N., & Ng, H. A. (2000), ibid.
16 Dane. E., & Pratt, M. (2007), ibid.
17 Williams, K. (2012). Ibid.
18 Andersen, R. & Cui, H. (2009), Intention, Action Planning, and Decision-Making in Parietal-Frontal Circuits. Neuron Review 63, September 10, 2009
19 Tversky, A & Kahneman, D. (1981). The framing of decisions and the psychology of choice. Science 211, 453-468
20 Bode, S., et al. (2011). Tracking the unconscious generation of free decisions using ultra-high field fMRI. PloS one, 6(6), e21612
21 Soon, C. S et al. (2008). Unconscious determinants of free decisions in the human brain. Nature neuroscience, 11(5), 543-545.
22 La Pira, et al. (2013). Validating nonlocal intuition in repeat entrepreneurs: a multi-method approach. Journal of Behavioral Studies in Business, 6.

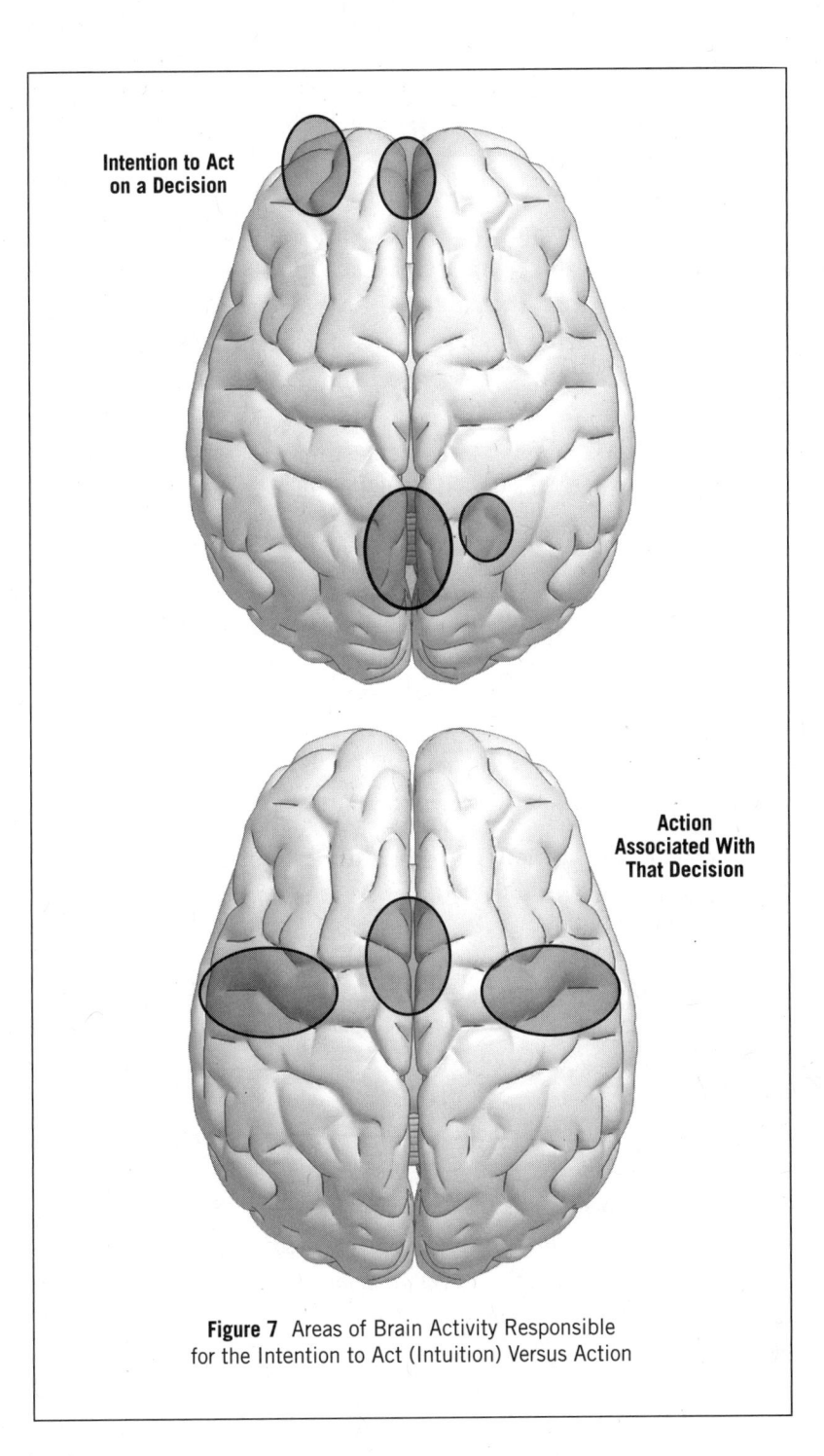

Figure 7 Areas of Brain Activity Responsible for the Intention to Act (Intuition) Versus Action

Intention to Act on a Decision

Action Associated With That Decision

For Don Johnson, the speed of his intuitive ability and the associated execution was an experience he was quick to share during the interview.

GUT!

Don Johnson is a member of the advisory board of BMO Capital Markets. He received the Order of Canada in 2005 and was promoted to Officer in 2009 for his key role in helping change Canada's tax laws to eliminate the capital gains tax on gifts of publicly traded securities to registered charities, and for his support of health care research, the arts, and social services.

Don talks about a quick intuitive decision that helped a Canadian company restructure on a tax-efficient and financial basis.

"I was on a British Airways flight from Johannesburg to London back in 1997 and I read the Financial Times of London. The banner headline was that "BAT[23] Industries Announces De-Merger." BAT Industries was a conglomerate which was in the tobacco business as well as financial services and other businesses. They announced that they were going to become a pure play tobacco company. I knew that they owned 42% of Imasco, a Canadian conglomerate. Imasco owned 100% of Imperial Tobacco, Canada Trust, and Shoppers Drug Mart."

Given this information, Don's intuitive thinking instantly worked out a financial and tax-effective way for BAT to become a pure play tobacco company in Canada.

"I knew that since they were going to become a pure tobacco company, logically their objective would be to somehow exchange their 42 % of Imasco for 100% of Imperial Tobacco, their core business, and sell the non-tobacco businesses.

"When I got to the Four Seasons Hotel in London I dictated a letter to my secretary and she put it on my letterhead and emailed it to the hotel. I then had the hotel courier the letter to Martin Broughton, who was the president and CEO at BAT Industries. It was a 'cold call.'

"I congratulated Martin on his decision to convert back to a pure play tobacco company. Obviously, in Canada, you want to exchange your 42% of Imasco for 100% of Imperial Tobacco and sell the non-tobacco

---
23 British American Tobacco

businesses on the most tax-effective basis. That began a dialogue that went on for two-and-a-half years. Essentially, the most tax-effective way for them to achieve that objective was to take Imasco private, bump up the cost base of the non-tobacco businesses to fair market value and then sell them. This structure was developed by our Mergers & Acquisition team with essential advice from corporate tax lawyers and accountants."

By purchasing the remaining 58% of Imasco, and subsequently selling Canada Trust and Shoppers Drug Mart, Don was able to show how BAT could convert its 42% interest in Imasco into 100% of Imasco with no net capital investment.

"It required $10 billion to take Imasco private and they realized over $10 billion on the sale of Canada Trust to TD Bank and Shoppers Drug Mart to a consortium of institutional investors including KKR and the Ontario Teachers' Pension Plan and paid no capital gains tax on the sale."

"That whole process took a few years, but the initiation of the process was strictly an intuition on my part on this flight from Johannesburg to London."

GUT!

This intuitive speed is a common aspect in every interviewee's experience. There are some that, despite the instant intuitive thought, still need to go through a logical, deductive process or consult with others, which may take some time.

Why was Don able to formulate such a quick solution to a complex problem?

The answer lies in our ability to learn on an implicit and explicit basis, and how these learning methods inform our intuition. For Dan Polakovic, this learning was crucial in getting him off the streets homeless and into a stable career with a loving family.

CHAPTER 14

Implicit and Explicit Learning

Intuitive decisions are not just pulled out of thin air. They are dependent on specific experiences that we learn from as we age. In particular, our intuitive decisions are informed by a combination of two types of learning: implicit and explicit.

Implicit learning is defined[24] as the absorption of information without conscious intent or awareness. Through implicit learning, knowledge is gained through continued conscious and subconscious observation of our surroundings and experiences, and those of others.

Implicit learning begins at birth as the brain absorbs information via observations and experiences on a continuous basis. This type of learning is also shaped by our own personal interpretations of decisions, our actions, and our behaviours, in addition to those of others. What we learn from our family values, the type of environment we are raised in, and our social interactions also contributes to the ongoing implicit learning, which then informs and shapes our intuition.

Explicit learning is a more formal learning method where we learn from three main sources: formal education, informal education, and professional experiences.

Formal education allows us to gain knowledge by attending schools, seminars, and any other formal methods. We learn by reading textbooks or related educational material, from teachers, lecturers, professors or seminar presenters, and any other supporting material.

Informal education is that which is gained through the reading of magazines, books, online content, social media, and other such sources.

---

24 Yang, J., & Li, P. (2012). Brain networks of explicit and implicit learning. PloS one, 7(8), e42993.

We typically learn from these sources out of personal interest or at the suggestion of others. Through this content, we gain knowledge from others and their experiences, retaining information that seems interesting and relevant to us.

Our professional experiences are another form of explicit learning. As we move from childhood into adulthood, we take advantage of employment opportunities, where we gain skills, knowledge, and experiences from our various roles and responsibilities. We are selective in retaining what we think works best in these professional experiences such as processes, evaluative criteria, particular management styles, etc. We gain confidence in those experiences that have a positive outcome and leave behind those that did not seem to work well.

Implicit and explicit learning are not mutually exclusive and can occur at the same time. For example, while we may be gaining skills and adding to our professional experiences in a particular employment opportunity, our brains continually absorb information consciously and subconsciously.

Although they may occur at the same time, they each have different neural pathways and access different parts of the brain, as was shown in a 2012 fMRI study[25] (Figure 8).

Although both types of learning inform our intuition, implicit learning is clearly a preference. In the same 2012 fMRI study[26] cited above, there is considerably more brain activity in those exhibiting implicit learning, which occurs in the area of the brain responsible for cognition.

In addition, in a 2013 research article[27], researchers showed that experienced individuals without formal training or professional backgrounds made poorer judgments after relying more on rational thought than when relying on intuition, suggesting that an over-reliance on explicit learning actually hampers our intuitive ability.

For Dan Polakovic, although he was able to obtain a real estate license to enter a career in that industry, experiences gained through implicit learning led to his continued success.

---

25 Yang, J., & Li, P. (2012). Brain networks of explicit and implicit learning. PloS one, 7(8).
26 Yang, J., & Li, P. (2012). Ibid.
27 Dijkstra, K., Van Der Pligt J. & Van Kleef, G (2013). Deliberation Versus Intuition: Decomposing the Role of Expertise in Judgment and Decision Making. Journal of Behavioral Decision Making, 26: 285–294

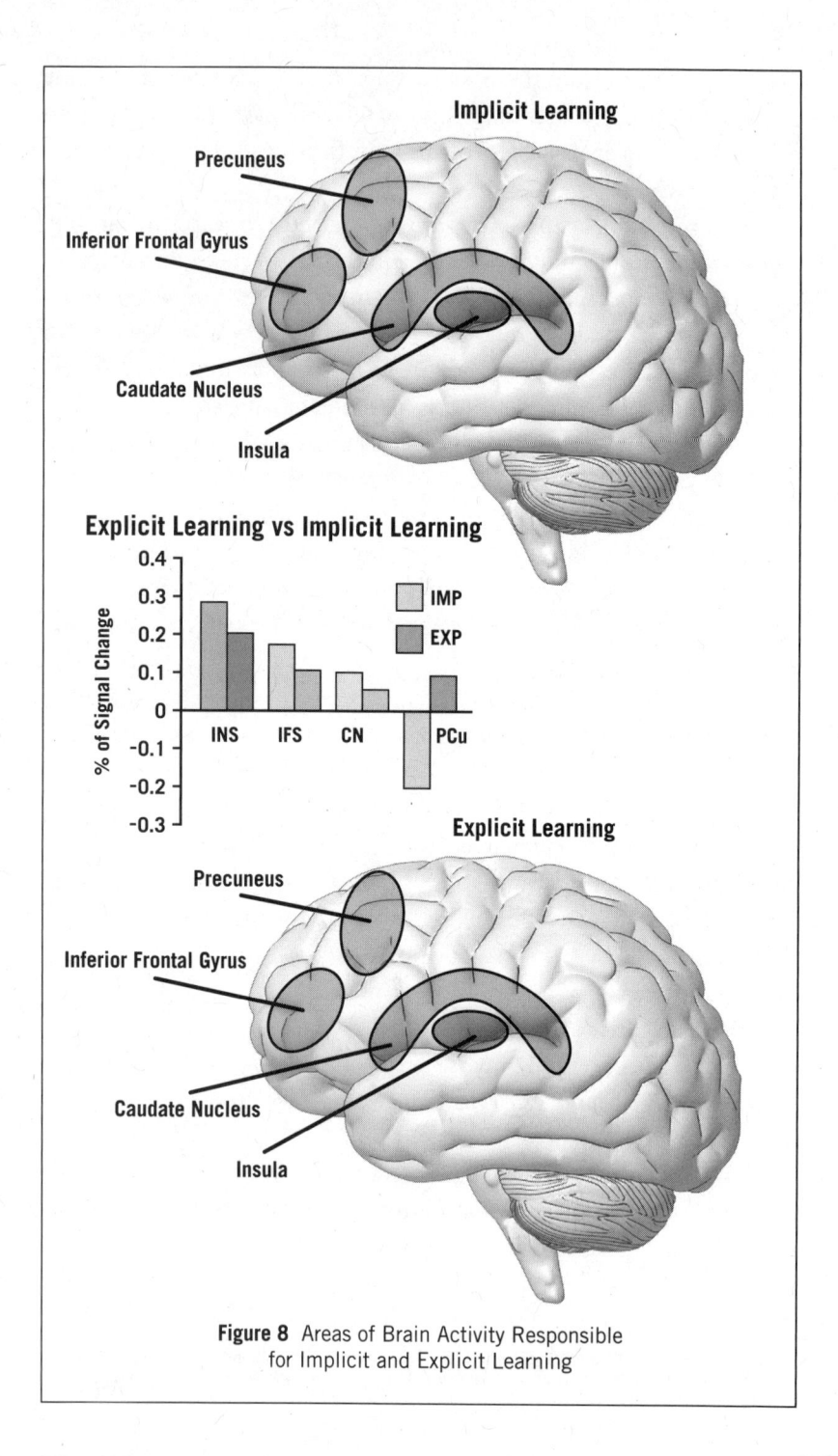

Figure 8 Areas of Brain Activity Responsible for Implicit and Explicit Learning

GUT!

While stopped at a red light, Dan Polakovic, just 13 years old, opened the back door of his parents' car and walked away forever, never looking back. Being homeless was the only way to escape an abusive household. All Dan now needed to do was to figure out how to survive.

The struggle to survive meant that Dan had to use every skill he had to fuel the basic parts of life, such as eating, finding shelter, staying healthy, avoiding dangerous situations, and making the right connections to move ahead. Making these connections meant that Dan had to be strict when choosing who he associated with, an instrumental part of his implicit learning skills.

Rachael: You're good at reading people. You can read people and understand what they're thinking. It's something that you have, you can tell if someone's bullshitting. That's intuition. You catch it right away. So you've learned over time how to manage a situation, and you know when to walk away from a situation, particularly in a home-buying situation. When you're dealing with somebody, you know within the first couple of minutes.

Dan: I can adapt to any situation. I've learned to have a thick skin. I can put up with a lot of nonsense. I can get treated awfully. It doesn't bother me. I can just get through it. I tried to figure out what was right all the time. I knew the things I was doing were wrong, but it was the right decision. Go left here, go with these guys, or go down here on my own.

The reality of making these choices was difficult, but it was about taking two steps forward, one step back, three steps forward, one step back, and so on.

Dan: It was over a long period of time. Slowly changing my life, you know. Even getting away from all those people and all those things. I still always had one foot in the door. I'd see old friends and hang out with them, and do things I probably shouldn't do, but then that wouldn't happen for six months.

With Rachael's positive influence, Dan was able to permanently move away from the negative influences.

Dan: She used to be like, 'We can't go and hang out with those guys.' And once I kind of realized, once I stayed away from there, everything was great. Everything away from that is awesome. Because I'm great at that. I'm great at life over here. Why are you going back over here to cause issues, right?

Both Dan and Rachael knew that if they were to have a good life and a family, they had to move away from a certain lifestyle and negative influences. They then embarked on an ambitious mission – to buy their first home when they were in their early 20s.

One of their key positive influences was the real estate agent that helped them look for houses. Dan and Rachael enjoyed looking at houses with them and became enamoured with the real estate industry.

Dan: She was awesome, we had so much fun. I wasn't sure if we were going to buy a house anymore, we were just going to have fun every weekend, and look at some houses. She got to the point where (she said) we're buying a house this weekend. We realized how much fun it could be and we thought, 'We can do that.'

Being so young, there were a lot of naysayers along the way.

Dan: Being 24 years old, I mean so many people, everyone I knew, like seriously, 'You think you're going to sell real estate? You think you're going to do well?'

Rachael: People said to us, 'You can't buy a house when you're 22.' My mother said that to me. 'You're too young to buy your house.'

Although both were fully employed, Dan and Rachael had limited finances and a chorus of naysayers. Yet, their decision to buy a house was undeterred. To achieve their goal, they turned to another implicit learning tactic that helped them get to this point – a hard work ethic.

Rachael: We always used to say to each other, like we've said in many scenarios in our lives, it will work because we're going to make it work. And I said, 'It's going to work because we're going to make it work, because we want to make it work.'

Soon after buying the house, Rachael became pregnant with their daughter, and their life's purpose took on a whole new meaning. Both were working in average income jobs, Dan in a factory and Rachael in an administrative position. Their intuition kicked in, and they both knew that real estate was the solution for them.

Dan: *I didn't really think about kids or anything like that, but when we had our own kids, that was when we were like, 'Okay, this is where I get to make my difference: it's with them.'*

Rachael: *It's so true. Remember, when she was first born, we knew something had to be different in our life, because we could not make the same the choices that we were making. So we owned our own home, but we were still having fun and hanging out with our friends and having parties and everything, but when she was born, it was like a life change.*

We both had jobs that were okay, but we saw how my parents' lives were a struggle. And I said, 'I want to be happy, and I want her to be happy, and I want to do something else, I want to make a difference. I want to look back and say, wow, I did that. I want to do something different.' And so we said, 'We can't afford to leave our jobs and go to school to find another solution.' So real estate was our solution.

Despite both working full-time, Dan and Rachael began buying and selling houses and also enrolled in courses to obtain their real estate licenses.

Dan's ability to trust his intuition in moving into real estate full-time came at a point when the factory he was working at was being shut down, with an offer to work at another factory at another location with more pay.

Dan: *I had a choice to take a buy-out from the company or transfer to another facility, making more money, which would be better anyways, or go at this. I said to myself, 'We're going to make more money.' I said to Rachael, 'You know, if it doesn't, which I know 100% it will, I can always find something else. I can always call my old boss, he's already told me he can get me a new job.'*

So I took the choice to go at this, with my buy-out. I had to cash in my RRSPs at the time, which wasn't much, a little bit of money, but it got us through the first couple months of trying to get this to work. We got married, and we didn't take a vacation, a honeymoon, because we used the money we had for a honeymoon and our vacation time to pay for our courses and take them.

Diving into real estate full-time, not only did Dan not have the security of a paycheque every two weeks, but he and Rachael were now expecting their second child. In addition, Dan's time on the streets also meant that he did not have some of the technological skills others had, which became apparent when he walked into his first office.

Dan: I remember walking into the office that day and I walk in, and I was like, 'So what do you do?' I had no idea, and no one was really there to help me, except for someone by the name of Sam. He showed me how to log on to their systems and do different things like that.

Rachael: That's how it seems to happen all the time. Like he had no computer background, he didn't even know how to use a photocopier, but because we were like, 'This is what we're doing now, we're just going to do it.' He's calling me from the photocopy machine saying, 'I don't know how to do this,' and I'm still working at my job. And then, in walks Mary into the room, sees him there, helps him, connects with him, and then that moment changed our lives.

Dan: I was complaining because the photocopier, they were charging us 79 cents for a colour copy. But all I had was a little blue thing in the corner, the rest was black and white. I said, 'That's ridiculous, I don't even have the option to change it to black and white. You have to pay colour for that.' And she looked over at me, and said, 'Oh my God, I love this kid,' because it was one of her complaints as well.

This was a pivotal moment for them as they eventually joined forces with Mary and continued on their successful real estate career.

Listening to his intuition, Dan had launched into a career that provided him and Rachael with satisfaction personally, professionally, and financially.

Dan: Within a week, I got two of my own listings. I don't even know how I got them, I can't remember how I got them. What happened was, in two weeks, I got two listings, sold them both myself, and I made $37,000. I made huge money, and I was like, this is amazing. It was so good. That doesn't happen all the time. I wish that happened constantly. And from that point, that kind of got us going. Everything just started to flow and it was right.

Seeing that glimmer of success, Dan made a bold promise to Rachael that if he could make $100,000 in one year, an extremely rare feat for anyone starting out in the real estate industry, then she could leave her employment and join Dan.

Dan: So that year, I made $101,000. So I said, 'Hold on, you don't have to make this decision.' But then we said, 'No, we're going to both do this,' and Rachael decided to leave [her employer]. Every year it's grown since.

GUT!

Dan's incredible success in real estate drew heavily from his experiences while homeless. The ability to read people, the ability to sell yourself in various situations, and the hard work ethic in trying to survive from dawn to dusk helped inform his implicit learning. His explicit learning came from the real estate license he took in addition to the "teaching" of buying and selling when Dan and Rachael bought their first house.

When Dan's implicit learning and explicit learning came together, his success was a guarantee as long as he put in the work. The best way to summarize this is from Dan himself: "*It's kind of like, what we put in, we get back.*"

There are a variety of definitions of intuition, as one can see with a simple internet search. Because intuition is a seemingly intangible concept, it is difficult to pinpoint one particular definition. Based on the definition proposed in this book, which resounds with each one of the interviewees, there seem to be common misconceptions which differ from the one that we are using.

CHAPTER 15

Common Misconceptions

There are three main misconceptions on what intuition is: luck; being overly spiritual in nature; and rational decision-making.

The first misconception is that intuition is responsible for making decisions based on a lucky choice. Although this "lucky" decision may have resulted in a positive experience, there was little to no reasoning or past experience to support such a decision. We might as well have flipped a coin. None of the intuitive characteristics were present when making this decision; it was made as if we were "rolling a dice", such as selecting one of two restaurants where no prospective diners had previous experience eating at either of them.

The second misconception is that in order to tap into intuition, we must be overly spiritual in nature. Given that intuition occurs subconsciously, there may be a natural tendency to gravitate to explaining intuition from a more spiritual angle. This is further supported by some of us being able to access our intuitive thinking by meditating, which is the intuitive "medium" of choice (Part 3).

This is simply not the case. Many of us have been able to focus on our intuitive thoughts and make decisions or take actions based on intuition with no spiritual influence whatsoever.

The last misconception is that intuition is solely based on rational thinking, which relies on a clearly laid out process and the availability of data to support the decision, and pure deductive reasoning. In addition, the actions undertaken or behaviours demonstrated are usually habitual in nature. Although intuition does rely to some degree on rationality, it is not constrained by rational thought processes.

Research[28] has shown that athletes who had a preference for intuitive decisions made better and faster choices than athletes who had a preference for making rational decisions.

When intuitive decisions are being made, we do not go through any risk analysis, cost-benefit assessment, or weighing of alternatives. The decision is simply made.

Although there may be other misconceptions about intuition, these happen to be the three most common identified by many of the interviewees.

---

28 Raab, M, Laborde, S. (2011) When to Blink and When to Think: Preference for Intuitive Decision Results in Faster and Better Tactical Choices. Research Quarterly for Exercise and Sport; Mar 2011; 82,1

CHAPTER 16

Not all Positive Experiences

Although intuition generally guides us to good opportunities and positive personal and professional experiences, some interviewees experienced negative situations that were guided by their intuition. Although not pleasant in nature, these experiences were essential in helping shape their intuition, role, or purpose later in life.

These are not experiences that were due to a lack of judgment or overly emotional decisions. These were experiences that the individual knew he or she had to go through, with an intuitive purpose only discovered later in life. Such was the case for David Williams.

GUT!

David K. Williams is the Chief Executive Officer of Fishbowl, a private company in Orem, Utah that produces inventory management software called Fishbowl Inventory. Williams wrote a book for business professionals entitled *The 7 Non-Negotiables of Winning: Tying Soft Traits to Hard Results* that discusses lessons from David's experiences as a business leader. He also contributes to *Forbes*, *Harvard Business Review*, and *Inc. Magazine*, and has been recognized by a number of publications and companies including Inc. Magazine, Deloitte and Mountain West Capital.

David was CEO of Franklin Quest's Canadian division from 1989 to 1991 when he was recruited by Stephen Covey to be a part of his leadership team for The Covey Leadership Center. In 1996, Franklin Quest was looking to merge with The Covey Leadership Center, and David decided to leave before the merger as he did not see a great fit with his skills and the merger entity.

David and his family moved to Utah, and David became interested in an old steel mill located in Utah County because of his concern for a yellowish haze in the air that the mill produced, which caused David issues.

"Man, that's ugly! You could smell the sulfur, but we all just put up with it because it was there. And, on an intuition, I decided I was going to buy it and tear it down. Somebody's got to do something with that thing to get rid of those smokestacks and get rid of the roller mills. There was not much more than just getting going and starting it."

Although David's wife thought he was crazy, the least he could do was to stop the operation of the mill, clean it up, and sell it to other developers.

This mill was built during World War II and was used to make steel for ships. Because of competition overseas, by 1999 this steel mill had gone through two rounds of bankruptcy. There were only two creditors left after the Chapter 11 bankruptcies. The first was the US government that backed Citicorp bank because it was a steel mill and $550 million of unsecured debt.

"For three years I poured in all of my money. I bet the farm. I sold everything. I put $2.2 million into it of my own money. Plus, other people saw me making progress and wanted to be in on it – people who had worked for me or knew of me – wanted to be a part of it, and I said sure. So I had some private documents drawn up and raised another $1 million through that."

It took three years to clean up the land. David also had a local venture capitalist who raised $60 million and had some political connections that could help get a "pass" on the property and get it re-zoned. He sold the rolling mills to Japanese interests, and, a year-and-a-half into the cleanup, the yellow smoke had stopped.

The farmers in the area were also interested in investing in the property as they were lured by the possibility of a developer buying up the land, and David drew up some contracts for their investments.

In the three years David spent cleaning the property, he incurred hundreds of thousands of dollars in legal fees, involved engineers, architects, those involved in construction projects, and so on. Once David cleaned up the property, it was worth close to $3 billion.

And then the floor dropped on David, the property, and the investment money that came with it.

"Unbeknownst to me, the 'debtor in possession', a legal term for the person who was anointed by the court to manage the asset, was an attorney from Denver. In the last meeting, this attorney from Denver pulled out this other contract. And, all this time I was doing this work, he was duplicating everything and copying everything because I was kind of an open book and was transparent. And I thought they were being transparent with me.

"And they said to me, 'We will do exactly what you proposed. So therefore, thank you for all your work, we're going to go ahead and do it. We've already talked to the courts and we'll retain possession and do what they have approved for you to do.'"

Within 30 minutes, three years and all that money was gone and David had absolutely no recourse.

"So, something that was just a gut feeling to do turned into a horrific financial debacle for me. I was unemployed, probably in debt for the rest of my life and I could not get out of bed for the next two weeks."

A good friend of David's, who had put in a lot of legal time in the venture without getting paid, suggested that David go through bankruptcy. David talked to other attorneys who also gave him the same advice, and reached out to others who had gone through the bankruptcy process.

This might have been an easy route to take, but David's intuition was telling him that bankruptcy was not an option.

"I had this feeling that I just could not go bankrupt. I cannot live in this little valley or bump into people and try to hide and go to a restaurant and see somebody I owed money to, because I went bankrupt, did not get paid. I did not want to hide.

"After agonizing for days and weeks trying to figure out what to do, I just had this feeling come over me, this intuition – ask for time. People hear things all the time or have a vision. I don't. I distinctly had those words come into my mind at the time."

David had 176 people that he owed money to that ranged from a few thousand dollars to hundreds of thousands of dollars. He had 80 credit cards as well. Up to that point, he had never missed a payment on anything.

"So, I started to call every single one of these people, from credit cards to banks to lease companies to individuals I owed money to. And you know what? They all gave me time. I told them I can go bankrupt and you get nothing and you can write it off, which is better for you. Or, if you can give me time, I will start making the minimum payment this month. If it's $10 this month I will try and move it to $15 and then to $20 and then $50.

"As soon as I made that commitment, I started getting calls from all sorts of people that wanted consulting work done. I all of a sudden had all of these opportunities on being a consultant."

David began getting a number of clients, allowing him to earn enough revenues to start paying some of the creditors.

"Within three years, every one of the creditors was paid back."

A medical supply company had invested in a company called Fishbowl. After three years and several millions of dollars, nothing had come from its investment. In 2004, the owner of the medical supply company asked David to close it down.

David was able to turn the company around, pay off all of the debt, and grow the company at a 10-year average of 35%. Along the way, Fishbowl continued to win several honours and awards, including MountainWest Capital Network's Utah 100 each year from 2007 to 2013, recognition in the Utah Business Fast 50 from 2008 to 2010, ranked in Deloitte Technology's Fast500 from 2008 to 2013 and making the list on Inc. 500 from 2008 to 2011, among others.[29]

"If you stream all these things together, my intuition went from coming back to Utah to be with Covey, which was a good experience, my intuition to leave at the right time because I did not want to work when they both merged, and this silly notion to bring down this steel mill that led me to learn how to lose everything to then not going bankrupt and working uphill with people to eventually pay them off and then led me to an opportunity to do a turnaround with Fishbowl.

"And all of that was based on, to your point, a gut feeling, the right thing to do. Even on paper, not the right thing to do."

---
29 https://www.fishbowlinventory.com/awards

David uses these past experiences to shape the hiring practices he uses. He interviews each candidate to find out how much "fire they have in their belly" and what their long term goals are. He ensures everyone feels like a leader and is paired with another leader for support.

"I am probably one of your most intuitive leaders in terms of not looking at paper to make my decision. I don't look at any reports. I don't look at any leading indicators. The only thing I look at is our financial statements. I just have enough feel and can put my finger on the pulse of the company to kind of know if it needs a little bit of an adjustment here or there.

"I have given away 49% of the company to the employees. I give clear direction as to where the boundaries are, and it's pretty wide open, and I say, 'You know what, you are being hired because we believe in you and you are an intrapreneur here. You go create. If you can find a better way to do it, then do it.'"

One of the most intriguing aspects of David's journey that remained unanswered before giving an interview for the book is that he is surprised that he is not skeptical or paranoid of people, given the emotional and financial turmoil he experienced.

When it was suggested that his intuition actually led him to trust people because each one of his creditors gave him a chance to pay the associated debt back, he found the answer.

"You are right, Sunil. Thank you. That is the tie in right there. Because all these people trusted me whom, all of a sudden, I had the inability to pay them. All I took was money from them. But I paid them."

GUT!

David's financially devastating experience, guided by his intuition, gave him the ability to trust people. Every creditor had a choice to give him time or begin exploring other avenues. In fact, one leasing creditor told him that going bankrupt would actually help his reputation. But because each one of them had faith in David's word, and trusted him, David was able to pull himself up from a deep personal and professional hole.

This trust is something he has for those he hires. Providing that they have the attitude to perform at their highest level within the company David leads, the employees are trusted with autonomy and respect for their decisions in making things better in their area of influence. This is how Fishbowl has been able to maintain its successful journey.

Trusting our intuition is crucial in making the right decisions and actions at the right time; it also allows us to take advantage of opportunities that are presented to us. But learning how to trust intuition is a process unto itself.

GUT!

PART 2

How To **TRUST** It

Your time is limited, so don't waste it living someone else's life. Don't be trapped by dogma – which is living with the results of other people's thinking. Don't let the noise of others' opinions drown out your own inner voice. And most important, have the courage to follow your heart and intuition. They somehow already know what you truly want to become. Everything else is secondary.

– Steve Jobs

CHAPTER 1

The TRUST Model

Although we all have the ability to tap into intuition, it is rare to be able to completely master this ability with no hiccups. Some of us can use intuition more effectively than others, seeming like intuitive experts. However, at some point, intuitive hurdles will happen.

Some characterize those who have attained a higher level of spirituality as more advanced in their intuitive capabilities. Yet, even they have some hurdles they need to overcome, such as Vivek Gupta, a Hindu "Acharya" or respected spiritual teacher.

GUT!

Vivek Gupta, respectfully known as Vivekji, is a respected spiritual teacher who has travelled the world to teach others about the practical means for spiritual growth and happiness, enabling them to become positive contributors to society.

In high school, he began taking classes to look at a career in medicine before switching to wanting a career in business. After finishing a degree in business, his intuition let him know that he had a higher calling.

"I got to live in a monastery in India. For those two and a quarter years, 18 hours a day, all I did was study my mind, in other words, study myself. The more I got to know my mind, the more I got to know myself. Some would call that intuition."

Vivekji elaborates about the particulars of his journey and how intuition helped him move to India to learn about himself.

"There are a few points, factors that are at play here. The first is an element of seeing what others did before you. I saw that people who were seeking found some sort of completion by going down this path, and if they did it, then I can do it too. I'm a firm believer that if one person can do it, anyone can train themselves to do it as well. So, what have others done?

"Another point is just an element of confidence. Whatever you do, if done with confidence, will help you grow. Intuition is bringing me to experience confidence. I'm not saying you should be a rogue and do evil things and wicked things. Generally, if I'm confident about this path, and generally people are good people, then that's the right path.

"The third is an element of risk. That you just have to try, and as you try, you keep on adapting or even letting go of that path that you've chosen, becomes a reality.

"I think about what I've done in the last six years, in regards to developing my inner self and the work that I do. On this path, as one becomes more powerful one becomes gentler. I've sought the advice of those people who've done this before, who have built up great inner strength and are leading other people to do the same. Then I am confident that I have great potential, just like everyone does.

"The beauty of being wise, the beauty of intuition, is that it's humbling. Not the other way around, because when one becomes more powerful, one becomes more humble. Whereas corrupt power leads to arrogance."

Vivekji articulates his thoughts on what intuition is from a spiritual angle, a large part of which is about getting to know ourselves.

"As we get to know more about ourselves, intuition has to break away from logic, because logic is limited to experiences. I can't just learn from my experiences, I have to learn from your experiences, and even an experience that never happened, I still have to be able to learn from that. It rises to that creative aspect.

"Our fundamental nature is awareness, and we've drifted from that. Studies have shown that with driving, 90% of the time we are unconscious. My nature is consciousness, but I'm just not identifying with my nature, so I don't apply my nature. When someone starts to practice awareness more, they're realigning with their infinite potential. The more I am tune in with awareness, the fewer mistakes I make.

"Intuition manifests when the mind and intellect are fully efficient, are fully effective. The perfection is inside. And even if there is inefficiency or ineffectiveness, one is not limited by this."

For Vivekji, the hurdle that he encounters in operating at the highest level intuitively is that, as one moves to a higher level spiritually, the time required to attain that level increases exponentially.

"I'm finding that the learning curve is becoming steeper and steeper. Let's say the change from being an angry person to a less angry person requires 5 years and 5,000 hours. To go from a less angry person to 'non-angry' person is going to take 50 years and 50,000 hours!

"The steepening learning curve demands that one practice awareness constantly. If you want to be an Olympic swimmer you have to practice every day, skipping even one day is not an option. If I only want to be a high school swimmer, sure I can practice a few times a week. For myself, the aspiration is to tune into perfection and nothing less will be satisfactory. Nothing else is worth the effort; it's perfection or not. This is becoming more challenging, and I'm aware this means I need to work harder. I need to practice constantly. I need to be more aware of the way I'm thinking, speaking, and acting, and my attitudes and motives behind these expressions."

For Vivekji, this journey to reach a higher level means there are opportunity costs when choosing one path over another.

"The challenge of prioritizing is becoming difficult, thereby inhibiting further developing this intuition. Everything in life is an opportunity cost. You talking to me is an opportunity cost, which means you can't talk to someone else, and vice versa. When one is clear about the need for intuition, one makes that a priority, and that means one has to let go of complacency, whether it's a vice, whether it's an indulgence, whether it's a vacation, whether it's sleeping in, whatever it is.

"But, to hold on to the higher, you have to let go of the lower, and that's difficult, especially since we're so used to this. If we believe this is normal, if we believe this is functional, then it's hard to see the light that, I really do need to let go of the lower to grasp onto the higher."

GUT!

Vivekji has dedicated his life to reaching a higher purpose in life yet, even with greater internal understanding, he encounters hurdles.

We are no different. Despite each one of us having intuitive ability, we will all experience hurdles that will dampen our abilities to tap into intuition effectively.

The ideal situation is to minimize the intuitive hurdles. Although this is a work in progress, we hope that we take many steps forward and only a few steps back. To limit the number of "back-steps", we should traverse each of the steps in the **TRUST** model.

Tune Into Ourselves

Remove Hindrances

Understand Our Intuitive Drivers

Sense the Internal Indicators

Take Notice of External Indicators

CHAPTER 2

Tune Into Ourselves

We all have the ability to establish a cognitive connection to our intuition regardless of the circumstances in which we may find ourselves. Furthermore, sensations, feelings, and other such personal triggers, called indicators, help provide a message that intuition is "telling us something".

Even when intuition and associated indicators try to help guide a decision or action, some of us still find it difficult to recognize intuitive signals, primarily due to a lack of self-awareness, which prevents us from recognizing that intuition is at play.

Research[30] has shown that being self-aware or mindful showed brain activity in the Dorsomedial Prefrontal Cortex and Posterior Cingulate (Figure 9), parts of the brain that are responsible for planning complex cognitive behaviour, personality expression, decision-making, and moderating social behaviour.[31]

Further research[32] has shown that if we are more self-aware, we can inhibit the neural pathways that lead to depression and anxiety, reduce mental suffering, and amplify the neural connections that enhance our mental well-being.

Being self-aware through proper mindfulness training should make us better at changing the neural pathways that hamper some of the

---

30 Lanius, R., Bluhm, R. & Frewen, P. (2011) How understanding the neurobiology of complex post-traumatic stress disorder can inform clinical practice: a social cognitive and affective neuroscience approach. Acta Psychiatr Scand: 124: 331–34
31 Yang Y & Raine A (2009). "Prefrontal structural and functional brain imaging findings in antisocial, violent, and psychopathic individuals: a meta-analysis". Psychiatry Research 174 (2): 81–8.
32 Siegel, D. (2007) Mindfulness training and neural integration: differentiation of distinct streams of awareness and the cultivation of well-being. Social Cognitive and Affective Neuroscience. Dec; 2(4): 259–263.

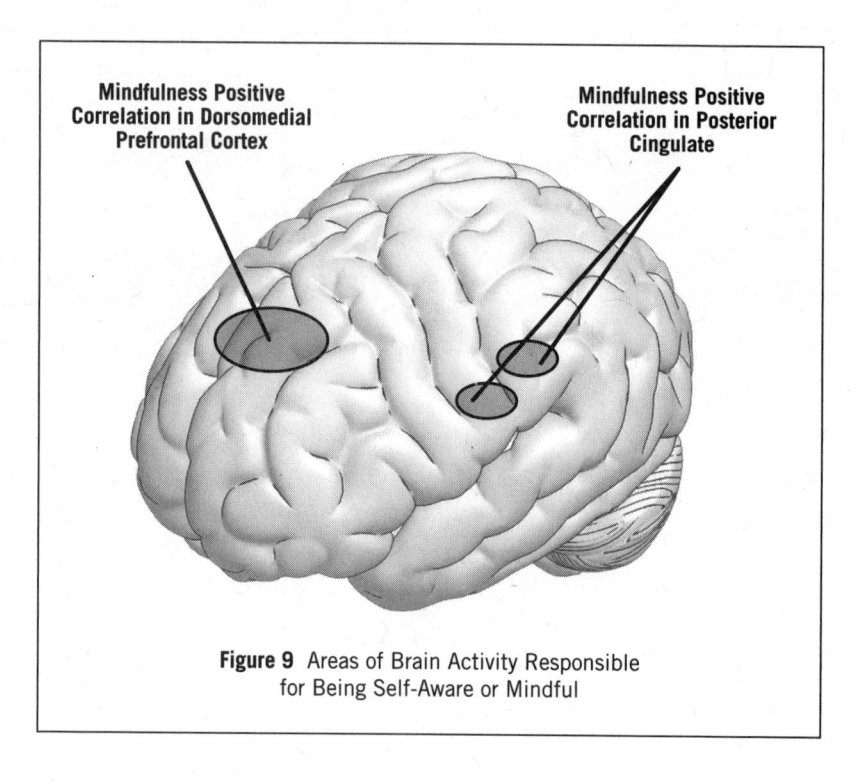

Mindfulness Positive Correlation in Dorsomedial Prefrontal Cortex

Mindfulness Positive Correlation in Posterior Cingulate

Figure 9 Areas of Brain Activity Responsible for Being Self-Aware or Mindful

intuitive processes and allow intuition to fully express itself. This self-awareness is an important part of Al Katz's comedy routine.

GUT!

Al Katz is a comedian who has headlined comedy clubs for over twenty years and has had numerous television appearances, including Showtime Comedy Club Network, HBO, Comedy Central, The Oprah Winfrey Show, and The Today Show. More recently, he has been a regular part of the entertainment on cruise ships.

Each performance is unique. The venues may be the same, but the audience members are not. Al gets one chance to assess what type of crowd he will face. Getting this wrong may result in a lackluster performance with the wrong type of jokes or a chance he may offend someone, both of which have ramifications for his career.

"It's like on stage, I look at the crowd immediately. The thing is I have to do it off stage from behind the curtain because when the lights hit me on stage, I can't see anybody. So, I react off of sound. I'll look at a direction when someone's talking. Every show is different. How do you get a standing ovation on one show and the next show you're doing the same material for a different group and people are heckling...why?

"Like last night I had to read that audience in a split second and put on my blinders because if I react to it, it could backfire. So, my gut tells me, stay away. Don't go to that section. If I even look there, it gives them permission to come in."

In essence, his comedy routine can only start when his intuition lets him know that he is comfortable moving ahead. He talks about how this intuition manifests itself. If Al is not self-aware, he is not able to pick up the signals that are telling him that either he is okay continuing with his routine, or that he should change direction to deliver a great performance.

"It's a gut feeling and then your hair stands up on end and you're like, 'Wow I can't believe it.' That's what gut feelings do. Something sends a message to your brain and you've got to do it, there's a reason for it. I took it into the entertainment profession.

"Johnny Carson used to say, you do things in three. You do a joke, you can do the punch line and you can do a tag on the punch line and a second tag, there's your three. If you keep pushing it to get more laughs within that string now you're stretching it and your laugh factor goes down. You've got to learn to read that correctly and there's times when my gut's saying, okay stop at three, that's the thing, that's the magic number and then you over-read your own feelings and you can feel where the laughter hits on a one-to-ten.

"It hits that ten and you're feeling great and you say, 'I'm going to do another one' and then you feel oh, wow that was a seven and what does your gut say, stop at three and you learn your lesson. It's the same if there is a problem with an audience and someone says something and you throw a jab at them and you get a good laugh on it and you come back with a second one and a third. Once you hit that fourth one your insides say no don't do it, stop. And then you do it and now the audience turns on you because you're pushing it, now you're the jerk. That's one of the magic numbers."

If Al does make a mistake when reading people, it could backfire.

"It's same with Bill Cosby. If there's a guy sitting with his arms crossed and maybe not even giving me eye contact, he calls it the face. Look at the face. Your ego wants everyone to laugh – "why aren't you laughing" – and you go after him and it ruins your show. Bill says, don't go after him. Leave the face alone. You don't know if they're having bad days. That's the hard part, you don't know what people have gone through before the show.

"I looked out the curtain last night, I saw four people sleeping. They were 'zzz'd' out, mouth open, one lady had her shoulder on another lady's shoulder. The stage crew was panning the audience and they were picking out people. We have a camera, a TV in the back and they panned in on this lady and she was 'zzzz'd'. She was out. Now, are you just resting before the show starts? If I walk out and I see that then I have to call attention to it. It's a laugh, it's a cheap laugh but what are you sleeping at my show for? You have all day to sleep and you come to my show, you sit in the front row and sleep? I don't get it.

"One gut says leave them alone, let them sleep, the other gut says scare the heck out of them. Or just jump out and scream in their ear, teach them a lesson. I have different thoughts with different audiences. You can do it to a younger person and have fun with it but if I'm on Holland America and they're 80 years old and if I would have the same reaction I could cause a person's death. Gut feeling says leave them alone.

"I walked out one time at a show on a Holland America and I had five people in the front row, mouth open, they were out. Thank you for napping during my show. You make attention to it and you move on. But you see my mind goes like that where I have to react off the reaction and it's got to be in a split second and I usually know what's good and what's bad, but that's also experience."

Al's ability to listen to his intuition is crucial for preparing for the audience, but he also uses it in his business affairs.

"I'll give you another example of what I consider was a gut feeling. I was represented by an agent for colleges and she's doing really well and got me a lot of dates for colleges. The money was great.

"This other agent, who I became friends with, wanted to represent me although I was on a contract with the other person. He called me up out of the blue and said, 'I've got a show for you,' and I said, 'Okay, see my agent and you guys do a split on commission.' You're allowed to do that. Instead of giving one agent 15%, if someone else finds me a job I can still do it but you have to do a 7 ½% split. He didn't want to do that. He wanted to prove he could get me work and steal me from my agent.

"Something inside said there's something wrong with this.

"He knows I'm under contract. He's going backwards to do this and it's wrong. Here's how he stated it to me: 'I've got this show. Will you do it for $1,200?' Well, yeah, I'd do it for $1,200 if you're making $1500, because then that's your commission, the $300. I said, 'Yes, I would do it if you're making $1,500.'

"He said, 'Well, are you going to do it?' I said, 'It depends on what you're making. If you're making $5,000, I'll give you $450 and I'm making the other $4,550.' He says, 'So you won't do it for $1,200?'

Al's ability to be aware of himself and recognize the intuitive indicators tipped him off and he instantly knew that this new agent was lying to him.

"Yes, I would do that for $1,200 but you're scamming me. In a heartbeat, I knew he was scamming me. I don't know how badly. I end up booking another show in the area and so, you know what? The $1,200 would be good. So, I went ahead and took the job.

"I drove from Chicago to New York to do the gig and he's not letting me know where my hotel is. I'm having bad feelings. He actually didn't have a hotel. He put me on his couch. Although I was upset, being this way was not the way to go into a performance, and as a pro you have to blank it out and go on with the show. Afterward, the people at the university handed me an envelope and said, 'We forgot to mail this to your agent. Can you bring this to him?'

"I open the envelope. $2,500, not $1,200. He scammed me.

"I ripped up the cheque and put it in another envelope so he didn't know I'd opened it. Although he kept asking for the envelope with what he thought was a $2,500 cheque, I waited until I got my $1,200 first before giving it to him. I wanted him to go through the hassle of getting his money. I gave my agent her full commission and I explained to her what happened and we basically blackballed the guy – lesson learned for him.

He scammed me and went behind the rules. I just couldn't believe he did that. It's just bad business.

"That type of thing, that's your intuition. You know what they are going to say; you're a partner. You can tell when the same partner turns around and screws you that way because they did something and you're used to a pattern and that ignites something inside your body that something is wrong. There's a spark that goes off: I don't feel right."

The example Al gives above shows that being aware of his intuition allowed him to leverage his strength in relational intuition. This has also given him the ability to listen to his situational intuition.

"My agent and her brother stayed over at my house in Chicago. Something happened in the house and we reacted: 'Something's wrong.' And we looked outside, something made us look out the front window. My agent's brother had a tour bus and it was on fire. Something made us look. We didn't hear noises. I said, 'Hold on, something's wrong.' They're like, 'What?' 'I don't feel right, something's happening. Something's happening right now,' and we looked out the window and we caught the thing just in time and we saved his bus. He was like, 'You got to be kidding me.'"

GUT!

Al's ability to tap into his various types of intuition is an integral part of not only his personal situations, but also his professional success. When he is self-aware, he is aware of his intuition. He listens to it, trusts it, and then acts on it.

Others have the same ability to tap into their intuition on a regular basis. What stops them from doing this from time to time is the intuitive hindrances that they are not able to remove.

CHAPTER 3

Remove Intuitive Hindrances

As mentioned previously, research[33][34] has shown that an intuitive decision occurs much earlier than the associated execution, with both intuition and associated execution affecting different areas of the brain.

Before we execute on the intuitive thought, the intuition goes through an emotional filter, showing up in the Amygdala and Ventromedial Prefrontal Cortex[35][36] (Figure 10) before an actual decision is made, which shows up in the Ventromedial Prefrontal Cortex part of the brain[37].

If we are able to control our emotional filters, intuition can be fully expressed. However, if we hinder our intuitive thinking, we ignore what intuition is telling us and we either do nothing or do something at odds with our intuition's suggestion. This often leads to uncomfortable situations such as not feeling happy internally, not feeling in control, and possibly experiencing some difficult situations.

There are four culprits that hinder our ability to make intuitive decisions: fearing failure, being overly emotional, having a big ego, and being overly rational.

---

33 Bode, S., et al. (2011). Tracking the unconscious generation of free decisions using ultra-high field fMRI. PloS one, 6(6), e21612
34 Soon, C. S et al. (2008). Unconscious determinants of free decisions in the human brain. Nature neuroscience, 11(5), 543-545.
35 Seymour, B., & Dolan, R. (2008). Emotion, decision making, and the amygdala. Neuron, 58(5), 662-671.
36 Winecoff, A., et al. (2013). Ventromedial prefrontal cortex encodes emotional value. The Journal of Neuroscience, 33(27), 11032-11039.
37 Ronningstam, E., & Baskin-Sommers, A. R. (2013). Fear and decision-making in narcissistic personality disorder – a link between psychoanalysis and neuroscience. Dialogues in clinical neuroscience, 15(2), 191.

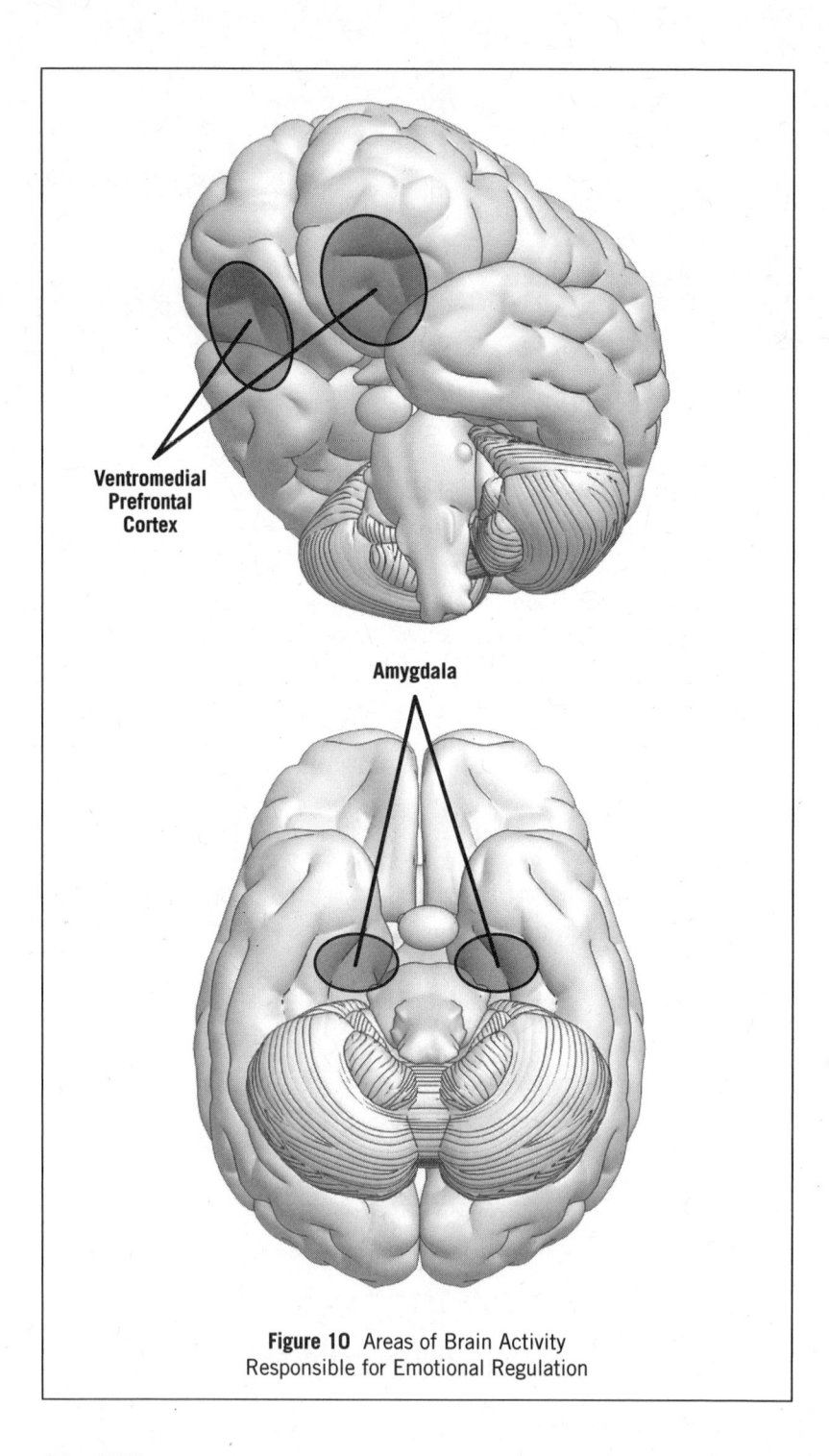

Figure 10 Areas of Brain Activity Responsible for Emotional Regulation

3.1 Fearing Failure

Fearing failure is a hindrance that generally overrides intuition. Even though intuition tells us that we should make a certain decision or act in a particular way, sometimes we doubt ourselves. This fear or doubt, which research[38][39] has shown manifests itself in the part of the brain called the Ventrolateral Prefrontal Cortical regions (Figure 10), questions the intuition and we begin to make excuses as to why we should not act on it, creating a lot of unnecessary chatter in our heads.

This constant chatter leads to self-doubt, which creates a number of issues, such as believing that we lack the necessary skills or confidence to move the intuition forward even when we know that the intuitive thought is correct.

This self-doubt resulted in Ambrose Duncan losing her bakery.

GUT!

After graduating from university with a Bachelor of Commerce degree, Ambrose Duncan was keen on working right away. She did not have substantial work experience, going into university right from high school, and she had no preconceived notions of where she wanted to work.

"I was strolling along a particular street in my neighbourhood and stopped in a coffee shop to get something to eat, and to think about what I wanted to do next. I ordered a large coffee, picked a chocolate chip muffin, sat down, and began to think about what type of business I wanted to work in. I bit into the muffin, and it was the best chocolate chip muffin I had ever tasted. I finished it so quickly that I had to go up to order another one. I finished the last one so I decided to try the banana loaf instead. I sat down again, took a bite, and it was extremely tasty."

After finding out the name of the bakery supplier, Ambrose paid a visit and began ordering bakery items directly from the supplier. Over the next few weeks, she noticed that the workers were always in a rush, so she casually asked the owner how busy she was.

---

38 Torrisi, S. et al. (2013). Differences in resting corticolimbic functional connectivity in bipolar I euthymia. Bipolar disorders, 15(2), 156-166.
39 Asp, E., et al. (2012). A neuropsychological test of belief and doubt: damage to ventromedial prefrontal cortex increases credulity for misleading advertising. Frontiers in neuroscience, 6.

"She pointed to a paper with close to 20 names of businesses on it that were all part of a backlog for that day. It was clear that she was understaffed and since I was looking for a job, I asked if I could join her company. She was more than happy to bring me on board. I gained a tremendous amount of baking skills over the next six months."

Not only did Ambrose succeed in the back, but she also excelled at the customer service side of the business.

"I had noticed that when customers came to pick up their orders, the other team members who were baking with me did not smile or ask if they wanted anything else besides what they were picking up. My intuition kicked in every time this happened. I would get this sensation in my head that would tell me that I should be the one talking to the customers. It was clear that the others did not seem comfortable doing this anyway. So, I asked the others if I could take over dealing with the customers, and they all looked relieved when I asked, letting me know that they would help pick up the slack in the baking area if I got busy."

After Ambrose began working the front area, sales started to climb.

"It was really quite simple. I talked to customers like they were my friends. We would also share some stories of what happened on the weekend and go into some family stuff and things like that. I found out the things that their family liked to eat and so I began making suggestions that they buy other baked goods that they had never tried before. And they were more than happy to try them."

Amber was adept at the customer relationship side of the business, and began taking an interest in the business side as well.

"So I asked the owner if she could take me under her wing and teach me about the business."

The owner appreciated the offer and took Ambrose under her wing, allowing the owner to concentrate on getting out of the bakery to generate sales.

After seeing the growth in the customer orders, experiencing how the operations worked, developing new baking products, and reviewing the financials from time to time, Ambrose became interested in running her own bakery.

"One day, I woke up, and on my way to work I was thinking about the bakery. And when I turned the corner, I looked at the bakery sign, and within an instant my gut told me that, you know what, I could do this. I could run my own bakery. And my mind was already telling me that I already knew how to order supplies, bake a variety of items, ask customers to order more, and I could see how well this bakery was doing financially. It was that quick. So, why am I not that confident? And this was a back and forth kind of thing. My intuition is telling me that this is so natural. And I feel very calm with those thoughts. But then, my mind begins to wander, and I don't feel very confident."

Ambrose began arguing with herself.

"On the one hand, I know I have all the skills. And I know that my intuition is telling me this. But when I reflect, I somehow question my intuition. What if this happens, what if that happens, what if, what if, what if. I feel so crazy."

Ambrose approached the bakery's owner and asked her opinion.

"I actually thought she was going to fire me for asking her for her opinion, but, in fact, she was so supportive. She kept telling me that I would be good in sales because it was all about relationships. And she reminded me that I had my fingers in every part of the business. Then she took my shoulders, sat me down, looked in my eyes and asked me what my gut feeling was. And I told her. So she said good luck and, with a smile on her face, she told me to get the heck out of the store."

Although the owner would be losing an excellent resource, she understood the entrepreneurial spirit and wished her well.

"I knew that I had to be located close to the opposite end of the city so that I had access to a new set of customers. I took a drive out that way and saw a really nice place that was close to a number of small offices. I took a bit of a drive around and noticed some coffee shops in the area. I knew that I could market to both of the coffee shops to get them to sell my baked goods and maybe provide the offices with something in the mornings. So I signed the lease on the space, dipped into my savings and also asked some family members to help pitch in, which I would pay back in the first year."

Ambrose started with a small oven at first and began to bake in the afternoons while spending the mornings visiting potential customers. Slowly, over the course of the next four to five weeks, she supplied her baked goods to three coffee shops and also delivered coffee and baked goods to a few offices around her building.

"Things were going well and I was getting busy, but my time was being spent running around trying to fill orders and find customers. I also needed some help baking as I spent literally no time making new products. So I put a 'Help Wanted' sign in the door, and pretty soon I had five people come into the store to talk to me about a job."

She hired three of the five who approached her and put them to work right away, freeing her up to spend more time outside the bakery to woo more customers. With her customer relationship talents, she signed on a few more offices, but these required more effort because of the time spent delivering the baked goods and picking up the trays at the end of each day. She needed to get more coffee shops carrying her product, which meant that she had to travel more, which increased her travel expenses, including gas and meals.

Despite her intuition telling her that she would have no issues gaining customers, she had this fear that she just could not do it. She feared that she would fail.

"I had fun going to these offices and asking for their business. But I started to feel bad about asking them to buy other bakery products. There were no complaints about my prices, the food taste, or the delivery. In fact, I was talking to an office which had over 50 employees and met some of them. They were telling me about some of the other bakery items they liked. And, instantly, my intuition told me to tell them that I can make the items they wanted and have them delivered on a regular basis. But I stopped myself. Why? I don't know.

"There were other offices who asked me for my suggestion, and I gave them a smaller order to start with. My intuition was telling me, 'Hey, why are you giving a small order?' And I was fighting my intuition. And when I left the building, I began mentally kicking myself that this could have been a bigger order."

Ambrose needed these larger orders as her bank account was

dwindling. After being pampered with a decent bank balance, she now faced a thinner one as her travel expenses, employees, and marketing expenses began to take a toll on the cash balance.

"I was used to having a good bank balance every month, but now with the wages, it was very hard to write those cheques because bringing on those three people really drained the bank account. But I needed those employees because I needed the business to grow and I needed to bring in more customers, which seemed to be going well. Plus these brochures really set me back and I was starting to see the bank balance get down to less than $500 on some days, and this really worried me."

One of the larger coffee shops in the area made a deal with Ambrose, offering a one-year contract to carry her baked goods every day with the option of paying after 60 days. Ambrose became excited because she had an opportunity to sell a tremendous number of baked products to a busy coffee shop, bringing in much-needed cash.

She felt an incredible amount of relief with this order, but with a smaller bank balance, she got a feeling that the deal was not so rosy for her.

"I had this creepy feeling inside me, this mild burning telling me that this was not the right decision to make. I was imagining my bank balance and seeing it quite thin all the time. Once again, my gut kicked in to warn me. But I feared that if I don't do this, I would fail. I did not want to fail. I was scared of failing. Even though the better solution was to increase the size of orders and not stretch the bank, I did not pay attention to that solution."

Thirty days later, a lot of inventory went out the door to the coffee shop, but the cash from that coffee shop was still 30 days away.

"Yes, I did see a big increase in revenues and lots of baked goods going out the door, but the problem was I still had to wait another 30 days for that money to hit my bank account. Meanwhile, I'm sitting here writing cheques for rent, wages, utilities, flyers, and a whole bunch of other expenses here and there. My bank balance was now around $500."

Because of the lack of funds, Ambrose was reminded that her payroll deductions owed to Revenue Canada were due, but decided to put off making these payments so that she could pay her day-to-day bills – and she continued to put these payments off for a year. She knew her ship was sinking.

"I started to fight my fears of failing and began asking for larger orders. But I remember doing this very sheepishly. When I was working for my boss, I never felt uncomfortable in making more suggestions. I knew I had to do this again. It was a matter of survival now."

She approached one of her larger customers to ask for a larger order and started to walk in the office.

"I actually felt calm. It was as if I was in my element. I kept asking the right questions, and my intuition told me to suggest this and this. And pretty soon, I had a 50% increase in the weekly order. And I walked away feeling like this was going to work."

Unfortunately, this elation was short-lived. Ambrose had to invest in another oven, which required monthly lease payments. Additional reminders from Revenue Canada forced her to reveal the amount she owed to the government, and it was very high. There was still hope, but her fear of failure came back again.

"I had the confidence to increase the order size again. I knew I could get more orders. It was so natural. But I began to think about rejection and what if I was not able to make the right suggestions? I would be a failure in my customers' eyes."

After a painful phone call from Revenue Canada reminding her about her payroll deductions, interest, penalties and possible legal action, Ambrose consulted some family members to discuss the situation.

"They gave me a dose of reality: I had to throw in the towel. There was no way I could make those payments. What was even worse, which made me sick to my stomach, was that there was no way I could pay back my family immediately. The only way I could do that is to go out, get a job, and pay them whatever I could."

Ambrose tried putting the bakery up for sale by putting an advertisement in the paper as well as a sign on the door, but when a few people phoned in asking about the business in general, they never phoned back. Finally, one day, Ambrose stepped out of the bakery, turned around, and locked the front door for good. She then went home and called the closest bankruptcy trustee to begin the proceedings to file for bankruptcy.

"I lost it all. I kept putting things off and the amount that I owed to the government just kept getting bigger and bigger. And it was not as if I could just ignore the government. They were going to get their money at some point. I guess I didn't grow the business fast enough. But now I have an incredible learning experience. I hope there are others reading this story that will learn from it."

Ambrose eventually went to work for another company unrelated to the baking industry. She was a natural salesperson and continues to do well in that role today.

GUT!

Ambrose's intuition told her that she had all the skills and knowledge necessary to succeed in the bakery business. Yet, her fear of failure and self-doubt curtailed her ability to increase order sizes, which would have increased her profits and her bank balance. She should have trusted her intuition all along.

To trust our intuition, we need to control our emotions. Out of control emotions hinder our ability to tap into our intuition that helps guide us to successful opportunities, or move us away from painful situations, such as the one Howard Payne found himself in.

3.2 Being Overly Emotional

When we express our intuition, it must go through an emotional filter before we can act on it. We need to control our emotions in order to take the appropriate decision or action.

If we allow our emotions to evaluate intuitive thoughts, we will begin to question the intuition and the associated actions. Eventually, we become overly emotional, and the questioning leads to a mistrust of the intuition, and we fail to act on it.

As discussed previously, the Amygdala and Ventrolateral Prefrontal Cortical areas of the brain are responsible for emotional regulation (Figure 10). In addition, research has shown that over-emotion was responsible for biasing certain future decisions and reducing any perceived risk, which would cloud our ability to make the proper decisions given the situation.

When we are in control of our emotions, we feel less anxious and better able to make the appropriate decisions or take the appropriate actions based on our intuitive thoughts. This level of control was shown in a research article[40] where the heart rates and skin conductance levels were much higher for decisions based on chance when compared to decisions made more intuitively.

When we fail to control our emotions, we hinder our intuitive abilities, which leads us to take a different decision or action. For Howard Payne, an overly emotional decision led to a personal and professional disaster.

GUT!

Howard Payne is a business development and operations professional with over 15 years of experience working for start-up technology companies. He completed his MBA degree and began working at a business where he was brought in to help commercialize a breakthrough patented technology by establishing key contacts with investors and companies who could provide the proper financing to commercialize the technology.

Although Howard did not have a background or experience with this technology, he did have a substantial rolodex of potential financiers and commercialization partners.

Over the next two years, Howard organized a number of collaborations worldwide, gaining deep knowledge in technology transfer and commercialization.

"I was able to bring a couple of my past colleagues to the bargaining table that would have given us a great financial shot in the arm as we still needed some more money to finance the ongoing research and development. We spent some money finding out what the company was worth so that when the investors were looking to give us money, we were able to see how much of the company we would have to give up."

---

40 La Pira, F., et al. (2013). Validating nonlocal intuition in repeat entrepreneurs: a multi-method approach. *Journal of Behavioral Studies in Business, 6.*

The investors were looking to put in $2 million and to get 25% of the company shares in exchange for that amount.

"This was an absolutely fair exchange of value."

However, the founder was not convinced. He was more interested in keeping as much of the company for himself as possible. At a particular bargaining session, the negotiations went from warm to frosty.

"We all sat down and after some time with idle chatter, I presented the proposed financial offer from the investors who were colleagues of mine. They wanted 25% and the owner wanted 10%. Initially there was laughter, but the smiles quickly went away when the owner looked serious. There was no way that he would get such a valuation for the technology. His delusion over the value was so far from reality."

This is when Howard's intuition was triggered.

"I knew that I had to convince the founder that he had to rethink the whole deal. The valuation was a very fair one. If we did not get this financing, there were a lot of things at stake – the survival of the company, the relationship I had with my colleagues, and my future at the company. The owner needed to see the difference between owning a patented technology that is going nowhere fast given how much we were spending every month, and getting the $2 million proposed so that we could continue looking for a larger company to buy the company out. The owner would make a significant amount of money by giving up a little piece of the pie."

But Howard questioned himself.

"I started to think about the consequences of asking him to rethink his version of the company valuation. Maybe he would get upset at me. Maybe I would be fired. Maybe I could ask my friends to reconsider."

With the negotiations going nowhere, the potential investors exited with the firm offer remaining on the table for another 30 days. Howard entered the owner's office to try to get him to reconsider the value of the company.

"The owner was very unwilling to budge from his valuation. I gave him a very quick reminder that we needed the money to move forward.

Otherwise we may not have the ability to recover financially and would need to sacrifice more of the company if our financial backs were against the wall.

"He just looked at me and smiled. He told me that he could not let go of his 'baby' that easily. I reminded him that commercialization would reap financial rewards for him. He just needed to be fair at the table. I also reminded him that the investment community is quite small and if he was not going to provide proper valuation for the company shares, my rolodex would begin to dry up.

"The owner thanked me for my advice and told me that he would apply for some small loans to keep us going. It was at this point that I had this strong feeling, which had to be my intuition, that I had to leave this company. My efforts were not going anywhere."

Even though Howard knew he had to leave, he began an emotional chain of excuses justifying why he should not leave.

"I was concerned about the employees and what would happen to them if I left and the company was not able to find financing. I also felt that I still could fix things, that I could bring back my two colleagues at maybe a valuation in the middle and that I could keep the owner happy. My wife, Clara, was very upset as well because I was bringing a lot of the stress home and it would affect my relationship with her and the kids. I found myself staring at the ceiling and the walls, trying to work out a solution in my head."

Clara had known what the best route was for Howard.

"Clara told me that I, personally, knew what the right thing to do was. I was too concerned with others and their feelings who had no relevance to my situation."

Despite the pleas from his wife, Howard continued at the company with the goal of finding financing at a lower valuation and trying to source a commercialization partner.

The owner paid an unexpected visit to Howard's office.

"He looked at me, raised his arms in the air, shrugged his shoulders and told me to bring back my two colleagues. I had this instant feeling of *gratitude and happiness come together. In that instant, I no longer felt that I needed to think about moving on.*

"But the owner asked me to deliberately change some of the financial information so that we were able to get the $2 million for 10% of the company. My intuitional antennae went off like crazy. I think I even smelled smoke coming from my ears. I knew that I needed to move on. But, instead of getting up and walking out, I made another dumb suggestion. 'Let's hire another CEO to move this negotiation forward.'

"I don't know what I was thinking. My gut reaction, twice now, was to leave. And here I am trying to find nonsensical solutions for an owner who clearly will not be able to move his company forward. I honestly pinched myself because this did not seem like reality. But it was."

Surprisingly, the owner agreed to have a CEO join the company. He found an individual with some industry experience who was also ready to provide some capital funding to help relieve the financial pressure.

"I was relieved. We not only had a pool of funds to move forward with, but I now had someone who should be able to see my side of things to move the company forward."

For two months, Howard worked side by side with the new CEO making various investor pitches around the country and was then asked to concentrate on attracting commercialization partners, which he was more than happy to do.

During this same period, he also received numerous senior management employment offers from large companies. These were lucrative contracts with a high base salary and stock options.

"Clara kept telling me to take the offers because the owner of the company could not be trusted and the CEO, who is a friend of the owner, may not be trustworthy as well. My intuition was almost forcibly telling me to take each one of the positions I was offered. But, once again, I questioned the intuition. I kept thinking we have a new CEO and we are getting investor attention and things will be great, and yes, I shut out my intuition. Absolutely."

One year passed and while in another city attending a conference, Howard received a strange call from one of the investors that he brought to the table.

"So he calls me up and congratulates me on the increase in business we had in the past year and was in the process of signing the paperwork to close $2 million in financing for 10% of the company. He was to meet the new CEO and open a champagne bottle, and asked if I was going to be there.

"At this point, my spidey senses are tingling big time because we had no increase in business. In fact, our revenues declined slightly. I had to say something at this point because now things seemed criminal to me."

Howard told the investor that he should walk away from the deal immediately as someone "cooked the books".

Howard returned to the city that night. The next morning, he tried to enter the building and his card key would not work. He tried calling a number of employees, the owner or the CEO, and nobody would respond. Suddenly, security personnel asked him to leave the property and told him that he could collect his things at the security office the next day.

Howard was fired.

He picked up his things the next day, which also included a letter from the employer. In the letter, it stated that Howard misled investors with erroneous financial information and that he was solely responsible for any future financial debacle the company may find itself in.

"There was a final cheque written to me with no additional amounts added for severance pay or holiday pay, and in the description line, it said 'Thanks for nothing.' Clearly an immature move. I packed everything in the car, drove home, and had an emotional meltdown."

Howard had to be treated for depression for six months, and it took another six months to find employment.

"Had I trusted my intuition at the beginning and not gotten into all of this emotional thinking and wafting, my employment situation would be entirely different. Being too emotional and not trusting my intuition came with a huge personal and professional opportunity cost."

GUT!

Howard had several opportunities where his intuition was telling him to get out of the company and move on. Yet, his emotional thinking got the best of him, and he did not allow himself to trust his intuition. Not only did this get him fired, but he suffered both mentally and financially after being forced out of the company.

Emotional thinking acted like a barrier, preventing Howard the opportunity to act on his intuitive thoughts. Ego does the same thing as well, as Sharon Brennan discovered.

3.3 Having a Big Ego

According to the Merriam-Webster dictionary, ego is defined as *"the opinion that you have of yourself "*.

Not only are we concerned with how we see ourselves, but our egos drive us to be concerned about how we project ourselves and the impressions we create on others.

This seems natural; we are social animals after all. Philosophically, we may argue that we are not concerned about what others think of our opinions and actions. However, how we actually conduct ourselves in social situations might contradict such arguments.

Ego hinders our intuitive capability when we place an overemphasis on how others perceive us. Research[41] has shown that a significant difference between our actual self-esteem compared to what we prefer to project hinders our intuitive capabilities.

Our intuition may tell us to do one thing, but we will try to predict how acting on the intuition will be perceived by others. If our intuitive decisions defy common logic or go against what the majority of people believe, for example, we may face negative reactions and adverse comments or we could be seen as unpopular.

Ego also becomes hindered when we portray ourselves as someone different from who we really are. We make statements or buy certain items to portray a certain image. If this image is congruent with where we are in both our personal and professional lives, then intuition will not be affected.

However, if there is an incongruence, then we might ignore our intuition to maintain the image we wish to portray. We fail to share our true opinions, make the right decision or take the right action, much like Sharon Brennan.

GUT!

---

[41] Jordan, C. H., Whitfield, M., & Zeigler-Hill, V. (2007). Intuition and the correspondence between implicit and explicit self-esteem. Journal of personality and social psychology, 93(6), 1067.

Sharon Brennan is Vice-President of Affiliate Development and Programs at Habitat for Humanity, Heartland Ontario. She is also the owner and creator of "There's An Elephant in the Room Cards".

She has spent considerable time in the music industry, as manager for Alan Frew from the Canadian band Glass Tiger for 10 years, and currently as a partner in Jeans 'n Classics.

Her earlier pursuits tapped into her entrepreneurial skills.

"I worked in the electrical wholesale industry. That was my first job when I was 15. This kind of plays into the intuitive thinking. When I was about 24, I decided I was going to open my own lighting stores. They were going to be ultra-modern.

"My dad came over to our house one day and I had this big piece of paper. I was married at the time already. I had this big piece of paper and I was mapping out what these stores were going to look like.

"My dad asked me, 'What are you doing?' I told him, and he said, 'Well how are you going to pay for that?' I said, 'I don't know, I just know I'm going to do it.' I had no money and I had a little girl. But sure enough, my dad actually stepped up and he became my partner.

"Three years later, we had 10,000 square feet and three stores. Intuitively, I knew I could do that. The problem was, I didn't have the business background to support my intuition. Yes, the city needed a modern lighting store. Yes, I could put it together. But once it got up and running, I didn't have a clue what I was doing. That was my business degree. Just from the intuition side of that, there has to be common sense attached to this whole intuitive thing."

Because of her age and lack of business experience, Sharon's ego got the best of her and completely blocked out her ability to use her intuition.

"I'm not sure how much intuition you actually can use when your ego is that wrapped up – oh, look at me, I'm 24, I own three lighting stores. They're the best in town. I'll give you a great deal. Come on in. I'm going broke. Look at my Miata though, it's the first one in London. I was young. The enthusiasm of youth and ego sometimes make you think you can skip the basic steps that lay the foundation for a solid business plan."

Since that incident Sharon has put aside her ego, and through her various experiences she ensures that she listens to her intuition and expresses it. She has relied on her intuition to move in and out of certain opportunities.

"I worked for the orchestra and I stayed on the straight and narrow. Then, when I was about 39, I thought, 'I'm pretending I'm happy, I'm pretending I like all this, and I really don't. So I'm going to leave and I'm going to work on Jeans 'n Classics.'

"I was only at Jeans n' Classics for about a month before Alan called. When he called, I said no immediately because I thought, 'Okay Sharon, learn your lesson. You don't know about managing, or the band. You don't want to get on a tour bus.' But he was very persuasive, and intuitively, I knew I should work with Alan, and I was right. It was a great ten years, and I learned so much about life and business."

Working with Alan Frew had its advantages, but Sharon also realized that she needed to tap into her creative processes.

"I learned so much with Alan. I got to be in a lot of high places, and I got to meet a lot of strong personalities. I learned that I was often too eager to put my heart and my soul into someone else's creativity, and let my own take the backseat. That's very easy to do with a lead singer, to let them take charge. They have to have that confidence in order to be able to stand in front of 30,000 people and sing. Alan gave me a tremendous gift by making me fight for my own creativity.

"Maybe for the first time in my life, I had to actually fight for my own space, instead of just waltzing in and having it. That was a good lesson."

After 10 years with Alan, he and Sharon parted ways, a part of a natural evolution, as Alan pursued other songwriting initiatives and Sharon had other interesting areas to explore.

GUT!

Being young in a career, Sharon's ego got in the way of important business decisions, which resulted in the lighting store closing down, but her intuition has been strong ever since.

Sharon also makes the important distinction that intuition is not about "wanting" or "hoping", which brings about anxiety. Instead, intuition is effective when we are "striving", but we need to watch for the sign posts.

In some cases, being overly rational can blind us to the intuitive sign posts. Bobby Umar missed his intuitive sign posts when he uncomfortably conformed to the career aspirations his parents wished he followed.

3.4 Being Overly Rational

One last hurdle hinders us from tapping into our intuition: being overly rational in our thinking or actions. Relying too heavily on social, societal, and cultural norms and expectations, and support from data, processes, or the experience of others, hinders intuition. Intuition may tell us one thing, but rationality mutes it.

Intuition will tell us to go through experiences and fulfill roles in which we would be most comfortable and content from both a personal or professional perspective. Yet, societal and cultural norms and expectations hinder our intuitive thoughts, and we make decisions or take actions that leave us unhappy.

This was the case for Bobby Umar as he followed the "traditional" path that many parents wish their children to take.

GUT!

Bobby is a four-time TEDx speaker, internationally published author, Huffington Post contributor and Leadership catalyst. With a background in brand marketing, engineering, and the performing arts, Bobby draws on his diverse 20-year career to lead Raeallan[42], whose mission is to discover, inspire, and develop leadership in Gen X and Gen Y. A champion of authentic connection, 'lost leaders' and heart-based leadership, thousands of people have felt a deep connection with Bobby's energetic keynotes and funny personal stories on personal branding, networking, and social media. With over 250,000 followers on social media, he has been ranked the fourth biggest leadership influencer on social media and the second best business coach to follow on Twitter.

However, Bobby wasn't always so successful. Early on, intuition was hindered because his choices had heavy influencers.

"My career was driven by what other people were telling me I should be doing, right? I was given the whole path to success as defined by my parents. Later on corporate entities, or academic professors, or even the people around me defined it. Finally, the biggest influence is our society.

---
42 www.raeallan.com

Society said go, get a degree, get a job, get a house, get 2.1 kids, and you know that's what success was. Oh, you're successful.

"But I know tons of people with a nice big house, two cars and two kids and they're unhappy. They have a big corporate career and they're miserable."

Bobby's intuition had him asking about his "Why" based on Simon Sinek's TED talk.[43]

"My big 'why' is there are lost leaders everywhere. Every person, every leader sometimes feels lost personally, professionally, academically, socially, spiritually, and I'm here to help them. That's what my mission is all about."

Looking back, Bobby was also lost.

"I was lost back in my undergrad and when I worked for four years as an engineer. I did it because I was good at math and physics. Could I say I loved it? No, not at all.

"The first intuition I got that I was in the wrong place was when we used to go for lunch with my colleagues. We would talk about 'Did you hear about the latest jet from Rolls Royce? Yeah, the X9000? You know, the Short brothers from Ireland are developing this really cool application, blah, blah, blah.' And I just didn't care.

"I said, 'Did you hear that Brad and Jennifer, you know, are having trouble? You know, Jennifer Aniston broke up with Brad Pitt! I can't believe it!' That's what I was talking about (I was 24 then remember).

"So that was the first inkling I had that maybe I was in the wrong place. I'd end up pushing and pushing to be successful there until finally I was let go, and this was four years in.

"In fact, that's almost always been the way it's ended up. So after the second time with my MBA and brand marketing career, I really thought about, well how do I fit? Where do I fit in? And so that's when I started being more aware of my intuition."

Bobby talks about sharpening your intuition with experience, not age.

"It doesn't get better as you get older. It gets better as you're more aware of it because there are people with 50 years' experience who know diddly

---

43 https://www.youtube.com/watch?v=u4ZoJKF_VuA

squat, right? And there's someone who, with two years of experience, knows a ton. So it's by focus. It's by practice. It's by harnessing that intuition gets better and better."

Bobby's intuition has become very good with making connections.

"For me, my big ingredient is the connection piece. I've always said that. To me, if anything we are disconnected, which definitely affects trust, which definitely affects intuition, which definitely affects a lot in relationships. Just like the child's intuition, the child's trust, and the child's connectedness to the world around us. It is very, very high. But over time we start to lose that connection."

Bobby's intuition is particularly strong when it comes to the connectedness between people.

"Do I trust my intuition? I would say very much so, yeah, I think for the most part, particularly when it comes to connections, like people that I know, relationships. For the most part I have a good sense of how a relationship will be.

"A lot of people worry about the failed relationships they had, and I have them, too. But, you know, look at it from the positive sense. It's just like the unemployment rate. The unemployment rate is six percent, but the employment rate is 94 percent. So my failed connection rate is like, you know, 10 people out of 10,000. That's pretty good if you look at the successful ones."

GUT!

Bobby's intuition was able to express itself when he aligned himself with the experiences and relationships he wanted, not those dictated by his parents, other companies, and society. This will differ for others, but for Bobby, following his intuition has helped him be personally successful in inspiring others.

After removing our intuitive hindrances, we need to take notice of our intuitive drivers. We all have intuitive drivers that, when aligned with our roles, responsibilities, and experiences, allow a strong expression of intuition. With our intuitive drivers aligned, we can take advantage of the opportunities to which our intuition guides us. However, we first need to understand what drives our intuition.

CHAPTER 4

Understand Our Intuitive Drivers

Intuitive drivers are conscious and unconscious influencers of why we do what we do. Using these drivers as a template, we evaluate every situation we encounter, relationship we develop, or role we take on to see if it aligns with the intuitive driver most important to us.

When we make decisions or act in ways that are misaligned with our personal intuitive drivers, we hinder our ability to express our intuition.

There are three intuitive drivers that, when aligned with our experiences, allow us to take notice of our intuitive thoughts – values, purpose, and personal vision.

4.1 Values

Values are those characteristics such as beliefs, trust, ethics, and morals that play a vital role in how we conduct ourselves in life and how we expect others to conduct themselves. We may use a number of these values as a general guide, or different values could be used as a filter in different situations.

If we surround ourselves with people and environments that are aligned with the values we uphold, intuition is better able to express itself. However, if there is a misalignment between our values and those of others, or we find ourselves in particular situations that seem to go against the values we hold, our intuition is triggered, letting us know that there is a possible value mismatch.

Intuition is hindered in the latter situation when we choose to ignore the intuitive triggers and continue surrounding ourselves with people and environments that are not in the best intuitive interest, as Bruce Croxon experienced.

GUT!

After co-founding Lavalife in 1987, Bruce Croxon served in many roles with the company – as partner, chairman, and CEO – guiding it to the position of category leader and achieving revenues of close to $100 million prior to its sale in 2004. Bruce currently runs Round13 Capital, a company dedicated to incubating and investing in digital start-ups.

Bruce attributes Lavalife's success to intuition, which played a pivotal role in its infancy period.

"It's good that we're talking about intuition in a way because, you know, the way I looked at it early on we used our intuition a lot, like everything was gut, right? Everything, without process, without formal strategy. It was really all about street-level gut and that's how, I think, a lot of small businesses get started.

"So I think when businesses start out, it is a lot about gut and intuition. What does your intuition or gut tell you? I think as companies grow the thing that separates companies that stay as founder-led companies versus ones that are able to scale and get bigger has a lot to do with the ability to pick up what's important from your intuition and formalize it into what we call vision and values. And what kind of company do we want to be as we grow up, right?

"And the ability to take your gut and intuition and put it into a place where other people can understand it, and adhere to it or add to it or to part of it, I think, separates the companies that are forever destined to be a sole proprietorship or a small company versus ones that are able to build a culture and, through attracting like-minded people, build that culture to a point where it can perform without relying solely on the founder's gut or intuition. You know, the gut becomes institutionalized in a sense."

Bruce's reliance on intuition was instrumental in shaping Lavalife's core values, which were clear about being collaborative in a team-based environment.

"That's what core values are. You know, my intuition always told me, for example, that team work – more people in on a decision – makes for a better decision. And partnership and people collaborating, trying to achieve consensus, is an environment that provides a lot of support. It *provides better decisions. It's not always easy, so you've got people to share the burden. So I'm a big believer in partnership and what it can do.*

"I think that value of being open-minded to consensus and collaboration, the ability to take that intuitive feel and turn it into, in this case, a core value of the company and then actively screen for people on the way in because people aren't going to change. We all have developed our own intuition and skill and way of being. My belief is people don't fundamentally change past the age of 10.

"So bring in people that are, in this case, team-oriented, i.e. absence of ego, willing to work with others, (with) no need to accept the glory, and can issue words like 'I don't know, geez, never thought of that.' Those were the characteristics we used to find in people coming into the funnel that would result in a team-oriented culture.

"But that all came from an intuitive sense at the very beginning as to what kind of culture would be best to try and go to a hundred million, which was always our modest goal for a small, medium sized business."

Once these values were established for Lavalife, driven by intuition, every resource brought on had to have their attitudes and own personal values filtered through the core values of Lavalife. The one time this was not done, the result was disastrous.

"I found, in my career, that the mistakes that I've made have inevitably been made when I have compromised on core values. This happened once when I prioritized technical skill – I don't mean technology, I mean technical competency – that was compromised over core values. An example of that would be when we underwent a large technology transformation at Lavalife, which was a critical project.

"I found that the team, although very technically competent, got sidetracked into issues that involved ego, the antithesis of open-mindedness when trying to problem solve. Really, in hindsight, for a good number of months, we were getting updated at the board, being told that everything was on track, and everything was fine. But in fact it took us a while to figure it out that everything wasn't fine and the project wasn't on track. A large part of that was a lack of transparency and unwillingness to look bad in front of the board, right? And it was a lot of blaming between team members and why it was not on track – all the things that would add up to be opposite of working as a team."

Because of this dysfunction, the team wasted a lot of time having unproductive discussions, which took their focus off the original goal: completing a technical project on time and on budget. This lack of focus cost the company a significant amount of money.

"The budget for the project was supposed to be $20 million over two years, and it turned out to be $42 million over four-and-a-half years."

The situation reached a tipping point and one day Bruce got a sudden call and had to fly back from Whistler, where he was living at the time.

"The board called me up one day and said that we were burning $1 million a month and you are coming home. I came back to take the helm at the request of the board and I fired the entire senior team in one day."

Sacrificing these core values was a mistake that Bruce vowed to never make again. He now has a high bar when it comes to trusting somebody's ability to execute as an entrepreneur.

"My gut told me that this person could do it, but my gut was wrong. It was wrong gut, bad gut. I've learned about what my gut has told me. The bar is now higher for me on the people side."

GUT!

Bruce was clear in defining his values when bringing people into the company. A small stray away from them not only cost the company significantly in production time but there were significant financial ramifications. If we all maintain our own set of values and filter our experiences through them, tapping into our intuition should not be difficult.

The same can be said for some of us who find out what our purpose is in life. Once that is defined and we move through life with that purpose in mind, intuition helps guide us, much like it did for Kelly-Sue McDiarmid, whose purpose was to love.

4.2 Purpose

Some of us have a singular purpose in life that guides us, leaning on internal or intrinsic qualities. We support this purpose by allowing ourselves to go through experiences, both positive and negative, that are related to that purpose. Our purpose in life may also change after a major life event unfolds and personal priorities change.

With a purpose as a singular focus, intuition will help guide our actions and decisions to support this purpose, and will provide specific warning signals if decisions and actions might sway us away from our personal purpose.

Kelly-Sue McDiarmid's purpose was to love, which she provided to two special needs children, throwing away both a six-figure salary and a marriage so that her love could continue undeterred.

GUT!

Kelly-Sue McDiarmid had the optics of a perfect life – diplomas from colleges, a university degree, married and pregnant with a son on the way, a job with a six-figure salary, and a beautiful house in a lovely Ontario town.

Growing up, she knew what her ultimate purpose was in life. Her intuition was tied to her strong sense of love and care, which started when she was very young.

"My intuition is that I'm continuing to help people all the time. It's a matter of, who else can I help along the way?

This purpose drove Kelly-Sue throughout her life. Her intuition played a significant role just after her son was born.

"When we discovered that he had issues, he was nine days old and he was dead for three minutes and 39 seconds. So, we were looking at a feeding tube, mute, deaf, blind, quadriplegic.

"A few weeks later, I was staying at the hospital and they called me and it was 3:26 in the morning. They said, 'You need to come right now.' And I walked in and there were a bunch of people around my son and someone was pumping his heart and they had slit open the side of his stomach and his intestines were out and they were draining on the floor.

"Somebody said, 'Get her outta here.' And somebody else said, 'That's the mother. She needs to be in here.' And for me it was like I was watching the whole experience outside of myself."

With no hesitation whatsoever, her intuition kicked in.

"It was, okay, what do we need to do? Well, you need to call the father right now. Uh, no, he's an hour and a half away and I'm not going to have him drive under these circumstances and there's really nothing he can do, so what do we need to do?

"The doctor said to me, 'You know, put him in a home, forget you had him.' Uh, no, not an option. 'Well, he's a quadriplegic. He's never going to communicate. This is what you have. You have a vegetable. Do you not understand that?' I'm like, 'Oh, okay. I get it. So what do we need to do?' 'Put him a home right now.'"

This advice did not deter Kelly-Sue's intuitive thoughts about taking care of her son.

"No, we need to work with him. You don't do that to somebody. You just got to do what you go to do as it comes. The neat thing about intuition is that if you are in tune enough with your surroundings and open to, okay, everything happens for a reason, I was put here to help people because I get it. I understand, you know, but if I didn't go through the crappy background I went through then I wouldn't be able to deal with him because he has so many deeper issues and anybody else would have just put him in a home."

The first thing Kelly-Sue did was leave her job to be home full-time with her son.

"I quit my job. I was making six figures. I was making a lot of money. It was intuition that I had to be with my son. I didn't bargain with God as to what kind of child I would get. I asked for a child. I was blessed with a child and this is what you do."

Kelly-Sue relied on her education, training, and personal skills to bring life to a home-based career to support her and her son.

"One of my degrees is sports medicine, so I know all the physio and the kinesiology and all that behind it. So I figured I can work with him. At the time I was just opening a gym on the side, and it just came to me: Why am I putting in 50, 60 hours a week when I'm going to put more hours into this gym and then have this child that is going to get nothing from me?

"So I realized that the gym is where it's at because I can make my own hours. I can hire people and tell them what to do and work it from there.

So instead what I did is I quietly opened the gym and then started to build clientele in the area and get people's trust because I'm not from here, and then work in another gym. And then, once I had people that knew that I was the cat's meow, I left and they came with me.

"But my whole thing is then, okay, what can I do for my child? So for Brandon I needed to make money and I needed to make money fast, and what do you do besides rob a bank or win the lottery?

"And we're talking $55,000 I needed as quickly as possible. So without ever doing it before, I ran a massive fundraiser and there was a dinner, a dance, a silent auction, and I invited everybody in town and we had 500 and some people come to it. We didn't have enough food and we raised over $60,000.

"So then I went and I put him in hyperbaric oxygen chambers and I took him through therapy that's from Hungary, Budapest. And we lived away, just him and I, for three months at a time to get the therapy and then come back. And I'd run the gym, and then I'd hold another fundraiser, and I'd make more money, and I'd go back again, and we just kept repeating it.

"I got him to a point with the hyperbaric oxygen that he finally had sight. His hearing became so acute that if you clap or sing happy birthday, he cries. He has a little bit of speech. He can say 'Mom', 'yeah'.

"So we've come a long way. He can use his right hand to use a mouse. He can use a computer device. He can use a speech device. He eats. He got off the feeding tube. It took two years to get him to drink out of a straw every day, just practice and practice and practice and encourage. You just do what you got to do and you go, okay, well how does our body work?

"And you break it down in your head and (figure out) what I'm going do for him. He's going to do push-ups because he needs to hold his own head up and he needs upper body (strength)."

Kelly-Sue's intuitive decision to help people and her experience with her son inspired her to sign up to be a foster parent. After several foster children came and went in her life, she had a girl dropped off at her doorstep that filled a hole she had felt all her life – her desire for a daughter.

"I really wanted a baby girl. I really wanted more children.

"My daughter came along. We got her at five months. She was totally addicted to cocaine. They didn't have anywhere else to put her. No one would take her. Again, I could save her. The mother was incarcerated, five fathers came forward and said they were the dad. None of them were. Can you imagine? Well, she's going to end up in foster care. She's going to end up in this nightmare world.

Kelly-Sue's first priority was to get her new daughter, Katelynn, off of her cocaine addiction.

"I'm not feeding a five-month-old baby cocaine. And I handed them the bag of coke back. I said, 'No, I'm not doing that. I will take her through withdrawals.' So for five days, you go through the withdrawals and you just are with them and hold them and do what comes natural, I think, to a mother.

"She made leaps and bounds. She's a serious miracle child just like my son is. I've been super, super blessed with my babies. She now talks incessantly. She looks exactly like me. She's brilliant."

After Katelynn turned one year old, she was scheduled to be moved to another foster home. But Kelly-Sue was not going to allow that to happen.

"When we went in at a year old, they said, 'We have a home for her.' And I said, 'Yeah, my house. I took her through this and I'm going to keep her.' 'Well, I thought you just wanted to be a foster mother.' 'Well, no. I was actually put in this situation to do this, so I'm keeping her.' I adopted her when she was two because that was just the right thing to do."

Kelly-Sue's love for her two children affected her marriage. Her ex-husband's inability to understand Kelly-Sue's deep love as well as his infidelity broke the marriage up.

"He hated every minute of it. He really had a problem with the fact that I wanted to help other people and he said, 'You know, why would you go back to your past and have to dive back into and have flashbacks just so that you can help some little girl?'

"He had real difficulty with the fact that I wanted to adopt her. 'Oh, she's on cocaine. She might even be worse than fetal alcohol. You have no idea what you're going to deal with. You want to make a decision here, like our marriage is already breaking down.'

"I said, 'Our marriage is gone. For me, I'm in this position to get this beautiful child and that's what I'm going to do and if you're threatening me already to walk, you're going to walk regardless, whether it's now or five, ten years.'

"The neat thing about intuition, I think, is that if you are in tune enough with your surroundings, everything happens for a reason. If you are in complete contact with your inner self and being able to listen to, okay, this is the path you're supposed to take, no matter whether your husband's going to leave, or you know, it's going to cost you a career or whatever it might cost you, there's another path and you need to listen to it and just go to it."

With the marriage on the verge of being shattered, Kelly-Sue's ex-husband decided to present divorce papers on Christmas Eve. With an almost dead-pan reaction, Kelly-Sue's intuitive desire to make others happy took precedence at that moment over dealing with the process of kicking him out of her life.

"With the divorce, he came to me on Christmas Eve. I knew he'd had a couple of affairs and he said, 'I want to give you a Christmas gift.' And I hadn't had a Christmas gift in years because I'm the one that worked and he hadn't worked in seven years and he said, 'I've been having an affair and I'm in love with her and I'm going to her.'

"So I sat there for a second and I went, 'Okay, first of all we're not ruining everybody's Christmas. We're going to continue. We need to hit the women's shelter because I have presents and their Christmas dinner. These need to be delivered. We've got three families in town that we do. We need to hit the Children's Hospital because I have teddy bears for all the children and I have angels for all the babies in the neonatal unit. We've been doing this ever since he was a baby. We are doing it.' I said, 'This is what we need to do. Right now.'

"So, again, intuition played. What am I going to do? Am I going to sit down and have a flipping good cry that, oh, my God, you want to be with somebody else? No, I've got things to do. That's unfortunate.

"So when we came back we had Christmas together and then went to his family. Christmas Day night he said, 'I really want to be with her.' And I said to him, 'Would you like me to help pack your bag?'

"He's like, 'You've got to be kidding?' I said, 'I'm not going to beg you. I am a successful, educated, cute girl. I do NOT need to beg anybody. So if you found somebody else and you've already slept with her, you need to go to her and I will gladly help you pack your bag.'

"So again intuition played. Bye.

"And it sounds like it was easy. Trust me, it wasn't. I've been single for two years. You know, once in a while you go, 'This sucks.' It's lonely, but I'm looking forward to the next chapter and I know that again a door's going to open."

Just before Kelly-Sue helped her ex-husband pack his bags, she was notified that she had cancer. While going through this tremendous ordeal and being told she had a short time to live, she began questioning everything she was doing.

"He left knowing I had cancer. Oh, yeah, that was a blessing, are you kidding?

"As soon as they said, you know, you got two months, two, three months max, like this is not good.

"Three quarters of my body was cut in half from cancer. I kept second guessing, 'What am I doing? What am I doing? What kind of treatment do I want? Do I really want to do this?'"

Once again, Kelly-Sue's intuition aligned with her purpose of loving others, particularly her children, which gave her the strength to overcome her fears and push on.

"Again with the intuition, it was so clear for me at that point because it wasn't a thought of me. It was a thought about my children. I'm now a single mother of two challenged children. I don't have time for this. Let's find out whatever therapy you think I need right now. I'll do it. Let's fight it.

"I finally came to grips with the fact that you have got to listen to your intuition in the beginning because it's always right. So stop second guessing because you're worrying about things that are out of your control and they're not going to happen anyway.

"The last diagnosis was two months and I said, 'Well, that's not going to happen.' That's what they told me two years ago."

Kelly-Sue's intuition has not only helped her keep a family together despite the experiences and circumstances each one has gone through, but she has been able to excel on the business side as well.

"So in the meantime, I'm building another company that I just purchased. I ran a nutrition company that made me substantial money. I utilize everything and anything that I have. I have a pool out back, I teach aquafit out of it. My entire basement is a gym. People come to my house so that I can just be home with my children. I have the sports medicine background, so I train hockey players, I train football players, I train police officers. I do whatever I can do.

"But the neatest thing about that is I'm continuing to help people all the time. So it's not just a matter of me bringing in money. It's a matter of, who else can I help along the way.

"I'm loving my children. My relationship with my children's never been better and with the past two years I just live on the intuition of, okay, what do I do next? So I constantly go, you just point me in the right direction."

GUT!

When Kelly-Sue aligned her intuition with her true purpose in life, the incredible hurdles she faced – quitting her job, starting a new career, raising money she did not have, sacrificing her marriage and overcoming a two-month life sentence due to cancer – were overcome. Her love for her children and others was so strong that nothing could stop her.

If there is a misalignment, then we may find that our intuition is hindered and we may lose out on certain opportunities. In Kelly-Sue's case, the stakes were higher than her own happiness; two high-needs children could have suffered a worse fate had her purpose and her intuition been misaligned.

Much like our purpose, when our personal vision is in alignment with our intuition, we find success in the endeavours we pursue, like Jeff Duncan.

4.3 Personal Vision

For Jeff Duncan, the common connection between most of the experiences he had was simple: he was told that he would not succeed in any venture that he had no experience in. Surprisingly, overcoming these doubts from others by doing things differently defined his personal vision that fueled his intuition.

GUT!

Jeff Duncan is President and CEO of Habitat for Humanity Heartland Ontario. Jeff had an early start as an entrepreneur, and has been successful in every venture with which he has been involved. This success has always been driven by following his intuition, which is aligned with a personal vision: a belief in pushing oneself and finding a way to do things he is told he cannot do.

"Well, for me it was what can I do to take me beyond my comfort zone and then surprise those people who said I couldn't do it. I have been lucky as there has always been someone who inspired or pointed me to the next opportunity along the way. I remember people telling me I shouldn't do the restaurant because it was too risky. To borrow $100,000 at 20 years old, people think you are out of your mind."

The experience Jeff alludes to occurred when he bought Walker's Restaurant. With its initial success, he then began expanding by opening a delicatessen, Between the Bread, and Walker's West, a catering business. In 2003, he sold Walker's, exiting the restaurant business. By then he had already made a career change to work in the non-profit sector.

"I had been involved in the non-profit community since 1989 as a volunteer in a variety of roles with various organizations. In 2000 I had owned the restaurants for 16 years and was about to turn forty. The experiences were great but I wanted and needed a change.

"It was time to make a decision – gear up and expand the business or get out! I feared I would be working long hours every day until I retired. It's a good but hard business with little time for leisure and family. I wanted new experiences, opted for change and started looking around. I was familiar with the Boys and Girls Club and knew the Executive Director. He said they were searching for a senior manager and I decided it might make sense for me to work there."

With no work experience in social services, Jeff applied and joined the Club's senior management team, where he managed the facilities and social enterprises for seven years. In 2007 he knew it was time to leave the Club and return to being self-employed.

Jeff had renovated homes for years and managed construction and enterprise projects.

"It seemed natural to start a renovation and consulting business. The business was a one-man operation and took off right away. In two years it was time to invest in it by hiring staff and really growing it. My wife and I made the decision to take that next step in the spring of 2009."

In May 2009 he got a call from Habitat for Humanity London about an opportunity. They needed a new executive director to lead them through some major changes. He found it a tough decision at the time.

"I had to think about working for someone again and it took two weeks make a decision. All I knew about Habitat was they built houses for families and Jimmy Carter was involved. I was the typical person on the street with a limited understanding of the organization.

"I researched and loved the business model as well as the mission and values; it is a non-profit with an entrepreneurial approach to finding solutions to poverty, housing, and community development. Wow, I was fascinated and this appealed to me at my core. My business was going great with lots of new opportunities, but something drew me to Habitat. I committed to an interim role for six months to help the board make the changes they wanted, and I would return to the business once they hired a CEO. I worked weekends to finish projects and put some work on hold. Within three weeks of being in the interim role I knew this was the place I needed to be. The problem now was I had to apply for and earn the CEO role as the search had started. I did win it and we wound the (renovation) business up and I have never looked back."

Jeff's destiny once again put him in a role where there was little to no definition, an environment in which he always thrived.

"When I started at Habitat there wasn't a how-to binder and little in the way of orientation. No one had the whole picture of the agency and executive director's role. It was going to be a real learning curve. It was May of 2009.

"On day two I was at the Habitat Canada conference in Winnipeg. That helped a lot as I didn't initially have a clue about the topics in some sessions but there were lots of people willing to share. There was a need to get up to speed quickly as the board had high expectations. Our business is diverse with retail stores, land development, home construction, mortgages, volunteer and social services. I knew how to do some things and *figured out the rest relying on all those years in business. We have now enjoyed major growth and become a regional affiliate."*

Part of Jeff's personal vision included often doing things in a way that differed from the ways of others, including no formal post-secondary education, which he regrets even though things have worked out well. He started forming his vision early on, as well as his entrepreneurial career.

"The intuitive moments I had started early. I wanted to work and make money. I was intrigued by wealth and a lot of my friends' parents were successful business people. My parents were great, they worked hard and built a good life but I wanted more. I was 11 and a friend caddied at the Hunt Club. It made sense to get paid for caddying and meet wealthy people, so this would be my path to success.

"I started by asking the pro for a job. He said no at first but said I could hang around and clean clubs for free. A few weeks later I was carrying a bag that weighed as much as I did, listening to the stories of successful people while they played and did business between shots.

"I thought the whole job was cool and I worked my way up to being a double-A caddy. One day a golfer was complaining his Globe and Mail delivery was always late. I was 13 and I don't know why but looked into it. It turned out they couldn't find enough paper boys. The routes were small with meager return for the effort. I was used to a long walk with a bag on my shoulder so a week later I began delivering newspapers. We always had extra papers and I didn't like returning them every day so I started buying and dropping them off at homes of people I knew. The promotion worked and my route doubled in a couple of months.

"I really liked a Cadillac a friend's dad had and he knew it. One day he asked if I wanted to make extra money washing and waxing it. I was 14, loved cars and wanted a Mustang. With no idea what to do I started detailing his car. Eventually I had six customers and had started my first business. I did get my Mustang. He became a lifelong friend and mentor.

"A while later I saw a sign saying that the Jade Palace restaurant was hiring. The early mornings caddying were less appealing and I liked the idea of working after school. I applied for the job, they told me I was too young so I went back every day for two weeks. The manager relented and I eventually became a driver and prep cook. When he later left to work as GM for a large hotel, he hired me as a cook. A couple of years later I followed my chef when he left to manage the best restaurant in town. Along the way my dream formed to owning my own place some day.

"What lessons can be learned from these early years: you walk across a guy's line on the golf green, not good but that's the only time you will ever do it. Instead of buying lunch midway, if a golfer offers you a sandwich and you can't stand baloney sandwiches, you smile and eat it. You are up at 5:30 am delivering newspapers to make a few dollars and washing dishes every weekend while your friends are out having fun. It's easy to dismiss this stuff but the more you think about it, the more you can learn from these early work experiences that apply when the time is right. Following my initial ambitions that were guided by my intuition, there was a point as an adult that I stopped worrying about how much wealth I needed to accumulate and focused instead on my role and performance.

"My belief is if a person understands the rules of etiquette, respect, sacrifice, perseverance, hard work, and humility, one builds the discipline and character needed to be successful. All along the way our work is scrutinized closely, but if we do our best with enthusiasm and a willingness to learn people notice and opportunities happen. Great decisions can be made by being practical, listening to our inner voice of reason, and applying those life lessons when one doesn't have all the skills necessary. Balance always seems to be the toughest thing to achieve and you really need to listen and pay attention to all these same things to get there."

GUT!

Jeff's intuitive experiences were guided by his personal vision, resulting in varied experiences early in his career, each of which were linked. The thrill of getting into situations he wanted to tackle but was told he couldn't or had little to no experience in spurred him on. He was able to create processes and procedures or modify existing ones to be more efficient, leading him to better productivity, outcomes and progressively better opportunities and quality of life.

When intuition is being expressed, there are indicators that inform us that intuition is at play. Some have that feeling in the gut area, others have heightened senses, and for Drew Green, his internal indicator is when he senses omens.

CHAPTER 5

Sense the Internal Indicators

When intuition is triggered, internal indicators will help us recognize it. These internal indicators are unique to each of us, although some of us may share a common one. The two most common internal indicators which we seem to sense are "gut feeling", which manifests within the stomach or intestinal area, and a "spidey sense", which is similar to the hairs on the back of our necks standing up.

When we feel our intuition trigger and internal indicators "tell us something", we have an opportunity to take the appropriate decision or action to support the intuitive thoughts.

For Drew Green, his internal indicator comes in the form of omens.

GUT!

Drew Green is Founder, CEO and Chairman of SHOP.CA, one of North America's fastest growing e-commerce businesses. Drew began his entrepreneurial career at 19, when he started his own personal training company, and then later started a company with his now-wife Andrea in his mid-20s, a company that continues to grow to this day.

Having spent the majority of his professional career connecting online audiences with retailers through digital media, marketing solutions, mobile marketing and marketplace platforms in the United States, Drew turned his focus to his homeland in 2010, with a vision to significantly improve the online buying experience for the millions of Canadians who shop online.

Drew became a member of SHOP.COM's executive team in 2005, where he led the sales, merchant operations, and business development departments during his tenure. Prior to SHOP.COM, Drew held sales and sales leadership roles with Flonetwork, (acquired by DoubleClick) and DoubleClick (acquired by Google).

Prior to founding SHOP.CA with Trevor Newell, Drew served as Senior Vice-President of Sales & Marketing for Vibes Media. In this role, Drew was responsible for defining, implementing, and leading the execution of Vibes' sales, business development, and marketing strategy. At the end of this journey, Drew's intuition began guiding him in a different direction.

"I refer to journeys a lot in my life. Right at the end of my time at SHOP. COM, my intuition played a role in where SHOP.CA is today. It's that experience that created a burning desire to turn a vision into reality. I also recognized that at that point in my career I was fortunate to have helped a few special entrepreneurs and executives create a tremendous amount of value executing their ideas, and frankly, learned a lot about what to do and what not to do when starting and growing a company. It's certainly not a perfect science, nor can it be done without tremendous sacrifice and resiliency.

"While I loved each of the journeys my career provided, it was time for me to start really thinking about what I needed to do and what change I could make, given my experiences and passions. So I looked home and found inspiration.

"I'm from Canada, but I had been in the US for the majority of my career and my intuition told me that there was going to be this massive behavioural change in the Canadian consumer.

"It's only funny now, but when I first started talking about my dream most would try and dissuade us from the vision we had for change."

Drew did not listen to these naysayers. His intuition told him that Canadian companies needed to make an investment for the long term, which might have explained why Canadian consumers were not typically buying online.

"My intuition told me that there was a dynamic that was missing in the market that should have been growing much, much quicker. After research, I found that one of the dynamics was fairly simple. Retailers had not yet invested in e-commerce like their US and international counterparts, and if retailers weren't investing in great e-commerce experiences

how could the consumer invest their time in buying online from them vs. their US competitors?

"In any large consumer market opportunity, in any rapidly growing business segment, unless there's a massive investment from visionary companies, consumer behaviour simply does not change as quickly as it could or should. For a lot of people, you know, they look at it and they say, 'Well Canadians just don't like to buy online.' That was incorrect in our opinion, that just wasn't what was happening or at very least, should be happening.

"What was happening in e-commerce in our country was we weren't investing for the long-term and back then (2010) there wasn't a Canadian-based company I could see that was saying, 'Hey, we're going to make a big and right bet on Canadian e-commerce. We're going to stick with it because it's not going to be easy or inexpensive to truly compete.'

"Several large retailers tried and then shut down. Several large retailers tried and pulled resources back.

"Any new venture with massive potential, especially in a new segment of an economy, takes massive investment to get to scale. It takes massive investment to change consumer behaviour. And it takes execution for staying power."

Successful US-based companies made large investments with significant growth being rewarded in the long term, which was sorely missing in Canada.

"I was lucky because being in the US I saw Amazon go from almost where SHOP.CA is now to a $200 billion dollar company. Living and working in the US I saw that evolution fist hand. I also saw that they understood that this was the first inning of a nine inning game in terms of e-commerce. And so they continued to invest in what it took to wow customers, they continued to get market share and they continued to grow in every way, brand, transactions, et cetera.

"No one had done that in Canada, not even Amazon.ca. And so, while Amazon's an amazing company, and successful in Canada, I still felt there was room for a home grown market leader position missing in Canada."

Not surprisingly, Drew's intuition "knew" that despite the challenges he would encounter along the way, he had a winning thesis for a business idea called SHOP.CA.

"My intuition said, 'Let's form a thesis.' Our thesis was that if the right groups of skilled, resilient and enthusiastic people were brought together, funded properly, we could have a chance to create a special company, a company built to last. There are no guarantees in business, and you're definitely going to have to overcome a lot of challenges. But the thesis was that there was this window. We wanted to try to tackle that."

Drew relied on his intuition to get him from idea to formal concept to execution.

"Intuition was a big part of the challenges that we overcame in terms of getting an idea to an actual concept because we had to go through a lot of finding out who to work with. Intuition played a big role into why Trevor Newell, my co-founder, and I partnered. He's a very special person with extraordinary capabilities. Someone I admire as a person, and as a business person.

"(After) about nine months together my intuition told me that we had done enough work and were ready. Trevor and I had a call and said, 'Okay, time to go all in, brother. Time to go for it.'"

Drew talks about his internal indicators being "omens".

"Intuition, to me, comes in a different form. It comes in the form of omens. I don't have a gut. I don't think of myself as having, 'Oh, what does my gut feel?' I try and take my time on big decisions and I look for omens. I try to look for omens because even when I'm not making a decision, often I find omens can show me the way or at least show me what I might want to consider."

Drew delineates a spiritual link with omens versus the ones he experiences.

"I think the word 'omen' is spiritual to a lot of people. [For me], it's not. It's a flow. There's this fulfillment, whether it's small or big, just being able to notice it and feel it. It's a fulfillment. It's a happiness because I feel like I'm in the rhythm. You're just happy that you're getting a sense of clarity, you know, you're getting a path.

"If I'm not reading omens and I'm maybe not clear of head because I haven't been able to, it's not a great feeling. I certainly go through times like that.

"When you're having a conversation, you'll hear somebody say something and to me that's an omen. It's a happiness. Or, the rhythm was telling me that there is something I should but I didn't do because I tried to use logic more than trust in the omen.

"I believe that omens are meant for us all. They're meant to drive us all towards what it is we should be doing in our personal legend. Personal legend sounds big but it's actually from one of my favorite books, The Alchemist. Personal legend is more about what are you supposed to be doing, your purpose. To me it meant, just do that and if you miss that you're really not going to be happy".

Drew's omens have helped his company attain early and rare success.

"As we sit here, we're one of the fastest growing e-commerce companies in North America, and we ONLY sell to Canadians – that is incredible to me.

"Intuition's played a role in overcoming, not only daily, weekly and monthly challenges so far – but we have a lot of work ahead to accomplish our mission."

GUT!

Drew's omens draw upon a number of internal indicators such as a happiness, flow, or rhythm, which remain difficult to pinpoint because of their intangibility. They have informed Drew when making salient business decisions, catapulting the company forward to early and continued success.

External indicators work much the same way as internal indicators, with one exception. External indicators are cues that are shown to us in the environment in which we find ourselves. Noreen Kassam's external indicators were responsible for possibly saving her life as she found herself alone late at night, tired and hungry in an Eastern European country.

CHAPTER 6

Take Notice of External Indicators

Similar to internal indicators, external indicators are found in our environment. When there is an anomaly in our external environment, our intuition is triggered. We use our senses to focus on various characteristics of our environment such as the activities around us, the speed of movement, the busyness around us, and so on.

Our intuition may tell us that we are in a "safe" environment and we can then continue operating within it. If we find ourselves in a precarious situation, then we need to move to a safer environment, which is what Noreem Kassam had to do.

GUT!

At an energetic whim, Noreen Kassam decided to travel to Europe unannounced. This is where Noreen recognized and tapped into her intuition.

"I started backpacking alone when I was 21. I didn't tell anyone I was doing it until I left because I knew I'd be denied. So I just packed a bag of clothes and I didn't know where I was going. All I knew was I had a Euro Flexi Pass or a rail pass where you can go from Canada to Europe and you can take ten train rides in a period of this long and you paid this much and it didn't matter where you went or when you went.

"So, I just went and it was the most magnificent experience of my whole life and that's where I can say I started paying attention to my intuition, and everything that happened subsequently to my trip happened because I learned to tap into my intuition."

Noreen gives one particular example of when her intuition told her to start running.

"I was tired. I had just taken a really long train ride to get into Prague and I checked into the hostel that I had booked the night before from another country. I got to Prague, I checked into the hostel and I was so hungry. I hadn't eaten in something in 12 hours.

"I went to the nearest restaurant, ordered food and it was probably the cheapest, most amazing food I had ever had in my whole life. Every bite surpassed anything I had ever eaten.

"So I'm sitting there eating. But the whole time I'm eating, the chef who made it was standing there and watching me eat the entire meal."

Noreen was not looking directly at the chef. A window separated the eating area from the kitchen. The way Noreen was sitting, she could see the window on the left side of her peripheral vision.

This was not the first time Noreen had had people look at her for a lengthy period of time. We have all had this happen to us. However, in this case, Noreen sensed that the way he was staring at her was different and dangerous.

"I was being stared at, basically stalked, while eating every bite of my meal."

To compound this uneasy feeling, in her peripheral vision, Noreen also saw the waiter staring at her. With two glaring uncomfortable stares, Noreen's intuition triggered her internal indicators that were letting her know that the situation could turn dangerous.

"I felt as though my heart started beating really quickly and my entire body temperature went up. It was like an adrenaline rush took over me and a voice in my head just kept saying 'leave now.' I couldn't really think. It was like another entity took over and saved me. I felt really strong and capable of anything.

"Obviously, I started eating quicker and quicker because I'm going to get out of here now, this is getting a little bit creepy. So I finished eating, paid the bill, and started walking out."

While Noreen began walking away, her intuition began signaling that the danger had not yet subsided.

"As I was walking out, I felt like I was being followed. There is this innate sense you get when someone's energy is intruding into yours. And I felt that energy nearing closer and closer as I walked out.

"Looking back to see it just visually confirmed what I had already felt.

"It was the waiter and the chef following me. And I was alone. I'd just got to the city. I had no idea where to go. I could barely remember where my hostel was because I hadn't slept. I wasn't with it. I didn't know anybody there. I was travelling alone.

"So I started walking faster. They started walking faster and they were getting closer and closer, and they were yelling at me and I couldn't understand what they were yelling. So I just kept going and going and going. And I started running. That would give them the hint that I'm not interested and I think that I ran straight for about ten or fifteen minutes before they gave up.

"And that was my first night in Prague and I was exhausted and I was tired and I wasn't paying attention to my intuition."

GUT!

Noreen's thought process, while running, went from being assaulted to possibly death. Her intuition led her to other women in Prague who she befriended right away, spending her whole time in Prague with them. With them as friends, Noreen felt safe during her visit to that city.

Being able to act on intuition 100% of the time is rare for many of us. Traversing the **TRUST** model helps to become aware of the blockades we put up. Once we become adept at removing these blockages, we can move beyond this model to find out how to actually use our intuition.

CHAPTER 7

Moving Beyond the **TRUST** Model

The **TRUST** model provides us with some guidance as to how we can minimize the various hindrances preventing us from tapping into our intuition. With time, we should be able to move from making a conscious effort to detect hindrances to a subconscious ability.

We need to recognize that removing hindrances on a continuous basis is hard to do. Some may be better at tapping into their intuition than others, whereas others will need to revisit the **TRUST** model more often.

The goal is to ensure that our actions and decisions reflect what our intuitive thoughts tell us. It is not a race or a competition. Rather, it is our ability to improve our lives.

Once we individually traverse the **TRUST** model and remove the hindrances, intuition will be free to express itself. The next step is to find out how to use it.

GUT!

PART 3

How To Use It

The only real valuable thing is intuition. There is no logical way to the discovery of these elemental laws. There is only the way of intuition, which is helped by a feeling for the order lying behind the appearance. The intuitive mind is a sacred gift and the rational mind is a faithful servant. We have created a society that honors the servant and has forgotten the gift. We will not solve the problems of the world from the same level of thinking we were at when we created them. More than anything else, this new century demands new thinking: We must change our materially based analyses of the world around us to include broader, more multidimensional perspectives.

– Albert Einstein

CHAPTER 1

Finding Our Intuitive Medium

We all lead busy lives and are bombarded by personal events, those of friends and family, and situations around us. Our brains are continuously absorbing and evaluating these experiences – through all that, our intuition must fight for our attention.

For a few of us, we can quell the "noise" around and give intuition the proper attention it needs. But for the majority, quieting the noise is not so easy. Most of us will need to situate ourselves in our intuitive "medium".

Our intuitive medium is that environment in which we place ourselves or an activity that we need to perform that allows us to concentrate on our intuitive thoughts and focus on the decisions or actions we need to take.

By reflecting on the times we have stepped away from the noise to think about issues at hand, we should recognize our own intuitive mediums. We are not restricted to one medium. Some may have a medium specific to certain intuition types or situations, whereas others may have multiple mediums that help them focus on their intuition.

The interviewees reported a wide variety of mediums, including taking a shower, walking in the woods, travelling, going for a drive, cooking, sleeping, performing a hobby, meditating, flying, skiing or sitting back and staring at the ceiling, to name a few. These intuitive mediums are unique for each of us. For Steve Groves, it was cycling.

GUT!

Steve Groves is CIO of GoodLife Fitness, a successful chain of Canadian fitness facilities. Although Steve has used his intuition before, it was more subconscious in nature. Only after joining GoodLife Fitness did he begin consciously thinking about it.

"One of the things we did at GoodLife about six years ago was the whole senior management team went through and did the Myers-Briggs psychological assessment. And mine came back as INTJ [showing a predisposition to an intuitive nature] and so I'm thinking what's this [intuitive nature] all about? And how does that compare with the opposite of intuition?

"Obviously, none of us are really introspective enough to know what makes them tick. We try to study it, we try to understand it, but at the end of the day, it's difficult. It's who we are. So I started to look at this idea of intuition. That was the first time that I really honed in on this idea that there are times when your gut tells you something and you want to pay attention to it."

To better listen and tap into his intuitive thoughts, Steve places himself in his intuitive mediums, cycling and running for the more creative decisions, and insomnia for the riskier ones.

"When it's something that's exciting to me, those things usually happen, more often than not, on the bike. Running sometimes as well, but when I'm out on my bike, it's usually for three hours. I think your brain needs time to get away from whatever has been bugging it, and that might take 45 minutes. When you're out on the bike, there's no other stimulus around you. I try never to have a headphone in or anything when I'm biking. I know that my best ideas come that way. It's normally when I'm out on a long bike ride.

"If I have something nagging at me and my gut's telling me that we're doing something the wrong way or I'm doing something the wrong way, generally what happens is that's when the insomnia kicks in.

"I have to capture the ideas and outputs of both. I have to capture the risky ones, just to get them out of my head and figure out what actions I can actually take on them when I wake up in the morning. Then for the creative ones, I get home from my ride and try to record as much of it as I can so that I can look at it later.

"It's in those moments when my brain is firing with all the chemicals that are obviously going through your body when you're active. That's when a lot of the decisions are made. I'm not sitting there analyzing stuff. I'm not sitting here reading a document. I'm not talking to people. I'm just stepping back and reflecting on whatever the challenge or opportunity is that's in front of us. Then you just have these gut feelings."

Steve talks about a series of significant events driven entirely by intuitive thoughts, consistently finding himself immersed in his intuitive medium on an ongoing basis.

"I graduated during the recession in the early 1990s. Probably the last fundamental gut feeling that I ever acted on was when the Internet and the World Wide Web felt like they were becoming things that businesses were missing out on or ignoring. I started my first business, which was an internet marketing, digital marketing agency. I sold that in 2002 to a company in Woodstock, worked for them for six months. Then the opportunity came up to basically start up the IT department at GoodLife. I saw it as a startup within the financial stability of a large organization. Not as risky as starting a business again from scratch, and doing it on your own shoestring budget.

"Then the feeling came again back in 2007, when I couldn't articulate to our business why we needed to start focusing on social media to better engage with our members and to better engage with even our own employees. This was concerning me. I took a bit of a leap of faith and I left the fitness industry entirely. Again, my gut told me it was the right thing to do.

"I went and joined a media company, The London Free Press, and later Sun Media. That was probably the most fundamental decision that I made in my career, purely from gut feel."

Steve's creative juices were able to flow at The London Free Press as management gave him an open field to play in.

"They were gracious enough to basically hand me the brand and say, 'We know we're moving into a digital world, we don't know what that's going to look like, go play. Take it, run with it and tell us what you think needs to be done.'

"Literally, for the first six months, I was allowed to just sit, think, plan and talk. There was no pressure to come up with a 12-point plan for the next three years, within a week. When you're the CIO, IT director, manager of IT, whatever you want to call it, there's just those day-to-day activities that you're forced to focus in on.

"I think one of the challenges that I see in day-to-day business, and I saw it at The London Free Press, was that so many people are forced to deliver on a regular basis. At The London Free Press, it was so obvious because you had a deadline. Every night at eleven o'clock, you had to put the paper to bed, and then you could literally, yourself go home and go to bed. Every day, they had a new 'product' that had to come out, so they're always focused on, 'What am I going to produce today?' It was nobody's job to step back and say, my gut's telling me one thing, but I don't have the freedom to go off and explore that.

"I was really lucky in that my gut was telling me something and I was employed in a job where I was allowed to also explore that idea, the notion that I had to figure out how to create a strategic plan around that. It was easily the most thought-provoking and fascinating time in my career."

Because the organization gave Steve an open book to play with, moving in and out of his intuitive mediums allowed him to reshape and shift the way news was told, moving from total reliance on printed paper to this "thing" called social media.

"We were able to recognize and articulate to the rest of the management team that we were really a multi-platform media organization. We were no longer a newspaper. The printed paper just happened to be the thing that we pushed out every night, but our news cycle was 24 hours.

"Accomplishment number one was when the editorial team, the newsroom, changed their model. Our reporters had to figure out that they didn't roll in at nine o'clock in the morning, have a coffee, figure out their schedule for the day, have their first interview by lunch, second interview by the mid-afternoon, start writing later in the afternoon, and then finish by their eight o'clock deadline. That was the typical news cycle up until that point. They said, 'Okay, we get it now, we need to change the way that we communicate with our readers and internally.'"

Steve was successful in getting The London Free Press to embrace communicating the news using social media tools in addition to the printed paper.

"Now, you had people who were basically on Twitter and Facebook, writing versions of stories for the web, and evolving those stories on the web before it ever went to print.

"The mantra I had was 'evolve the story throughout the day'. When somebody says, 'Okay, it's deadline,' just take whatever version of the story that you have, and that's the one that goes to print, then you keep working on it. When your day is over, you hand the story off to somebody else, they work on it through the evening. Stories aren't meant to be written with a deadline, then printed and sent off. They're constantly evolving.

"That was the first success we had from an editorial standpoint, was that mind shift. That translated over into a series of experiments that we did, where they thought, 'this looks interesting, let's start trying to do broadcasting, let's start trying to be a live video broadcaster.' That culminated in The London Free Press being one of the top ten news broadcasters in the world for online video live streaming for a period of time."

This use of social media became extremely significant during a horrific event when Tori Stafford, an eight-year-old Canadian girl, was abducted from Woodstock, Ontario on April 8, 2009, sexually assaulted and murdered.

"That happened when the newsroom had started to fully embrace the digital world. It was the most devastating day of my life as a father, but it was also the most fascinating day of my life from a professional standpoint. When the story really broke early in the morning, 12 hours before the traditional newspaper 'deadline.'

"'We found a body.'

"That newsroom just completely took off and everybody went out and started doing things in a very digital fashion. They understood that this story would unfold throughout the day online. If they waited to circulate any news until their newspaper came out the next day then the breaking news story would have already been told by the radio and TV journalists.

"The newsroom ended up winning a Canadian National Newspaper Award in the breaking news category for coverage of the Stafford story. It was because they were on Twitter, they were on Facebook, they were the only ones broadcasting live every day, doing a live press conference, feeding photos and stories from the field, from their Blackberries.

"They really started to embrace this idea. We had great success with it. We were considered to be pioneers, not only within the Sun Media chain, but within North America. We got the attention of a lot of internationally recognized newspapers, who were monitoring what we were doing. We were sharing ideas back and forth with them: Chicago Tribune, Boston Globe, different papers we were able to connect in with."

Steve eventually left The London Free Press to join GoodLife Fitness again. He still uses his creative thinking, but because his role as CIO is more operational in nature, he is more involved in the day-to-day operations. Yet he still misses his time at The London Free Press.

"There's not a day that goes by that I don't miss my time at The London Free Press. Best time in my career. The people at The London Free Press know that, the people at GoodLife know that. It was the most creatively stimulating…

"Do I miss it? Absolutely. Are there outlets for that at GoodLife? There are, and I'm kind of trying to carve a role for myself there. We have a relatively small department, I don't have to have 400 or 500 people in my department and six directors, where I can just leave it to them. I have to be there, hands-on as much as I can be. Do I dream of a day when I can step back, be more strategic, go into our clubs, spend more time with our CEO, and think creatively about how our business will be different in five years? Absolutely."

GUT!

Steve's creative intuition started expressing itself early on in his career. His ability to think differently had Steve constantly immersed in his intuitive mediums so he could focus on elevating the winning strategies and mitigating the riskier ones.

Situating ourselves in our intuitive mediums will allow us to focus on what our intuition is telling us. However, if we do not align our intuitive drivers with our experiences or situations, we stifle our intuitive abilities, despite situating ourselves in our intuitive mediums. For Michael Tait, following the herd into a financial career was optically popular and financially rewarding, but personally, he was not in a happy place. He needed to change his career path completely despite others questioning his decision. The change was essential for him in being a better person, a better father, and a happier individual.

CHAPTER 2

Alignment of Intuitive Drivers

To use intuition to its fullest extent, we need to align our personal and professional experiences with our intuitive drivers.

Situations in which we are "out of alignment" significantly curtail our ability to acknowledge and listen to our intuitive thoughts.

We need to gradually make appropriate changes to our personal and professional lives so that they are consistent with our own intuitive drivers.

Michael Tait found himself in a career that began to show signs of misalignment with his values, and his intuition guided him to make a complete career change, much to the astonishment of his peers.

GUT!

Michael Tait is a founding partner at SHOP.CA. His journey that resulted in him joining SHOP.CA began when he changed his professional career to align with his intuitive driver, being happy.

"I like to think about, more holistically, what do I want to 'be' as opposed to what do I want to 'do', and what makes me a better father and a better husband, because being a good father and a good husband makes me happy.

"That's my intuition and that's 'values,' and that's important to me and that's a good thing. I think it is important to dream an ideal and pursue this – I disagree that one cannot have their cake and eat it too.

"Your intuition wants you to be happy. I think people are realizing that. I don't like to think about any generation being unique from another, but I think that it is a very effective mechanism to stand back and say I'm going to 'be' the person that would make me most proud. My sense is this is easier to achieve when you are happy.

"That other stuff, I don't know what you call it. I think it's very manufactured by society and by what you **think** is going to make you happy, not what **is** going to make you happy.

"I see a lot of people galvanize themselves against their intuition sometimes. And you wonder what the world would look like if everyone just went with it. It would be interesting. There might be a lot more open and honest conversations and perhaps stronger relationships, I'm not sure. It would be an adjustment but communication as a whole would elevate."

Michael began a career in the investment banking area after completing his MBA. This particular choice was due mainly to "following the herd".

"I've spent several years in the financial industry, for example, and the reason I bring that up is simply because most of my peers in that world, when making key life decisions, made them for financial reasons. That was the extent to which critical choices were considered and weighed... where and how am I going to make the most money was the core of this contemplation.

"And everything else will just have to get out of the way. Many choose to work in an environment that makes them unhappy, or choose to work in a way that causes them to not be themselves at home, or choose to work in an environment where they are not able to see their family to the extent that they want to or ought to – all sacrificed at the altar of income.

"That's not a novel or a new thing. It's been going on for thousands of years probably in different ways. In my career, from the age of 25 to 40, I was in that environment."

Michael's overriding purpose of making money overrode his intuitive sense that, maybe, he was not happy. Once Michael made the jump to align his professional pursuits with his intuitive driver, happiness, and align it with his professional pursuits by joining SHOP.CA, he had difficulty explaining his decision to his colleagues.

"To work backwards and try to explain that to the linear mind of a financier was very hard. A lot of my friends and colleagues would look at me quizzically with one eyebrow raised and ask, 'What are you doing?'

"I knew that it felt right to me and in fact was quite natural. And that's why I did it. It was very hard to explain why I felt that way, partially because 'breaking' from the pack just is not any fun for those still in the pack.

"I felt a little uncomfortable sometimes going down the path of explaining that because most of the time I would just say, 'You know what, you've got to make your decision. I've made mine. Your choice is your choice, i.e. use your gut, use your intuition, make your own call. I've made mine based on mine. I'm not trying to sway you either way. I never would.'"

One of the surprising things that Michael has encountered is that people ask him to sway their decisions because they do not feel strong enough to move away from past choices and follow their own intuition.

"Most of the time, the people that are challenging you to explain your choices that are based on your intuition are often asking if perhaps they should be making the same choices – as they have similar intuition yet are searching for the potency to follow it.

"People often ask others to indirectly influence them in the direction of their own intuition – again, they want to obey these feelings because they intuitively know it will make them happier, but they don't have the courage to do so standalone."

The easy road is to keep following the herd or maintain the path we are on because we made the choice, even when we know internally that we have not made the right choice or the best choice for us. Michael talks about intuitive hindrances and our ability to openly justify the role we are in, even though internally we are unhappy.

"There's a capability in most of us to know what we should do, or want to do or ought to do based upon our intuition of who we want to be. If you really think why you'd ignore your intuition, I do think it's based in ego and fear. And it is not fear of the unknown – there is no such thing – it is fear of imaginary outcomes that are often not real, but it requires less courage to believe in these outcomes.

"When we let that fear take over and make decisions or choices for us, then we are incredibly adept at convincing ourselves and others that we made those decisions for honorable upstanding reasons. I wonder about that.

"At the end of the day, if you're not letting intuition guide you as much as perhaps you ought to, you're getting further and further away from who you want to be and likely happiness or peace.

"Instead of bridging that gap by listening to your intuition, people tend to bridge that gap, I think, by convincing themselves that they're making the right choices based on things that are less real, but work for the moment.

"It's much easier, obviously, to just do what everyone else around you is doing, and perhaps sometimes ignore your inner voice in the name of some very important things: in the name of my responsibility, in the name of a commitment to a company, or my family, or my mentors, or whoever/whatever. Unfortunately, 'group think' encourages such justification. If any of your readers have ever experienced the sensation and accompanying discomfort of justifying an action that is counter-intuitive, and watching their audience collectively nod their heads in agreement, they will know what I mean by this.

"There are a lot of justifications, very strong ones that help us make a case against our guts, against our intuition sometimes. And because intuition, just generally speaking, is a lot harder to explain in a world that requires a lot of explanation, I wonder if we spend a lot of time trying to figure out, justify, or explain things we're doing in tangible ways when we're doing them for intangible reasons."

While in the financial industry, Michael usually acted on his intuition and began to distance himself from certain situations in his career that went against what he thought was the right thing to do despite negative financial and career progression ramifications. These situations clearly went against his intuitive driver of being happy.

"I guess there would be three or four things during my career within finance that would be deemed somewhat controversial if you just looked at them through my optic lens. I've made some decisions on principle and feel. You try to make change and you try to do what you think is the honourable thing and best positions you to be that ideal you have dreamt.

"There's a substantial ethical quagmire that is well documented in the financial industry. It's such a transaction-based business that there are millions and millions of transactions happening every minute, whether it be in currency or bonds or equity or any security where there's a buyer and a seller. If there's a spread, and there's two views, and they're meeting in 'the middle', and there's a 'middleman', then there's lots of opportunity for, shall we say, moral freedom.

"I've seen a lot of things that just didn't feel right to me that you stand up for. Maybe that's changed in the past four or five years. Certainly, in the first 15 years of my career, no one really wanted to hear that. I'm sure there are tons of examples of this.

"What I'm really saying is that making choices based on what felt right to me, and the test that I give myself of how I felt about things, led me to sacrifice very lucrative outcomes.

"There have been a few times when you realize, behind closed doors, something untoward happens in a business. The path from realization to action is when courage is tested and unfortunately can be quite fleeting amongst large groups of highly intelligent people. What I have found is that when courage fails and intuition is ignored, it simply delays the inevitable – so it's best to go with your intuition in these situations and rip off the band aid, as they say.

"When these decisions based on fear are made and involve ignoring intuition, they are very difficult to explain, unsurprisingly – I have never heard an executive say, 'I didn't have the courage to follow my intuition – had I done so, this would not have happened.'"

Michael's career in the financial industry, although successful in one sense, was not challenging to him. With his move up the corporate ladder, his ability to use intuitive decisions in his position became less important in his role.

This intuitive "stifling" combined with his urge to realign his professional career with his intuitive driver resulted in him joining SHOP.CA.

"For someone like me who relies on their intuition quite a bit, you perhaps are attracted to do business with others who rely on intuition as well. You have to trust your intuition and you have to create the organizational structure that allows the intuition to be put forth and executed upon. That is part of the reasoning and appeal of a company such as SHOP.CA.

"I was on the front line in the financial industry where I was making split-second decisions and following my intuition constantly whilst making decisions for my clients in real time. That was great. But over time you become more and more involved in management and the next thing you know you're a managing director in a 75,000 person organization where intuition becomes irrelevant. There is a structure, and I get that, you're managing risk. When you're playing with hundreds of billions of dollars in shareholders' capital, how you feel about something becomes less interesting. That's where that industry became less interesting to me.

"I find that in an environment such as this, SHOP.CA, we're making real-time decisions. Drew[44], the team and I are constantly challenging each other's intuition. We consider facts but are really just causing each person to think about how they 'feel' about a series of options.

"When making key decisions, starting with an open and honest conversation is key, with little preamble. Efficiency is different from hasty – as careful is to reckless – so if an executive is 'feeling' conflicted and he doesn't know why yet, he is encouraged to 'sleep on it'. Whether it be a long walk, workout or a good night's sleep, sometimes intuition needs to be conjured to the surface.

"The move to SHOP.CA felt right because I liked the team. That was enough for me to know that given the opportunity, balanced against the analytical part of my mind, the prospects and enthusiasm were there. Being a part of building something offers tangible gratification that is otherwise elusive in business – and hence risk tolerance is higher when this gratification is present. This was a driving force behind this decision.

"Intuition allows us to move quickly and I think it requires a lot of trust in each other. The organization has to be responsive to intuition. Building an intuitive team is important, but as important is to create an environment where this intuition is valued and can be translated into an executable idea.

"You learn that, as time progresses, if you let intuition steer you, how others may feel about that becomes less and less important. From a career point of view and a personal point of view, you need to understand what exactly and specifically makes you happy – put differently, who do you want to 'be'? Just make a list.

"One of the only things that troubles me more than seeing somebody do something that they know they should not be doing, is somebody not doing what they know they should be doing."

GUT!

---

44 Drew Green – Founder, CEO and Chairman of SHOP.CA.

Clearly, Michael's desire to be happy was his intuitive driver. When moments in his career did not align with "happiness", he decided to make a change, despite the opportunity costs.

In the end, he joined SHOP.CA, an organization that runs on intuitive thought from senior leadership, right down to the front line employees, and whose core values have been filtered through intuitive thoughts. He is clearly in a happy place, professionally and personally.

For those of us who are not happy where we are, it is essential to find out where our current intuitive strengths are, where we would like them to be, and then do whatever it takes to make that shift. Hence, we shift intuition quadrants, realigning our Intuitive Zone of Influence to match where we really want to be. Once there, our intuition operates with much more efficiency.

CHAPTER 3

Shifting Intuition Quadrants

We may discover a desire to shift intuition quadrants when we find ourselves in situations where we are not as proficient in those intuitive areas that interest us individually. This could be because we find ourselves in personal or professional situations that seem to hinder our ability to make the intuitive decisions we wish to make.

Another reason to shift intuition quadrants is that we are moving further along in both our personal and professional endeavours, and the roles and responsibilities that we take on may require us to boost our strength in another intuition quadrant. This shift will enhance our ability to recognize the intuitive thoughts guided by that particular quadrant.

To successfully make the desired shift, two steps are required.

The first step is to find out where our current and desired Intuitive Zones of Influence lie in our own personal Intuition Quadrant chart. To do this, we would answer a series of questions[45] that take into account our personal thoughts on where we are, where we wish to be from a personal and professional standpoint, and any intuitive hindrances that we seem to have.

For example, Figure 11 shows an individual's Current Intuitive Zone of Influence who has good strengths in both situational and experiential intuition. Figure 12 shows this same individual's Desired Intuitive Zone of Influence, which indicates a desired strength increase in relational intuition.

---

45 The questions that produce an "Intuitive Improvement Score" can be answered at www.gutincorporated.com/INzone.

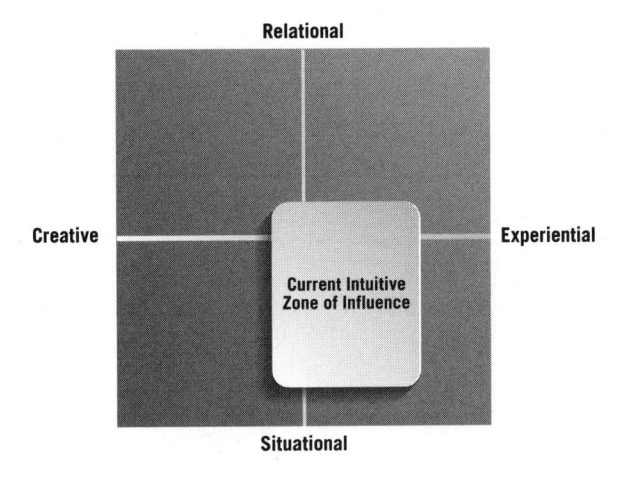

Figure 11 Current Intuitive Zone of Influence

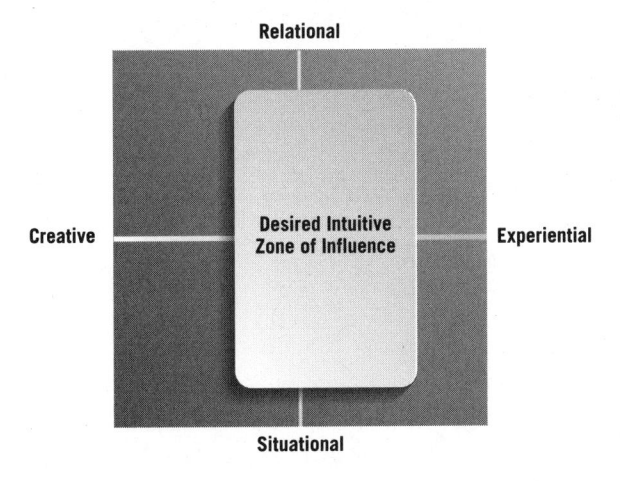

Figure 12 Desired Intuitive Zone of Influence

Once the respective Intuitive Zones of Influence are placed on top of each other, as we can see in Figure 13, we can quickly see where this person's intuition needs to shift.

In addition to these charts, a proprietary Intuition Zone Score (INzone Score) is calculated. With the ideal score being 100%, this will indicate how much relative effort we will require to reach our Desired Intuitive Zone of Influence. In the example above, the individual's INzone Score was 60%, based on the shifts in the Intuitive Zones of Influence. A higher INzone Score indicates how close we are to where we believe our collective intuitive strengths need to be. A lower score indicates that we may have some work to do to get to our Desired Intuitive Zone of Influence.

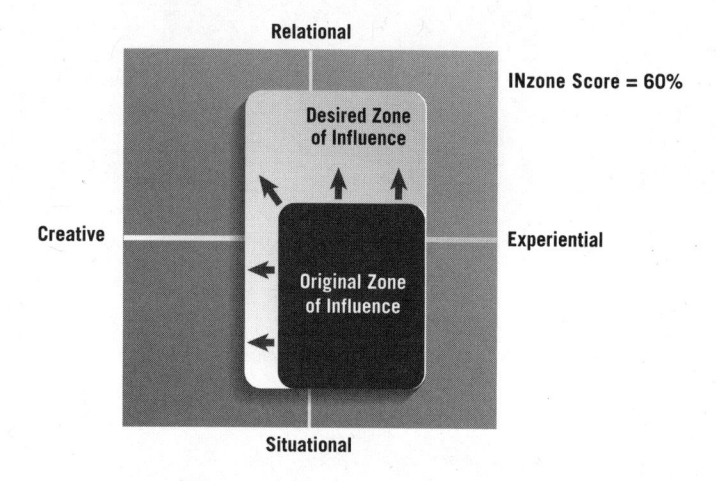

Figure 13 Shifting of Intuitive Zone of Influence and Intuition Zone Score

The associated Intuitive Zones of Influence and INzone Score will only be as accurate as how honestly we answer the questionnaire and may shift over time as we take on different roles and responsibilities that we enjoy.

The second step is to uncover the process of increasing our INzone Score. One way would be to immerse ourselves in those particular environments where that particular intuitive type is able to provide guidance. In the example illustrated above, this person clearly wishes to primarily improve his or her strength in relational intuition. This person should find a more social role in addition to relying on the support of peers who would help this person recognize some of the intuitive indicators that inform relational intuition. Over time, this person should be able to increase his or her intuitive strength in that quadrant, resulting in a closer alignment between the Current and Desired Intuitive Zones of Influence and an improved INzone Score. Another way would have us enroll in conferences, seminars, or courses[46] where we can learn practical techniques in how to increase our intuitive strengths in the other quadrants.

---

46 www.gutincorporated.com/events

144 GUT!

It is important to ensure that we honestly wish to move into a new intuition quadrant. There is no ideal situation in which quadrant(s) we need to be strong.

For some of us, the status quo is fine. We are happy with where we are in all aspects of our lives and have no current desire to increase our strength in any of the intuitive quadrants. In fact, we may even strengthen our intuitive capabilities in those intuition quadrants in which we are already strong. In this situation, our intuition is operating at a maximum level.

On the other hand, some of us may feel the need to strengthen our intuitive capabilities in the other intuition quadrants and are open to a change in our lives. We may not be happy in our current situations or we may see a natural progression for ourselves that we desire.

It is important to note that there is no "best-case" scenario. These choices are individual in nature. Our intuition will let us know if we need to stay on the same path or if we need to change. In some cases, certain aspects of life change. This could be a sudden promotion, graduation, complete change in industry, or a life-altering event such as a loss of sight, as Christa Nasser faced.

GUT!

Christa Nasser has had diabetes since she was 6 years old. She learned very early that she had a condition called diabetic retinopathy and neovascular glaucoma. Over time, this disease slowly begins to degrade eyesight. In Christa's case, this disease accelerated when she was in her early 20s.

"In my early 20s, I could still see at the time, but little things were starting to go. It was harder to focus on things, and it was harder to see at night.

"When I was 23, I moved out of my parent's house and went to Toronto and that's when it started getting really bad. I had a whole bunch of treatments – laser treatments and injections and surgeries. About a year after that, I was told that I was legally blind in both eyes and that they could do nothing about it. So, I moved back home in 2010."

This was personally devastating for Christa as she had to sacrifice a number of things she had built up.

"The first six months were probably the hardest. I had to give up my car keys. I quit my job. I left my first apartment and I moved back to my parent's home. It wasn't exactly the highlight of my life."

On New Year's Day that year, Christa told herself that she needed to take charge and move ahead with her life, despite her eyesight issues. Much to her surprise, she excelled in her course.

"I decided to enroll in school, which pushed me to be more comfortable travelling on my own and being independent and using a computer. I just really enjoyed the course and I had never done this well in school before.

"I started off in the office administration general one-year program and really enjoyed it. This was the best I had ever done in school. So why not stay for the extra year and get more experience and start doing the co-ops because I was nervous going back to work. This was the first time going back to work after going blind. I wanted to have an opportunity to spend four months at a company to realize whether or not this is what I am capable of before I try and get in somewhere for the rest of my life."

Before losing her sight, Christa was strong in relational intuition, and relied on her eyesight and hearing to watch for anomalous signals from others that might indicate deceit, dishonesty, and other such issues.

"Facial expression did help me. You can tell by the look in someone's eye. The way someone I knew acted, everyone sees them as this great person, great friend, not that they were a bad person. But, I had this feeling that when I was around them, it was not a good idea and it would turn into bad things. It was a feeling in my gut."

This person that Christa had a bad sense about acted in ways that ended up pulling Christa further away from a close friend, destroying that relationship.

After losing her eyesight, Christa could no longer rely on her eyesight to inform her relational intuition. However, her intuition made a sudden switch and she gained a tremendous amount of strength quickly in her situational intuition.

"My intuition comes into play a lot when I am travelling. I just know that either I have walked too far or I have missed a corner that I was supposed to turn. I am not necessarily lost, but I just know that I am not where I am supposed to be."

Christa is able to travel extensively because of Jorinda, a guide dog that is also her companion and has helped her in both her relational and situational intuition by providing certain signals that help Christa's intuition assess the situation.

"She's really good about different situations and people. There are a lot of times where I'll be waiting for the bus at Dundas and Richmond and, all of a sudden, she will get up and stand in front of me and stand really, really close to me. And you can kind of tell that maybe I should leave and go wait at a different bus stop. Or she is backing away from somebody else. I'd feed off of that. Maybe it's a good idea for me to turn around and walk in a different direction.

"There have been times where I'll be walking home somewhere in a completely familiar area. So we'll both know exactly where we are. And she'll just stop dead in the middle of the sidewalk and won't move and her ears go back. I'll just say, 'Okay, we're going to turn around and we are going to take the long way home' because it's always easier to get out of the situation. But, if she wasn't there, I would have never ever have known that."

Christa has had to rely on her heightened awareness of her senses to inform both her relational and situational intuition.

"I always tell people that I can't hear any better, I just listen better than sighted people. I just know how to listen better to what I am hearing. Walking down the street and crossing the road, if I know that a certain corner is supposed to be a stop sign, and there are cars that are idling, then I obviously must not be at a stop sign, I must be at a stop light.

"A lot of people are surprised that I can tell when Jorinda's even just turned her head and I know that she's not paying attention because I can feel in her harness that she has looked to the side."

Losing her eyesight has given Christa a chance to be much more self-aware and have a better sense of who she is. She has lost the ego one might typically have in their 20s and has developed a sense of purpose.

"I am much more self-aware. I know what I want and what I care about. I didn't have much ambition before. I didn't really care about my grades, I'd pull off a 70% and I'd say, 'Oh whatever, it's a passing grade.' But I still wanted to have the bigger, the better, the best things. I think I was just lazy. I think my ambition to do better had a lot to do with people telling me that I couldn't or shouldn't do things.

"Now, I don't really care so much about having the best things but I have the ambition to work harder and make myself better, push myself to do things that I would have never been able to do before."

This intuition quadrant shift has also changed Christa in terms of self-confidence and communication.

"I was more of a follower before, whereas now, I don't do that so much. I'm much more of a leader and make my own decisions. I don't let other people tell me what I should do or what I can do. I wasn't the type of person that would stick up for myself or defend myself, whereas now I don't really care about what people say to me. It doesn't matter what they think. It's what I can do, what I think I can do."

GUT!

In Christa's case, losing her eyesight meant that she had to go about life in a very different way. The visual indicators, instrumental for her relational intuition, were no longer there. She had to not only rely on other senses, but the cues from the environment aided by her companion, Jorinda, who has been instrumental for her situational intuition and in guiding her.

Her situation brought her closer to listening to her intuition than before as she became much more self-aware and gained confidence by consistently overcoming intuitive hindrances. This has left her in a position where she is happier on a personal level, and given her recent scholastic achievements, soon in a professional level.

In the comfort of the intuition quadrant we find that we are strong in, or as we make the shift from one intuition quadrant to another, we will find that, over time, we begin to make consistent intuitive decisions. The reality is that our intuitive decision-making abilities will face hurdles along the way. To jump over those hurdles, we would need to revisit the **TRUST** model.

CHAPTER 4

Revisiting the TRUST Model

Over time, we should become more adept at tapping into our intuition. Despite developing some "expertise", the reality is that we will likely experience one or more of the intuitive hindrances along the way. After shifting into a new intuition quadrant, we may also encounter intuitive hindrances because our nascent entry has not had the benefit of time or experience.

Because of the above issues, we might require a revisit of the **TRUST** model to remind ourselves how to better tap into intuition by effectively removing the hindrances.

All in all, by using this feedback loop, we will inevitably become effective at allowing our intuition to express itself. Furthermore, we will be empowered to take the appropriate decisions or actions that will help us be content in our experiences, regardless of the encounters, roles, or responsibilities we undertake.

Eventually, we begin to lead happier lives moving forward, leaving the past experiences, good or bad, behind us.

We can thank our intuition for helping us lead happier lives.

We can also thank ourselves for taking the steps to maximize our intuitive abilities.

GUT!

PART 4

GUT! Incorporated

Intuition is critical in virtually everything you do but without relentless preparation and execution, it is meaningless. I talked to people I trusted that knew me and they said, 'This is not what you should do.' It wasn't so easy. And people said, 'You know, you are just crazy. You are working for the top PC company in the world. How could you even think of doing this? You've lost your mind.' And yet that voice said, 'Go west, young man. Go west.' And sometimes you just have to go for it.

— **Tim Cook**

CHAPTER 1

Does Corporate Intuition Exist?

As individuals, we are all able to tap into our intuition.

A company, whatever the size, is a collection of individuals, and each of these individuals has an ability to tap into intuition.

Therefore, corporate intuition must exist, provided the individuals working in a company have the opportunity to use their intuition within their own corporate roles and responsibilities.

Bob Lutz, former President of Chrysler, recounts[47] that, despite mounting internal and external criticisms, intuition was responsible for his company producing the incredibly successful Dodge Viper. Not only did sales begin to rise substantially, but both public perception and company morale significantly increased, resulting in the company's turnaround in the 1990s.

Many celebrated people such as Richard Branson, Albert Einstein, Tim Cook, Steve Jobs and Oprah Winfrey, among others, run their personal and professional lives primarily using intuition.

There has also been a growing body of research on intuition within a corporate environment, which has credited corporate intuition with helping to form a corporate vision[48], ethical decision-making[49], positively affecting those outside of the firm[50] and making a significant competitive impact[51].

---
47 Hayashi, A. M. (2001). When to trust your gut. Harvard Business Review, 79(2), 59-65.
48 Kopeikina, L. (2006). The elements of a clear decision. MIT Sloan Management Review, 47(2), 19.
49 Woiceshyn, J. (2011). A Model for Ethical Decision Making in Business: Reasoning, Intuition, and Rational Moral Principles. J Bus Ethics (2011) 104:311–323.
50 Kaufmann, L. et al.(2014). Rational and intuitive decision-making in sourcing teams: Effects on decision outcomes. Journal of Purchasing & Supply Management 20 (2014) 104–112
51 Williams, K. (2012), Business Intuition: The Mortar among the Bricks of Analysis. Journal of Management Policy and Practice vol. 13(5)

Perhaps more importantly, intuition has been shown to positively affect a firm's performance in those business environments characterized by some uncertainty[52].

It may be safe to assume that intuition plays a major role in a company, from birth to maturity.

So, what is it?

---

[52] Khatri, N., & Ng, H. A. (2000). The role of intuition in strategic decision making. Human Relations, 53(1), 57-86.

CHAPTER 2

What is Corporate Intuition?

It is no surprise that corporate intuition shares similar characteristics with personal intuition. Executives themselves have mentioned that intuition is subconscious[53], essential for entrepreneurs when starting a company[54,55], instant in nature resulting in speedy decisions[56], and is supported by data, experience, and rational thinking[57].

In corporate intuition, as opposed to personal intuition, a collection of intuitive experiences come together to make improvements to processes, procedures, strategic direction, or whatever other characteristic within a company environment will benefit from intuitive thinking.

Companies are "born" with intuition as entrepreneurs starting a business from scratch leverage their own intuitive thoughts. As this company grows in size, more people are added, and the company begins to rely on their collective implicit and explicit experiences.

When taken together, the company becomes intuitive.

A company also has its own strengths in certain types of intuition, which can be mapped on a Corporate Intuition Quadrant.

---

53 Burke, L. A., & Miller, M. K. (1999). Taking the mystery out of intuitive decision making. The Academy of Management Executive, 13(4), 91-99.
54 La Pira, F. (2011). Entrepreneurial intuition, an empirical approach. Journal of Management & Marketing Research, 6, 1-22.
55 Sadler-Smith, E. (2004). Cognitive style and the management of small and medium-sized enterprises. Organization Studies, 25(2), 155-181.
56 Wally, S., & Baum, J. R. (1994). Personal and structural determinants of the pace of strategic decision making. Academy of Management Journal, 37(4), 932-956.
57 Burke, L. A., & Miller, M. K. (1999). Taking the mystery out of intuitive decision making. The Academy of Management Executive, 13(4), 91-99.

CHAPTER 3

The Corporate Intuition Quadrant

Much like personal intuition, corporate intuition can be characterized by four main types: strategic, operational, relational, or situational. The relative strengths for each intuition type and how it changes over time will be specific to either an individual or a group of individuals based on the requirements of that particular group.

For example, a group of employees who are specifically responsible for operations should have a collective strength in operational intuition. In addition, the supervisor or manager overseeing that group should be slightly stronger in relational intuition to ensure that he or she is able to bring on the proper resources.

As a company grows, the collective intuitive capabilities and related strengths of various departments such as engineering, sales, marketing, and so on can be mapped to a Corporate Intuition Quadrant, which will show the Corporate Intuitive Zone of Influence for that specific team or department.

The company as a whole has a Corporate Intuitive Zone of Influence that will be affected by factors such as the industry they are in (fast-paced technology software versus an operationally-driven distribution centre), where the company is in its life cycle (start-up versus mature) and size (small collective versus a stratified number of corporate levels).

Where the corporate intuitive strengths lie based on these types can be visually represented by a Corporate Intuition Quadrant (Figure 14).

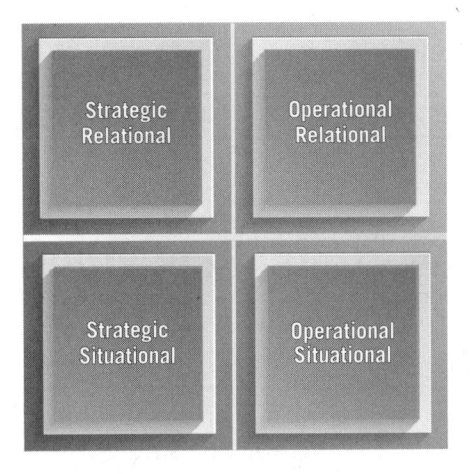

Strategic Relational	Operational Relational
Strategic Situational	Operational Situational

Figure 14 Corporate Intuition Quadrant

The first corporate intuition type, strategic intuition, relies on a keen intuitive sense for the long term strategy of a company or to be able to intuitively know how to position its products and services in the marketplace. Jean-Pierre Taillon's ability to transform how the market saw security services resulted in G4S Solutions Canada Ltd. experiencing tremendous growth under his leadership.

CHAPTER 4

Corporate Strategic Intuition

Those in a corporate setting who use strategic intuition tend to make decisions with little data, and rely on their past experiences and the advice and past experiences of others. The types of decisions affect the ongoing strategy of a company, such as changing a brand, introducing a new product, or starting a company. There is an inherent understanding that the underlying processes that support the strategic goal will be in place under the watchful eyes of members of the management team.

These individuals use their intuition to translate a vision or an idea into strategy to make it a reality. The intuition mainly goes through a creative process and uses a rational process for minimal support. The intuition makes the connection between the long term corporate needs with short term processes and goals to accelerate growth in a particular business area, much like the growth that G4S Solutions Canada Ltd. experienced under the leadership of former President and CEO, Jean-Pierre Taillon.

GUT!

Jean-Pierre Taillon, who presently heads up security provider G4S UK and Ireland as Regional Managing Director Central Government Services, had a background in the telecommunications sector before being asked to lead G4S Solutions Canada Ltd. (G4S) as President and CEO.

Jean-Pierre talks about how he used his intuition in a creative way despite being in a commoditized market.

"*Intuition is really about being a little more creative within the walls of* a commoditized product. I always called it the art of the deal. I found that when I was in telecom, everybody who is going to buy is going to buy and turn it into a commodity. You're buying minutes, you're buying bandwidth, you're buying pipes.

"What I used to like to do was see if you can turn it into some kind of solution. What problem are we trying to solve? How are you going to solve that problem? If it's telecom or if it's a network or whatever, that's how we're going to solve the problem, and hopefully put some magic inside of it and build some margins.

"We were doing virtual storage before virtual storage was even popular. If you're too small of a client, why don't you just buy a portion of that storage kit capacity and just pay for it in years versus buying a big hunk of hardware? Again, it was pure intuition, knowing that there's something there."

Jean-Pierre cautions that you can be visionary in your thinking, but in the end, there needs to be a business case to be made. Intuition will help build that bridge, but it needs practice.

"Intuition needs practice. It's whenever the rubber hits the road. In a lot of cases you may say, 'I've got this brilliant idea,' but it might be 10 years ahead of its time, physically and/or economically and/or reality. That's when the magic comes: when you actually start looking at these things. Every idea's got merit, but at the end of the day, which one will make profitable growth, which one makes sense, or which one can you live on?"

Jean-Pierre stresses the importance of having the right resources to help support your intuitive thinking once you have established what corporate strategy you are moving forward with.

"In a lot of cases, a lot of CEOs will see this. You've got to reflect upon what kind of company you want to create. What kind of brand do you want to create? Once you can figure that out, then it depends on the people that can rally around that brand and that environment.

"A lot of people end up self-selecting, which helps you basically guide the company. Folks that like a certain style of company, going into a certain market, delivering a certain market, will either be with you, quickly leave, or be a problem."

Jean-Pierre's strategy to make G4S successful had to follow the same intuitive guidelines that he used in the telecom sector – what do you have, what strategy will you employ, and who do you select.

When he joined G4S, he was already playing catch-up.

"When I took it over, we were primarily a small, $160 million company, Canada was a very little branch. It was this very limited brand, people didn't really know it.

"We had some aviation, but we lost the contract for performance issues, quality issues, and that type of thing. When it came time to even look at it, the global organization said don't even waste your time. Most of the people around me said the same thing."

The brand presence in other parts of the world were strong, despite the weak brand in Canada.

"It was a premier brand in the UK, it was a premier brand in India. Everybody knows G4S in India. It's huge employer down there. In the UK, well now there's scandals, but pre-scandals, it was a well-respected brand."

Jean-Pierre's intuition led him to formulate the corporate strategy he needed to continue to grow G4S's customer base.

"At the end of the day it is just gut thinking, saying, look, I know we can do this. I realized, in the security business you want to de-commoditize it and add value. From there, the thought process starts building itself.

"I've got the right people, they just need to be focused. The story was, we would take our capabilities from around the world, build a top-notch team, and basically just go from there. That was sort of the theme."

Jean-Pierre's intuitive decision-making was instrumental in G4S Canada being awarded a lucrative aviation contract, despite the company losing an aviation contract before Jean-Pierre took over.

"A good intuitive example was when we won the cash aviation contract, a billion dollar contract. Just knowing that we could do it, and then taking the time to execute, it was basically all gut despite everything just telling you that we couldn't do it.

"The indicators were that we couldn't even bid on this job because of past history and past issues we'd had, but my intuition had it so that if we can rebrand the company in front of the client and show them that we're a brand new company with new thinking, new talent, and new behaviour, and bring the world's capabilities to Canada and showcase that, we'd have an opportunity to win this deal."

To ensure that G4S was to be considered a serious contender for the contract, Jean-Pierre maintained regular communication with the client, providing extensive information on G4S's capabilities in similar contract opportunities around the world.

"It was pretty much all myself for two years. I would contact them quarterly, just to ensure they knew who we are, what we're doing, some of our capabilities around the world: Belgium, Schiphol, London-Heathrow. With that, they finally realized that these guys have a license to bid and be part of it. And we actually won the whole British Columbia tender. First time we ever even had a footprint in British Columbia."

Once the contract was awarded, Jean-Pierre had to execute on putting in place the structural elements to support the contract.

"I basically had to hire from scratch, find a location from scratch, build an office, hire everybody, build a team, and support the area with product."

Jean-Pierre also applies his creative intuition when looking at other business opportunities that leverage the corporate strengths G4S has.

"Right now, I'm in the middle of thinking about the next generation organizational structure, and we're thinking of calling it Advanced Services Delivery. This is kind of at the beginning stages of what we're doing,

"This would be stuff that has monitoring systems that monitor texts and tweets. So you're a company, you're doing something in the marketplace, you're worried about threats. We'll basically monitor that.

"Actually, I'll give you a great example. A worldwide large gold extractor just had an annual general meeting. This company does a lot of interesting work in North Africa, in Nairobi, in tougher places in the world. They wanted us to monitor the web, and monitor Facebook, and monitor Twitter, and monitor whatever you can in social media, to ensure that when they do their annual meeting, there's not going to be protests outside. And if there are, we know what people are saying.

"So that's the kind of thinking that we're looking into. And it fits in *nicely with what we do. It's an advanced service, it's very niche, small, not everybody can do it. But that's just one of the pieces that we're looking at."*

GUT!

Jean-Pierre's strategic intuition pulls from his ability to think creatively despite being in a commoditized business. Not only has he been successful in adding significantly to the revenues and customer base, but he has mapped out a healthy corporate strategy to continue G4S's successful journey.

In Kevin Higgins' case, his strength in corporate operational intuition helped him shift his new division's business model away from one he had used for the bulk of his career at 3M.

CHAPTER 5

Corporate Operational Intuition

Operational intuition in a corporate setting primarily focuses on making intuitive decisions in areas that are more operational and short term in nature. These types of intuitive decisions tend to rely on more data and deductive logic, although the related changes may have creative elements.

An operational intuitive decision is made by those who have filled operational roles in their careers and have some strength in creative intuition. The creativity needs to respect the underlying processes and procedures that are put in place or that need to be changed. Generally this type of intuitive thinking leads to improved procedures and processes that support the intuitive strategy put in place by senior management. Kevin Higgins provides a perfect example of how he used operational intuition to better a process.

GUT!

Kevin Higgins holds the position of Vice-President of the Industrial Business Group for 3M Canada. He joined 3M in 1980 as Marketing Manager and National Sales Manager for the copying products division. Since then, he has held marketing, sales leadership, and business management positions in a number of 3M business units ranging from engineering systems division to medical and health care.

Working for 3M, which is a data- and process-driven organization, has meant that in Kevin's leadership roles decisions taken rely on data. Despite this reliance, Kevin has consistently used his intuition in his roles, often using data as a supplemental tool.

"I rely on intuition all the time. We do live in a data-driven world, but it has to be tempered with what we know about the real world."

A prime example of how he used intuition to vastly improve a particular area of business occurred when he took over the medical business area, which shipped a variety of medical and surgical supplies such as tape, dressings, casting products, and monitoring products.

"We were shipping directly to hospitals, which allowed us direct access to the customers. Yet, in a 3M world, the majority of our business goes through distribution."

When Kevin began overseeing this division, he quickly saw operational inefficiencies.

"We were choking on it. The business hadn't grown, the reps were distracted from focusing on growth and new business acquisition as they were handling niggling issues about invoice clarity, returns, pricing updates, and so on."

Kevin talks about an example of an inefficient process where a hospital would order a small quantity of a particular medical supply item repeatedly throughout the day.

"I went to the distribution center and I'd see a picker go to a slot and pick 50 vials of A-test, a biological monitoring device that indicates whether a surgical tray has been sterilized or not. Essentially it tells a department whether its sterilizers are working.

"This picker broke into a full case and picked a box of 50, wrapped it in a huge packing slip with an elastic and put it in a bin, and it went by itself into the back of a full-sized transport truck.

"It was killing us, just thinking of boxes on the back of trucks going down there. The way hospitals work, you would get seven, eight, nine orders a day, all with one item, and sometimes we'd have eight or nine trucks going in."

This direct business model had been used extensively in Kevin's previous positions.

"I had come from the engineering systems division, where we shipped and billed a quarter of a million to million dollar systems for plants and for offices. We were direct. I'd always been in direct businesses."

Despite his deep experience using the direct business model, Kevin's intuition told him that this same business model was not right for the medical and health care products division.

"My gut kind of told me that this wasn't right. The data showed that we could easily cover the freight and warehousing costs of small orders with the increased net margins we enjoyed by avoiding a middle channel, but it didn't feel right."

Kevin began changing this division to using an indirect model by moving the ordering of products through a distributor. This would consolidate the ongoing multiple daily orders to a single weekly bulk order, saving a tremendous amount of time and cost in the supplying of products.

"We undertook to change that business, which was 95% direct, and levelled the playing field in our policies so that we didn't have subtle biases, so that end-users would want to buy direct. We shared part of our margins with our channel partners, which on paper looked like a stupid thing to do."

This change in customer buying behaviour freed the sales reps up to sell and acquire new business. The new channel dealt with the minutiae of direct shipments.

"We shifted from about 95% direct to about 60% through distribution. By the end of the next year, we were pretty much up to 90% indirect. At the end of the first 12 months, after three years of flat or declining sales, we actually grew top line sales by about 3%, and in subsequent years by double-digit growth rate, more than covering the supposed margin loss."

This shift in the business model and resulting turnaround was purely due to Kevin's intuition, despite his past experience with a different model.

"All the data would say not to do it, but we did it, and we created a model that is still pretty much used to this day in this business, and that was more than 10 years ago that it was done."

GUT!

Despite being immersed in a direct distribution business model, Kevin listened to his intuition and acknowledged that this business model was not right for the medical and health care division. Making that change produced tremendous results that continue today.[58]

In a corporate setting, operational intuition will more than likely focus on the processes and procedures that can be improved upon. If an improvement is required, a number of resources would be required to make the changes.

Hiring the right resources that can leverage their intuition to find improvements is essential for a firm to maintain its corporate intuition. If there are resources that are a detriment to this process, then they need to be identified using corporate relational intuition.

Once identified, attempts should be made to guide or train them. However, if they are still a hindrance, then they need to be removed. If they remain in the organization, corporate intuition is hindered.

Ignoring corporate relational intuition could result in unfortunate organizational circumstances, such as what happened at Hooplah. Leslie Hartsman, Hooplah's CEO, ignored corporate relational intuition, which would have resulted in a troublesome employee exiting early. Instead, the employee instigated the exodus of a business partner and a number of employees, leaving Leslie picking up the pieces.

---

[58] Kevin's intuitive decision to change the business model at 3M's medical and health care division has become the subject of a case study written by Fraser Johnson, a professor at Ivey School of Business who teaches operations management.
   Says Professor Johnson: "The case allows the students to understand the advantages and disadvantages of direct to consumer distribution versus using value added resellers. Kevin decided to outsource logistics to a third party so that 3M could concentrate resources on what the company does best, which is product innovation." https://www.iveycases.com/ProductView.aspx?id=44905

CHAPTER 6

Corporate Relational Intuition

Corporate relational intuition resembles the relational intuition we use on a personal level. This type of intuition is used during social interaction in a corporate environment. These social interactions primarily take place during employment interviews, internal meetings, or conversations with those outside the organization such as potential customers, suppliers, investors, and so on.

In employment interviews, individuals or groups are assessed to see if their values match the corporate values and culture, and are being authentic when they talk about their employment history or professional skills. In these situations, the intuition of those employees, managers, or consultants interviewing or assessing individuals watch for cues, such as facial expressions, body language or tone, and language that inform the intuition. If there is a disconnect between the actual interview and the representation of skills both verbal and in written form, this type of intuition should provide a warning to the interviewers that these individuals may not be the best candidates for the position for which they had applied.

Internal meetings or conversations happen all of the time when getting updates on projects, performing employee evaluations, or talking about the work being performed, for example. If an interviewee appears to be deceitful in these meetings or conversations, this type of intuition should lead to a deeper dialogue on the situation, with the possibility of further investigative action.

Some situations involve individuals within a company conversing with those outside of the organization. Corporate relational intuition will let an individual know that something may be amiss during these conversations. Depending upon the importance of that external entity and the potential impact to the company and its performance, further conversations or investigations may be needed to ascertain why negative cues were being given.

In Leslie Hartsman's case, his corporate relational intuition was triggered when his partner decided to form another company but tried to keep it a secret.

GUT!

Leslie Hartsman is President of Hooplah, a digital media agency focused on building and supporting brands online. He has built his company into one of Toronto's fastest growing digital media agencies with an award-winning client list that includes eOne Films, Rexall, Mobility, Nestle, Mazda, TIFF, and Roots Canada.

Leslie recognizes that both his intuition and entrepreneurial spirit started when he was young.

"I was intuitive at a very young age. I've been an entrepreneur since I was 13 years old. It was part of my need to communicate. Perhaps it is because I am an only child, but I always found a need to interact and engage with people.

"When you're by yourself with your parents, there is only so far you can engage. When you're out in the world, you can engage with people, swear once in a while, speak the truth, and hear some interesting things in return. That's what I enjoy most about being an entrepreneur: the great conversations I get to have."

While working for his father, Leslie received some life changing advice.

"I was working in construction with my father. I went and met with one of his suppliers, a good friend of his, and he pulled me into his office and said, 'Why the hell are you working for your father? Go out and earn your own stripes somewhere else and then maybe if you don't like it, come back. But go out and do your own thing.' If my dad would have heard that or found that out, he would have been furious, but it was the best advice I had ever received and I followed it."

Leslie's entrepreneurial ambitions started to flow and he knew he needed to start something. He made his first foray into the digital area when he was 26 years old, making iron-on name tag labels, which he sold online.

"I had been a longtime summer camp camper and staff and for years helped my mother sew labels with my name on them into my clothes. There were only a few places in town to get them and I thought, 'There are kids all over the country going to camp and school and need these labels. Why don't I make an iron-on one and sell it on the internet?'"

This was when Leslie launched his first Internet business, NameLabels.com.

"It was really my intuition to do something like this online, to create this e-commerce store because there was a need there. People never knew where to find these labels or buy these labels, or what they were called. I said, 'Well, the internet could be a good place for them to look for them.'

"I sold labels online for kids' clothing for identification purposes, so they wouldn't lose their clothing. I started in the basement of my parents' house. My Dad would come downstairs every day and check on me. He never understood how I was making money sitting in front of a computer, because he's an old school construction guy.

"After three or four years of doing that, I thought to myself, 'If I'm doing really well with this one product, maybe I could do this for three or four others.'

"But I couldn't do it by myself. That's when I had called my business partner and said, 'What are you doing at your job? Do you like your job?' And he's like, 'No, I really don't like it, but it's paying good money.' And I said, 'What if you could make the same amount of money, but do it in an office with me? We could hang out, listen to our own music, and just make money.' His answer was, of course, 'Yes, who wouldn't want to do that?'"

Hooplah was born.

"We continued selling products online and grew our company to include 30 different e-commerce websites. In 2003 when we looked at all of the stuff we were selling online, we realized that we had a developed a unique capability: online marketing. Driving traffic, driving people to an ROI based webpage. Whether it be professional services, professional product, novelty items, etc.

"So that led us to believe, maybe we should take this on the road and go and talk to people who are trying to sell online. Everybody's spending so much money on these websites, but they're not selling. They've been told that if you create a website, you will sell. But the truth is, if you build it online, people will not necessarily come. There was no rulebook on what we were doing because we were just applying what we had learned firsthand – we were pioneers in the industry."

Initially, clients for Hooplah's marketing services were friends and family, but with their natural talents in the digital arena, their client list began to grow.

"Over the years, more people were asking us about marketing, but they were also asking us about other web components: Can you build me a website? Can you help me with some video? E-mail blasts? Etc. At the time, it was a great idea."

Although the firm grew in both clients and staff, it was veering away from Leslie's original vision. It was now focused on providing a onetime service for clients, but he wanted to focus on creating recurring revenue streams.

"We now had 31 employees developing applications, websites, e-mail marketing campaigns. But something just wasn't feeling right to me. I wanted to be a service-based business where we would build relationships with clients and there were annuities and instead we were developing websites and never seeing the client again."

In 2009, Leslie's intuition was triggered by a sense that his other business partner was not happy and was looking to go elsewhere.

"I had a business partner who wanted to be all things to all people and provide any web service anyone would request but I was turning in the other direction, trying to downsize, trying to focus. In my gut, I knew I was in for a fight.

"I found out he was opening another agency behind my back. I just didn't know when. When everything was going on, I kept my head about me and followed my intuition. I didn't fire anybody or let on that I knew what was going on. I knew what was going on, right to the end."

Leslie describes the intuitive feeling and indicators that he picked up on.

"It was kind of a strange thing. But I could feel it. I started to feel a shift probably three or four months prior to that.

"I would bring very profitable opportunities to the table and they would be turned away because they were not deemed to be 'exciting' enough. In return, they would bring opportunities to the table that they believed were exciting but were putting the company at a financial loss. I thought to myself, 'This is where we're going to start drifting.' I knew something was going to happen. That's when I prepared myself."

Leslie recalls another cue he had about his partner leaving, an intuitive feeling about an employee who instigated the partner's leaving. Surprisingly, this was one occasion where Leslie ignored his intuition.

"There was definitely a third party involved in shifting my partner's thinking. Months before that my gut was telling me to fire this third-party actor but I never did. That was a valuable lesson for me on the importance of following my instinct."

By failing to heed his intuition to let the third party go, Leslie could not discourage the shift in his partner's thinking, ultimately resulting in the partner leaving and Hooplah going through a major change. After his partner left, Leslie restructured Hooplah; he reduced his staff, rebranded the company, and began doing what he did best – and clients followed.

"It wasn't a fight, it wasn't a blow-up. It was calm and collected. At that point, I realized what we could be, what we could do.

"We repositioned the company October 31, 2009 to be a digital media agency, an automatic new layer in the social media component. We were able to come in at another angle. Instead of coming in through the website angle, we were coming through the social and the digital media angles."

Although there were some initial pains getting the company back on its feet, ultimately, Leslie was able to take Hooplah in the direction he wanted with no dissenting opinions.

"It took about eight or nine months for me to pick up the pieces but it was well worth it. We grew exponentially from there.

"I feel great for it. I feel like we're a new company. Although we have the same name, the same brand, we have gone in a totally different direction and we are all better for it today."

GUT!

Leslie picked up on a number of cues that informed his relational intuition, sensing that something was not right with his partner. If he had not ignored his intuition and fired the one employee he had doubts about, perhaps Hooplah may have been a different company.

Or perhaps this situation was inevitable given the different strategic directions Leslie and his partner wanted to take. But because he clued into his gut, he was able to prepare himself for what lay ahead.

The success of a company relies on being able to look at its strategy and evaluate it against data-driven reports such as market share, competitive analysis, and so on. Where intuition plays a key role is in having management take a step back and evaluate what is going on without staring at reports and graphs. There may be cues from the overall environment that indicate something is wrong. This is exactly what Jim Treliving did when his intuition told him that Boston Pizza's expansion plans were not going as well as expected, and he made the difficult decision to pull back.

CHAPTER 7

Corporate Situational Intuition

Corporate situational intuition uses cues that come from the corporate environment. These individuals' intuitive abilities constantly assess the activities around them, the employment conditions in their particular area of corporate responsibility, and the internal and external reactions to a particular executive strategy, decision, or action.

If the corporate environment provides concerning cues, the problematic strategy, process, or procedure may be suspended and a further detailed assessment, decision, or action may be carried out to rectify the situation.

For Jim Treliving, suspending Boston Pizza's expansion plans was essential because the cues from the corporate environment showed a loss of control for the international franchisees and that the expansion plans to Eastern Canada were going awry.

GUT!

Jim Treliving is Chairman & Owner of Boston Pizza International Inc., Canada's number one casual dining brand. With Jim and his partner, George Melville, at the helm, Boston Pizza has been consistently recognized on Deloitte's list of Canada's "50 Best Managed Private Companies" and more recently as one of Canada's "Top Ten Most Admired Corporate Cultures" by Waterstone Human Capital.

Jim was a young RCMP officer in 1966 when he left to join "Boston Pizza and Spaghetti House" in Edmonton, opening his first Boston Pizza franchise in Penticton, British Columbia in 1968. From that small location, through hard work and dedication, Jim has expanded Boston

Pizza to over 350 franchise locations with almost $1 billion in annual sales today. Boston Pizza now has more than 325 restaurants from coast to coast.

The Boston Pizza franchise concept became successful in Western Canada, headquartered in Vancouver. To try to increase its brand presence, Boston Pizza became the official pizza supplier for Expo '86 in Vancouver. This turned out to be a winning move for the company. Jim talks about the successful expansion that took place just after Expo '86.

"After Expo '86 ended, and we were quite successful at that, we started to build after that year: 15 stores right away towards Eastern Canada. And at the same time, we opened in Taiwan and Japan and Hong Kong."

Jim began seeing situational problems in three particular areas, cues that his intuition picked up on: time zone differences, lack of controls on franchisees, and not understanding local eating habits.

The time zone became an issue with Boston Pizza's headquarters being in Vancouver, which made things tough operationally.

"The problem was that there was a three-hour time change, and it was a day's travel if you fly to Toronto and sell a franchise. The other way was also a problem: if you are training them back here and you send them back, a whole day is shot in just going back and forth. Also, if you are talking to somebody in Eastern Canada and you have a problem at nine o'clock in the morning, it's six in Vancouver. It was a real problem having the time frame, even in this country."

Meanwhile, without controls in place, a franchisee made unapproved changes to Boston Pizza's set menu.

"The franchisee began changing things when we weren't there. A guy would walk in and say, 'You know, fish and chips would work on your menu.' And the franchisee would say, 'Yeah, that's not a bad idea, why don't we try it?' We didn't have the controls we have today."

The final issue was in the difference in eating habits between Vancouver and Toronto. This time difference affected staffing and service levels. For a new brand trying to establish itself in Eastern Canada, this was not a great start.

"In Toronto, people generally work in shifts. People start work at seven, finish at three, go home, pick up their kids at four and then go out to eat at five or six o'clock. In Vancouver, you don't go out to eat at six o'clock. You're getting home at six, and then you go out to eat at seven or eight o'clock.

"We got our butts kicked in Ontario and were told to go home because we weren't ready. We weren't ready for the volume, and there was double the number of people than any of the other places in Western Canada. They eat at different times, they eat a lot, and they bring their families.

"So all of a sudden, we get hammered at five o'clock, and in Vancouver, there's nobody in our restaurants at five o'clock. Service was slow because we had the wrong ovens. We had deck ovens, so you're taking one thing out at a time or two at a time. We had to go to conveyor ovens to make it faster. People don't have two hours to sit there and wait. Some people got upset and would not return again."

Jim's intuition picked up on these situations and instantly had a solution. By having a local or regional office close to the franchisees, all of these major operational issues would be resolved.

"We had to sit back and rethink our whole way of doing things. I remember getting back on the plane and flying back to Vancouver saying to my partner, George, we made a mistake. We realized right away that we had to put people and structures on the ground first and then go back into those areas. We had to close those stores. We had to walk away."

All of the Eastern Canadian and overseas franchisee locations were closed and over the next four or five years, a new expansion strategy was developed. No expansion would happen without the inclusion of a local geographic presence in addition to the development of appropriate controls for franchisee owners. After rolling out this new expansion strategy, Boston Pizza returned to Ontario in the late 1990s, with Jim actually moving back to Ontario to open the head office.

"So the next time we went back east was in the late '90s. I actually moved back there and opened an office. And that is why it turned out to be a big success. You have people on the ground. You are seeing everything. You are not at a three hours or eight hours difference. That was a huge piece for us."

Despite the US going through two wars, the attacks on September 11, 2001, and a major recession, Boston Pizza has been expanding in the US for close to 14 years. Jim has established 50 franchises in the United States, slowing down the expansion during the big recession, and ramping back up today to continue the growth.

With the Canadian expansion model fixed, Jim moved down to Dallas to put the infrastructure in place for Boston Pizza to expand into the United States with as few hiccups as possible, and talks about the importance of having a local presence there.

"If I had not been there, we would have been forced to close down. Going to the US is going to another country with a different set of rules, regulations, the way they do business and the way they eat. Pricing is completely different, costs are completely different, and it's probably the toughest competition in the world. That's why it is number one in growth compared to everybody else."

Jim knew that when expanding overseas, it was critical to keep the menu as Western as possible. That's what the younger generation wanted, the ones who would spend money and return to Boston Pizza regularly for the next 25 years.

"The older people didn't come to the restaurant. It was all the younger people. That's what we wanted. Older people would be coming in with their kids. I remember walking in the store and the pizza would come to the table. And in those days, you had a knife and fork there, but they didn't know how to eat with a fork. They would use chopsticks.

"With the Chinese, you don't eat with your hands. And they don't touch the food. They would look at the pizza and they wouldn't know what to do with it. But the kids would pick it up with their hands and begin to eat it."

Jim talks about the success he has had in expanding to Mexico.

"We just opened in Mexico eight or nine years ago. We have five stores down there and we are building seven more in the interior. We are not in the tourist areas. Our stores are lined up every day.

"We did not go and make it Mexican. It looks identical to the one in Toronto. Is the guacamole better? Yes. It's fresher. Is the salsa better? Yes.

It's stronger. You and I can't eat it because they like it stronger. We didn't change the pizza formula. We didn't change the pasta formula. There's the menu."

That same Western-style menu was instrumental in ensuring a consistent brand experience anywhere in the world, with a few minor tweaks for culturally sensitive issues.

"What I've often said about people in those parts of the world, which is the same reason why people want to go franchise to places like India and all these other places is that you've got to look at it and say, they've got all the choices in the world of their own food, but what they're looking at is saying I don't want to be American, I don't want to be Canadian. I want to be Chinese or I want to be Indian, but I want to have the choices of looking and seeing that I can dress and eat Western food.

"When we opened up in Hong Kong and Taiwan, we were lined up for three or four hours. There's no sense in us competing with a Chinese restaurant. They wanted North American food.

"The group from India that we are dealing with said the first thing you can't do is have any pork. You can't eat beef. End of story. You have to then look at all kinds of substitutes for that.

"You do all of that ahead of time. And that's because you bring people in, you go ahead and put an office and a structure together, and then you go and get your franchisees and train them."

GUT!

Jim's situational intuition was able to take cues from the environment and find an appropriate solution to mitigate the increasing operational problems he was having. Although there was an opportunity cost in closing the expansion locations in terms of brand perception, intuitively, Jim knew that it was crucial to get the business model right. Jim listened to his intuition, and Boston Pizza has been a highly successful chain of restaurants worldwide.

Many of those in corporate environments display strength in multiple quadrants that are critical for their role within a company. Samantha Gamble used her strength in strategic and operational intuition to help a company expand and increase revenues, as well as fix a number of operational problems that unnecessarily increased costs."

CHAPTER 8

Multiple Quadrants

With our personal intuition, each of our respective Intuitive Zones of Influence maps will generally span across a number of intuition quadrants, so it would be expected that the same would also apply for Corporate Intuitive Zones of Influence.

The difference is that these Zones of Influence may be different for various departments, teams, or management levels, depending upon the intuitive ability of the decision-maker at that particular corporate level.

As we gain professional experience and take advantage of promotion opportunities, the Corporate Intuitive Zone of Influence begins to expand, and we can then reliably tap into intuitive decisions in the other quadrants on a more regular basis.

Some of us have been able to leverage these intuitive capabilities early in our careers, which has served us well in our ongoing corporate responsibilities, similar to Samatha Gamble.

GUT!

Samantha Gamble is a successful business consultant who specializes in turnarounds, typically becoming involved when companies are in financial distress. After making the required changes to turn the company around, she steps away, leaving the company's management team with the right tools to move the company forward.

In one particular consulting engagement, Samantha was asked to join a company that produced health care products. After negotiating the engagement fee, Samantha began exploring what the problems were. The first day typically entailed having a detailed meeting with the senior management to have an open and honest discussion about the most pressing problems.

"Through a referral, the CEO of the company expressed a lot of interest in bringing me on board as his company was clearly in trouble. The company started four years ago in Ontario and then expanded to Alberta after one year. Sales peaked at $2 million in the second year, and had been declining in the last two years, despite an increasing customer base. There was clearly something wrong with this company. My intuition was telling me that the business model was sound and that the revenues should not be falling like this.

"When I first talked to senior management, I asked them to articulate what kind of problems they had. The first problem discussed was in the order fulfillment area, where 30% of the orders were either missed, delayed, or sent to the wrong address. When asked what system the company was using to take orders, they mentioned that they had online and phone-in orders which were entered into an Excel spreadsheet. My intuition began yelling at me! $2million in revenues, and you have an Excel sheet?"

This shocking revelation triggered Samantha's operational intuition, and within an instant she knew she needed to revamp the ordering system and streamline the operational processes from start to finish.

"Just as soon as they had completed telling me about the operational issues, I could instantly envision a chaotic order fulfillment area that had people running around with no sense of direction, people clamoring over each other to get information, and so on. The only solution was to gather everyone to help map this process out and find out why these orders were getting missed and how they can correct these errors quickly because they were losing money each time this had happened."

After quickly forming a game plan to fix the operations, her strategic intuition perked up and wondered why there were no expansion plans.

"It was clear from the financials that their shipping costs were very high. My intuition instantly told me that this company had to either expand and open other distribution centres, or go through a distributor. Shipping product all across North America with only two offices is very expensive.

The freight expenses would be putting a significant squeeze on profit margins. It made intuitive sense to me that they needed to be closer to the customer.

"I asked the team if they had considered expansion or other distribution channels. With baffled looks around the room, it was quite clear that they never thought about this."

Samantha had her work cut out for her. Step one was to streamline the operations. Once that was done, she could then move onto step two, which was determining which expansion route made the strongest business case.

"The first thing that I needed to do was to walk the floor area where orders were being filled. Right away, I saw people running around and product going from one area to another with no sense of efficiency. Normally, you would want some sort of a path from order-taking to delivery that made physical and logical sense. I just saw a lot of people moving all over the place. Very chaotic. There was a lot of work to be done in this area."

Samantha watched the order takers fill out the Excel spreadsheet, and while they were busy filling in information from phone-ins and online orders, some employees tried to interrupt them because they were missing information that they needed to send the orders away.

"One of the employees was given the wrong address for an order and walked away. Thirty minutes later, the order-taker had run over to him to give him an updated address, but he had told her that he had already put it in the delivery bin, which was wheeled outside to a waiting van from a shipping company. This had to stop.

"After bringing the people together on a weekend and mapping out how orders were filled, we identified what information was required from order to delivery that could be centralized in an online database. If we did this, it was clear that many of the issues the employees saw would disappear.

"One of the employees talked about reorganizing the shelving to match product numbers and have labels not only on the shelving in the aisles but also on the ends, which would make her job much easier as it would drastically cut down the time to search for product.

"Finally, we discussed having the online program generate the *appropriate shipping labels for the various customers, and be able to select the right shipping company based on address.*

"So from order-taking over way down to shipping, the process became streamlined, in theory with everyone having a say."

Samantha investigated a number of software vendors who could provide the company with what they needed, and after six months, it was implemented. The first statistic to come out one week after it was installed: order accuracy was at 100%, which had never happened.

The next step for Samantha was to attend to her strategic intuition. She compared the overall profitability of opening a distribution centre versus having orders filled through a distributor. Opening their own distribution centre clearly presented a strong business case for the company.

"Once the expansion strategy was agreed upon by management, we began scouting distribution centre locations. I worked with the shipping companies to try and minimize our shipping costs through both reduction in shipping charges as well as investigating which cities to locate the distribution centres in to minimize overall shipping costs.

"There were two ways to open up distribution centres. One would be in a stepwise fashion whereas the other would be to increase the debt and open the five locations that were ideal.

"My intuition told me that it was much better to open up all five at once because the wasted time and effort in opening up in a stepwise fashion in addition to realigning the order-taking system just didn't make financial or operational sense. So, we negotiated with the banks and looked for existing locations."

Once the locations were set, Samantha had to ensure that the order-taking system would support the expansion by shipping the right amount of product to those distribution centres, given the demand that was expected from the customer base.

"Through some software customization, any orders that came online or through the phone would be routed to the appropriate distribution centre to get filled. I was able to work with the various shipping companies to integrate our order-taking management system with their electronic system."

After a full year, the company now had five other distribution centres in addition to the two existing ones and a very efficient order-taking and delivery system. Not only did revenues increase to $3.5 million the following year, but the cost to ship each unit went down as well, thereby increasing profit margins.

Samantha's job was now done, and she walked away extremely satisfied.

GUT!

Samantha's strength in both the strategic and operational intuition were critical not only for fixing the operations but streamlining them so that expansion was relatively easy and supported.

Over time, a company will grow and will then require different intuitive strengths. Along with this shift, those who are moving up the corporate ladder must also shift their intuition quadrants to match the positions that they fill. Bill Johnson had to make this shift as he moved from an operational role, using his operational intuition, to relational intuition, critical to ensuring that his intuition focused on ensuring that every franchisee he was responsible for got the attention they needed to operate as smoothly as possible.

CHAPTER 9

Shifting Corporate Intuition Quadrants

As our corporate experiences deepen and widen and we gain strength in other intuition quadrants, we may find that the type of corporate intuition we rely on most shifts from one quadrant to the other.

This does not mean that we lose any of the strength from the former quadrant; rather, this may mean that we tap into intuition from two of the quadrants on a regular basis or we support the move by relying on other corporate resources that would be responsible for making intuitive decisions in the former quadrant, much like Bill Johnson's experience.

GUT!

Bill Johnson started working at a McDonald's location in London, Ontario at the age of 18, flipping Big Macs and wiping tables. Through hard work, dedication, and focus, he rose through the organization, taking on multiple management roles in North America. In 2000, Bill became President of McDonald's Canada, and in the next five years, moved to the CEO position and eventually Chairman, before retiring in 2005.

Throughout his career at McDonald's, Bill could rely on his intuition to lead him to seek advice from mentors to help move his career forward. Bill talks about one of his earlier mentors.

"In 1974, I was a restaurant manager in Hamilton, and the Executive Vice-President for Eastern Canada at the time asked me, 'What do you want to do with McDonald's, at McDonald's?' And I said, 'I like your job.' He said, 'Really?' And I said, 'Yeah.' And he said, 'Okay. You have to do two things.' I said, 'What's that?' He said, 'Work hard and grow a moustache.'

I said, 'Grow a moustache?' And he said, 'Yeah, you have a baby face. You look too young to be in management.' So I grew a moustache for 10 years."

Although this seemingly funny story gave Bill a good laugh, he needed this type of frank advice to navigate his way up the corporate ladder.

Bill's intuition provided guidance on what positions he would be comfortable taking, despite his background and experience. In his usual way of doing things, he would check with a mentor to make sure that his intuitive decision was correct if he had a lingering doubt. And in some cases, he would make the decision himself.

"When I was a manager in London, Ontario in 1976, Toronto head office called me and said, 'We'd like you to come to Toronto to become head of HR.' So I thought, 'All right.' I didn't feel comfortable because I'm an operations person. And so I asked a mentor and he said, 'Bill, don't go near that.' I said, 'You know what, that's what I thought, but you just reinforced it.' So I turned it down.

"A month later I get a call again from Toronto. They said, 'Okay, we now want to move you to head up training.' And my gut told me, 'No, that's not who I am.' I asked the same gentleman and he said, 'No, Bill, you're right. Don't do it.' I called and turned it down. He said, 'You're turning down two promotions?' I said, 'Yeah, sorry. It just doesn't fit for me.'

"So they called one more time and they said, 'We'd like you to come to Toronto and be part of heading up operations.' I didn't even call this other guy. I said, 'When do you want me there?'

"So your gut tells you, but sometimes it's nice to have a little reinforcement from someone to say you're right. You're making the right decision or, no, don't go there. So I did that a lot throughout my career."

Bill worked in operations for some time before his intuition told him to shift gears and change roles, preparing him for a position that would help him strengthen his relational intuition as he began to be concerned about keeping the franchisees happy.

"One time I knew a gentleman who was a senior vice-president and was retiring from real estate construction. So I said to myself, 'You know what, I can do that.' Even though I was an operations person, my gut said to me,

'Bill, you'd be good at that,' even though I knew nothing about real estate, nothing about construction.

"So I approached the senior people who were making the decision and, literally, they laughed at me. They said, 'Bill, nice try,' but two months later they called me and said, 'You're right. You would be the right person to do this,' and they gave me the position and I did it for two years.

"Again my intuition told me I would be good at that. And you know why I was good at it? I knew there were issues between real estate construction and the franchisees. In real estate construction, when they would build a location they would hand you the keys and walk away, and there may have been issues going on over the next few months, just like building a house, right? And I used to see that.

"I said, 'You know what? That's where I will come in and fix that piece of it.' When I first took over, I let everybody in real estate construction and legal know, I wasn't going to interfere with what they did day-to-day. I wanted to build a relationship between them, the franchisees, and the restaurant managers. And it worked."

Bill continued in his position successfully until he got bored. His intuition was telling him that McDonald's would be expanding globally, and he wanted to be a part of that experience.

"My intuition told me that I was stuck at a glass ceiling. I always like to try new challenges, so I approached senior management and said, 'If you see something outside of Canada let me know,' because my feeling was that's where the world was going now. It was going global. That was in 1993, 1994. It was growing like crazy. I said, 'Let's do it while I'm young and I can handle the travelling.' Within weeks, they called me about Mexico."

Because Bill began changing roles, his intuition was guiding him to gain strength in the relational intuition quadrant, picking up on important cues along the way. He tells of two such incidences.

"When my wife and I got married, she worked for McDonald's in a different department. Within about six months, we could feel some people were getting uncomfortable because I was moving up in the company in the senior positions and she was at a different level.

"And she and I had a chat and our intuition told us, 'You know what, *people around us don't feel comfortable.' And she totally agreed that she had to leave McDonald's to just take that pressure off both of us.*

"McDonald's wasn't happy that she left because she was doing a great job. But we both knew we didn't need that stress every day, and we could feel it. She resigned and hasn't worked outside of the house since.

"And I'll tell you it changed overnight. Overnight I felt it. Everybody relaxed and said, 'Okay, now we don't have a little spy in the background,' even though she wasn't spying. But that's what they felt. Our intuition said the situation wasn't comfortable for anybody."

On another occasion, Bill's intuition hinted that a member of his management team was looking for employment elsewhere.

"He was my senior vice-president of marketing. The way he conducted himself, my intuition knew that he'd been out there looking.

"One day, he asked me to go in the boardroom because he wanted to chat with me. I said, 'Okay.' And he said, 'I'm leaving.' I said, 'Oh, you're leaving?' He said, 'Yeah, I've been offered a position with Magna.'

"So right away I got up and shook his hand. And he said, 'Well, you're not going to offer me something else? A counter offer?' I said, 'No, you've been looking.' So I said, 'Hey, good luck. Knock yourself out and really enjoy your new position.'

"And I knew it wouldn't last and eight months later he left Magna. So he came back and asked if I would re-hire him. And I said, 'Sorry, I've moved on and you're going to have to move on.' There was no trust there."

Even though Bill supplemented his intuitive thoughts with the advice of others, when he became President of McDonalds's in Canada, he needed to minimize the dialogue as much as possible for the quicker decisions.

"Over a period of time within a year, year and a half when I was President, my intuition was telling me that I needed to make some decisions quicker than other decisions.

"I had a regular officer team of 12 officers, and we would meet on a regular basis. My intuition told me that I did not have to call everybody in and have long term meetings. So, I formed an executive management team. I took four of the officers in the team of 12 with me so that if, all of a sudden some quick decision had to be made, I didn't have to get together with all 12.

"I'll tell you, it worked like a charm because I got together with a small group, it took 10 minutes and no one on the big team was insulted because these four were a part of the team. You do have to have long meetings, don't get me wrong. But I needed to make quicker decisions.

"I was the first one to do that at McDonald's, to have an executive management team, and it really worked well.

"There were a few situations that came up where we had to react quickly and make a decision. The officers started realizing, with my style, it's not going to be a long process, folks. We couldn't wait a few weeks to get the whole team together and have them fly in from across the country.

"Almost 80 percent of our restaurants are franchised. So I had to make sure I get information out to the franchisees very quickly because if they hear something is going on, they're going to wonder, 'Okay, Bill, what are you doing?'

"So I needed this group to get together with me very quickly and make a decision on something that was urgent. It could have been banking. It could have been a fire. Anything like that. My intuition was this had to be done quickly."

The quick decision-making style that Bill's intuition generated came at a crucial time for McDonald's.

"When we had the mad cow situation, it lasted only about a week and a half and it was fine. The executive team, the five of us met every day. We made the decisions. I did the press conferences, and all the franchisees stayed and ran the restaurants. We did not have to have any huge meetings."

With his relentless focus on the franchisee, Bill's intuition picked up on cues that something may have been wrong on the operational side.

"I didn't spend a lot of time in the office because I knew I had the experts in legal, experts at HR, and the experts at training, experts in finance. I was out in the locations visiting coast-to-coast all the time."

Bill would sense what the problems were by visiting the locations on a continual basis, and would return to head office to inform his senior management of what problem areas needed fixing.

"[Senior management] would wait for me to come home and say, 'Okay, is there something about finance that he saw? What's he telling us that we're doing wrong?' The only way you can find that out is by being out in the field, and I would see certain things.

"That's why I mentioned going into real estate construction. I'm not a real estate person. I'm not a construction person. But I knew by visiting and being out in the location, something was wrong. I knew there was an issue there. I said, 'Let's fix the issue.' And I had to fix it somehow.

"And so the intuition about taking over that guy's position in real estate construction when he retired, I'll tell you, worked out very nicely."

Bill's senior staff may have not realized why Bill was always concerned about visiting the franchises, but he got an opportunity to demonstrate this.

"My focus is relationship building with the franchisee. They're out there 24/7 and most businesses today, especially McDonald's, is 24 hours a day. So they're out there across Canada serving the customers and working with the managers. They are saying, 'Okay, Bill, what are you doing for me?' And I understood that **completely** years and years ago.

"Our CFO one day said, 'Bill, I'd like to go visit restaurants with you.' Fantastic. So off we go and get to the location and say hi to all the staff at the counter. I always go in behind and go to where the grills and the drive-thru are.

"The restaurant manager's with us, and the franchisee. Within three or four minutes I said to the franchisee, 'Where's our CFO?' He said, 'He's in my office looking at the books.' I said, 'No, no, no.' So I went and found him. I said, 'That's not why we're here. You can look at the books any time. You have to get a feeling of what's going on in the locations and then take that back and apply it to your senior staff.' And that's similar to what I did with real estate and construction.

"But he went out for one reason, and didn't realize why we really go out and visit locations. It changed his attitude overnight. And he did the same thing to those in finance."

Bill's intuition also picks up cues from the franchisee operations on how well certain menu items perform. An excellent example of this was when Bill eliminated pizza from the McDonald's menu.

"I am intuitive about the menu at McDonald's, okay? You have to know when to make changes and when not to.

"As an example, we introduced pizza three or four years before I went to Mexico. It was a huge success. And so I went to Mexico and I came back and worked at Vancouver for about a year, year and a half before I took over the country. And when I came to Vancouver, pizza sales were so low I couldn't believe it.

"Drive-thru sales went from 25 percent to 60 percent of sales and then stalled. And my intuition was telling me that what was happening was that pizza, which took six minutes, was slowing down the drive-thru. People didn't want to wait for it anymore. It just became a mess.

"And so I said to the franchisees in Western Canada, 'We're going to take pizza off the menu. The franchisees said, 'We're all going to lose money.' I said, 'Okay. If you lose any money, you show me, I'll write you a cheque.' They said, 'Really?' I said, 'Yes.' I took it off the menu and I never wrote one cheque.

"So then I moved to Eastern Canada into Toronto and the first thing the franchisees asked was, 'Are you going to eliminate pizza in Eastern Canada?' I said, 'We'll see. Let me take a look and feel it out.'

"I'm driving from Montreal to Toronto and we had a location near Kingston on the highway. And if you go in the drive-thru there, it's like a tunnel effect. There is a curved ceiling and you come in and you can hear people in the car in front of you talking.

"And there's a lady with two or three kids in the car and the kids are all anxious, you know, they're on the highway. And the lady is asking our employee how she wanted pizza.

"And our employee is saying, 'Now do you realize I'm going to have to park you and it's going to take me seven or eight minutes to prepare the pizza?' And the lady says, 'I'm fine. I'm okay with that.' And the employee's like, 'You're sure? You don't mind if you park?' What was happening was our employees were telling our customers that you don't want pizza. I could feel it.

"And my intuition said this was wrong. But people weren't picking up on that. Maybe they were telling us this on the surveys. I'm not blaming anybody, but nobody was picking up on it and it was just the same old, same old, same old.

"A big part of communication is listening. I was listening to that *employee and I could imagine what that employee was going through on a daily basis. It was a pain to try and serve people this product. It didn't make sense any more.*

"I went back to Toronto and eliminated pizza from our menu."

This same intuitive feeling Bill had for menu items continued. He spent millions of dollars having the Mexican McDonald's locations open two hours earlier to serve breakfast, which became 15% of sales. Bill's intuition told him to listen to a franchisee in Fredericton who had an excellent idea for a dairy product, resulting in the McFlurry being launched in over 40 countries.

GUT!

Bill's climb up the corporate ladder led him to shift his reliance on operational intuition, where cues from the franchisees came to him from the overall operations of McDonald's. He started relying on relational intuition, with which he picked up cues from the franchisees that informed him about issues involving operations and the menu. This shift in intuitive type was important for Bill's exceptional decision-making ability in the various roles he held as he moved from flipping Big Macs and wiping tables to becoming CEO and eventually Chairman. A shift in our intuition quadrant may also be necessary as we traverse through life and gain experience in the areas that truly make us happy.

If a company fully embraces intuition as a valuable decision-making tool, each person, regardless of corporate level, must be able to express his or her intuition freely. Corporate intuition can be stifled if hurdles exist within the corporate environment. The only way to remove these hurdles is to traverse the corporate **TRUST** model.

CHAPTER 10

The Corporate TRUST Model

A company must constantly change with a shifting external environment, changing strategies, additional product lines, competitive behaviour and constant turnover internally. Even with an established corporate intuition, these changes will inevitably introduce hurdles that curtail the expression of intuition in certain parts of the company.

To ensure that a company maintains or improves its intuitive capabilities, management must make appropriate decisions and actions to remove these intuitive hurdles. It must also put in place corporate values supported by processes and procedures to maximize corporate intuition.

To find out what hurdles exist to curtail or remove them, management must be cognizant of the corporate **TRUST** model.

Top Down Intuition

Remove Corporate Hindrances

Understand Corporate Intuitive Values

Select Appropriate Resources

Transform the Culture

CHAPTER 11

Top Down Intuition

How a company operates is directly affected by the leadership team in place. Senior management is responsible for setting the tone for the rest of the company to a large degree. Therefore, it is not surprising that if the CEO of a company uses intuition to guide his or her decisions, then from the senior management down, all levels of a company should have an appreciation for using intuition in making key decisions.

In fact, Ralph Larsen, former Chairman and CEO of Johnson and Johnson, and Richard Abdoo former CEO of Wisconsin Energy Corporation, both explain[59] that intuition is an essential part of decision-making at the top management level.

Hence, it is imperative that all members of the top management team have the ability to tap into their own intuition on a regular basis to help inform key business decisions, starting with the president or CEO.

Once the senior management team is operating at a high level from an intuitive perspective, those further down the management ranks must also be allowed to use their intuitive capabilities.

Over time, using intuition to guide decisions will filter from the CEO to the senior management team to larger teams and finally the organization as a whole. This process is essential in how an entire organization is able to learn.[60]

When this process is effectively put in place, individuals can make crucial decisions that may save the company from uncomfortable situations, such as one that Chirag Shah was able to help his company through.

---

59 Hayashi, A. M. (2001). When to trust your gut. Harvard Business Review, 79(2), 59-65.
60 Crossan, M. et al. (1999). An organizational learning framework: from intuition to institution. Academy of management review, 24(3), 522-537.

GUT!

Chirag Shah is a partner in the audit and assurance practice of PricewaterhouseCoopers LLP (PwC) working in the London, Ontario office.

Chirag provides services for a wide variety of public and private clients in industries including technology, life sciences, financial services, and education. He has provided services beyond the traditional audit role including public offerings, acquisition, and due diligence support.

Outward appearances might suggest that an accounting firm is all about checks and balances on paper with little to no room for intuition. Such an assumption started an engaging discussion with Chirag on whether intuition does exist in the accounting world.

"Probably 80 percent of the stuff we do is very much defined. It's governed by either regulatory pressures, rules, or methodology on how you investigate. There's a hierarchy of evidence that you would gather in order to substantiate certain business efforts.

"But, you know, when you introduced the idea to me, I was initially thinking, how much intuition is there really in our business? And as I stepped back and looked at some of the interesting projects that we've done and where we've driven them, there is a level of intuition, especially in a lot of our consulting, performance improvement, risk, and controls type of practice areas.

"So as you look at it, we will be engaged on a performance improvement project where our staff will come in with some ideas on where there may be opportunities to investigate to look at performance improvement for our clients. We will use a very empirical method of gathering information to validate those.

"But the core assumptions that you come in with, we do require a little bit of guess work, on saying that we suspect that there's going to be the best bang for our buck to move into this particular direction and we need to be able to gather that information, react to that, and then continue to delve further in order to end up with substantive recommendations that result in value back to the client.

"There's part of me that looks at that and asks, 'Is that true intuition, or is that business acumen? Is that a set of experience that we bring to the table and as a result of past experiences resulting in value added

recommendations?' There used to be an old adage of this term called CAKE: Cumulative Audit Knowledge and Experience. It's that experience side of it that tends to push you towards that intuition side.

"But as you get layered on with more and more experience, I think that that does allow you then to start looking at circumstances without necessarily delving in and gathering empirical data. You look for opportunities and risks in certain areas that can result in valued recommendations to the client.

"As I step back, honestly, yeah, I think there probably is a level of intuition that has to come into play."

To support this intuitive feeling within a corporate setting, there needs to be support from the senior management that acknowledges the validity of intuition as a decision-making tool in certain circumstances and at certain levels of the company.

Chirag talks about how PwC does this by ensuring that intuitive thoughts are listened to and appreciated by establishing open communication throughout the organization, starting from the top.

"If you want intuitiveness within your organization, you need to have flexibility and autonomy that's driven down through the ranks. People with their feet on the ground have to have the ability to be able to execute and funnel their ideas up and down seamlessly.

"If you don't have that level of communication, the flexibility, the ability to execute and the ability to have autonomy for authority, and the more you suppress that, the less intuitive an organization would be. You then suppress independent thought and you're just there to execute within this box and don't think outside of that box. The creativity of an organization is limited by certain policies and structures and how you set it up.

"We have a cultural environment that allows that feedback back and forth, yet we're limited by a regulatory environment and a procedural framework on a lot of methodology that it is very much framed as to how you'll execute. Yet we want to have nimbleness on the ground with our staff because if they're not able to think creatively on their own, we're not going to end up with valued opportunities and recommendations for our clients.

"So we are at odds with how we want to execute, and yet we drive a good amount of autonomy so that people are delivering great value on the ground.

"The feeling that you have a voice and that voice is being heard is a very significant component of that in driving the intuitiveness of an organization. If you know that that voice is going be heard by somebody, then you're willing to raise it and give ideas, provide creativity and voice your opinion.

"However, if you have no channel for communication, or if you have a channel but nobody's listening, you're much more reluctant to funnel anything up. There isn't an opportunity to funnel ideas up the channel or a desire by senior levels to have a funnel of that information come up.

"A philosophy that our firm has adopted is that we want people to continue to think outside of the box and bring fresh ideas and bring opportunities, not just internally for our organization, but really on behalf of our clients. For us, that's a key success factor at the end of the day.

"We coined a term, 'trusted business advisors', where staff members' goals are to be trusted business advisors to their clients. The only way they can do that is to have a robust understanding, be open to listening, have a dialogue with their clients and then be able to feed back creative ideas on solutions or issues that our clients are facing. I think that that is a critical success factor for us.

"I think that most organizations could take advantage of that. I think there's a number that don't. They've boxed themselves into what they're doing. 'This is how we do it and we do it very well and we don't want anybody changing the formula and we need to manage people within that box so that it doesn't mess up the formula that we've got.'

"I look at our industry. We have no widgets that we produce. We don't have a technology that is necessarily proprietary. We're not capital intensive as far as pumping out lots of product. At the end of the day we sell the knowledge of our people. So, for us, we have to be intuitive. We have to provide that autonomy. We have to allow people to have a voice and continue to grow their skill sets, and be confident in bringing up that great knowledge.

"We really want people to be sharing great knowledge. We want that interactivity. That collective knowledge will be much greater than any one individual trying to provide advice on any one particular topic.

Chirag provides an excellent example of how his intuitive thought, supported by his manager, resulted in a review of a client's situation, despite all of the checks and balances telling him that he could sign off on a set of financials.

"My example was in the very early stages of my career. It was myself and the manager as my partner on the job. I was the feet on the ground and his eyes and ears leading the team.

"We ended up uncovering a very unfortunate incident at a client. I was executing on the job at the time and there were some very unusual cash transactions going on back and forth.

"This client dealt with the commodities industry and they had a formalized hedging policy associated with their commodities. And we went through their position sheets and they had certain structures on where they were allowed to hedge and where they were not allowed to hedge. They weren't allowed to do speculative trading. The president's compensation was set up as an incentive over performance.

"We kept seeing transactions back and forth, cash transactions that really smelled funny. We went through the standard methodology, audit methodology and were unable to validate anything wrong going on.

"But you've got something in the back of your mind saying there's something we're missing. There was something in the backs of our minds and we said, there's just something going on and it doesn't smell right. It's just very unusual to get this level of transactions.

"We validated it through direct evidence on various different things back from a third party. We got all the paperwork and all the evidence that was presented to us by the client said that they were in a balanced hedge position with commodities held on hand. All the evidence points to saying that everything is fine. On paper everything adds up. Two and two equals four. So, you've got everything you need to say it's fine.

"We conferred with the partner on the job. If I had told him, 'No, we're good to go and this is why,' then likely we would have finalized it. I still remember sitting in his office chatting about this back at the time and I said, 'There's something here that I don't like. It just doesn't smell right.' It was very much a gut feeling: something's not adding up.

"The partner then said, 'I'm not going to release these. We're not going to finalize on these.'

"So we referred the matter back up to the client's head office and further investigation went on. We waited another month and a half, two months down the road."

Chirag's intuition that something was not right with the financial transactions was bang on.

"As this thing unraveled, the president was actually actively trading on the market at amounts that were well in excess of the risk that the company was willing to take on, and his benefit was that every profit he generated went into his bonus plan. So this was a really high risk, high reward situation and low risk on a loss basis. There were no repercussions, as long as nobody found out.

"Well, it turns out he had falsified a number of position papers that were being presented to us and it was at the very top level that they were being falsified. There was a lot of fraud involved and it was an unfortunate circumstance for that individual president and he did get terminated at the end of the day.

"It was one of those circumstances where I recall us going through this transaction saying, 'This just doesn't smell right. There's something wrong,' and thank God we didn't finalize on those. That's a very tangible example of that intuition coming in full force."

GUT!

Chirag's intuition picked up on transactions that seemed uncharacteristic of the previous trading history. Clearly, the partner supported his intuitive thinking despite the paperwork telling a story that should have given the team a green light to approve the financial reports. Without this support, the reports may have been approved and the client would have continued their exposure to the financial risk that the company's president had fraudulently undertaken.

In PwC's case, top-down support for intuitive thinking is imperative to ensure that those in the company can truly express their opinions. Senior leaders must allow their own intuition to guide corporate decision-making and must ensure that their senior leaders, managers, and employees also embrace intuition.

The fluidity of intuitive decision-making throughout an organization will ensure that corporate intuition becomes a valuable tool in its success in the marketplace. Ideally, intuition will always be tapped. The reality is that even those making corporate decisions will have intuitive hindrances that need to be overcome.

CHAPTER 12

Remove Corporate Hindrances

Much the same as the hurdles faced with personal intuition, there are four culprits that hinder a company's ability to make intuitive decisions: fearing failure, corporate ego, being overly emotional, and data-heavy decision-making.

12.1 Fearing Failure

Many companies today run on the fear of failure as they are overly concerned with short term thinking, such as quarterly results and immediate returns on investment. This type of thinking squashes creativity, when it could help accelerate the growth of a company. In an uncreative environment, employees function much like robots, which affects the company's overall morale.

Ted Rubin[61] is a leading social marketing strategist, keynote speaker, brand evangelist and acting CMO of Brand Innovators, and in March 2009 started publicly using and evangelizing the term ROR: Return on Relationship™, a concept he believes is the cornerstone for building an engaged multi-million member database, many of whom are vocal advocates for the brand. He recognizes that many firms operate out of fear, which drastically affects their potential for increased success, be it in employee morale, customer satisfaction or even corporate performance.

GUT!

Ted Rubin is the most followed CMO on Twitter according to Social Media Marketing Magazine, one of the most interesting CMOs on

---
61 www.tedrubin.com

Twitter according to Say Media, #13 on Forbes Top 50 Social Media Power Influencers, 2013, and #2 on the Leadtail August 2013 list of Top 25 People Most Mentioned by digital marketers.

"It's taken me a lot of years, but I have learned to trust my intuition. Emotion and intuition are completely different. And I think emotion often overrides the intuition that you should be listening to.

"The reason I love this topic is that, for me, I go with my gut. Intuition takes on everything that is going on around you. Intuition takes in the facts that you are seeing, the emotion that you are feeling, and without you knowing what is happening, it sorts through that stuff and gives you the heart of an issue that you might be missing by reading or looking or any of those things."

Ted talks about how corporations are operating out of a fear of failure, which hinders their ability to instill an intuitive culture.

*"Companies need to follow their intuition more. I think what's holding them back is **absolutely** not logic, it's fear. A lot of companies are run on fear. Everything is done not to fail instead of to succeed. Obviously, there are companies out there that do a miraculous job. Amazon is a perfect example."*

Ted Rubin cites Amazon's founder and CEO Jeff Bezos as one who sidesteps fear and operates with a long term view rather than a fearful short term view. In an interview with the Harvard Business Review[62], Jeff talks about investing his profits back into the company, and Ted expands on his corporate example.

"Jeff Bezos does not let fear get in the way of anything. He does not let any of the naysayers get in the way. If he believes something is going to happen 20 years down, he starts investigating it now. Every dime of profit at Amazon goes back into investment in the company. There are a lot of investors that are questioning that. But, it's what he's done all along.

"I wrote a post[63] on the future of retail, and in my opinion, in the next 7 to 10 years, Amazon will overtake Walmart in global sales in every aspect. Forget about whether it is in-store or out-of-store. I think Amazon is going

---

62 http://blogs.hbr.org/2013/01/jeff-bezos-on-leading-for-the
63 http://tedrubin.com/this-single-company-will-own-the-future-of-retail-via-openforum

to eat their lunch. I think Walmart, just like any other legacy company, is trying to hold onto what it has instead of moving to the future.

"Even if they don't mean to, most companies operate out of fear. The employees operate that way. They don't want to lose their jobs. They meet Sunil or they meet Ted with these amazing ideas, the way you should engage with your customers, and they sit there and they listen and they go, 'Oh my God. Amazing. Yes. Return on Relationship™, loyalty and advocacy and trust. The brass ring. Of course that will increase our sales. But…we'll increase them next week! Well, probably not. Well, then we can't do that.'

"I have to worry about my quarterly results. I have to worry about my shareholders. I have to worry about what my board is going to say. I have to worry about my job. Because that's the way I am being evaluated. Therefore, I am going to take the safe route because I have been doing that for the last four quarters. I have met my numbers for the last four quarters. Nobody gives a crap if I double my numbers. They only care if I don't make my numbers.

"Right? Think about that. You do get rewarded for making your numbers, but very few companies will reward bonuses for dollars over your numbers. And they usually punish you for not making your numbers.

"As much as people want raises and bonuses, what they are worried about is losing their jobs, especially today, especially with the lack of longevity and how hard it is as we get older to get back into the work force. I think people do most of their jobs to keep their jobs and not to get a better job after that.

"Intuition is being incredibly overlooked in business."

Ted provides an excellent example of how he used his cues that informed his intuition on what executives needed to hear to get a sale.

"A lot of people have it. You can see it. In a meeting, you can see it. You can see people getting it. You can also see them shut down. You can almost watch it.

"The lack of willingness to use intuition in business is hurting us a lot. Most companies don't encourage their employees to fail. When they say, 'I want you to fail,' it doesn't mean I want you to lose your job. It's just like what Robert Browning said, 'Your reach should exceed your grasp[64].'

---
64 http://dictionary.reference.com/browse/a+man%27s+reach+should+exceed+his+grasp

A company that embraces failure is a company that embraces employees that reach beyond their reach.

"When I speak, I talk about child-like imagination and how we have to reignite it in corporate America because right now it doesn't exist. We knock the creativity out of our children. We don't encourage outside-of-the-box thinking and encourage our kids to be creative.

"We teach them to be afraid to come up with an idea that someone else says is stupid. And I see this in companies all the time. I watch brainstorming sessions and see people afraid to share their ideas. Either they don't want their coworkers to say, 'Oh that's stupid,' or they're worried that the board is going to say that that was not the right thing to do.

"We have to begin to daydream again. We have to begin to doodle. We have to actually be able to think. I say next week when you are in your office, sit down at your desk, and just stare straight ahead and think. See how long it takes for people to come up and ask if you are okay. And when they come up they are going to ask if you are okay and you'll say yes. And they will ask what are you doing? And you are going to say, I am thinking. And they are going to go, what? What are you thinking about? I'm just thinking. We don't give the opportunity to people to think anymore.

"If you are at a children's museum and are watching the kids build blocks, they sit down with each other. They might suddenly try and build a bridge without any support just by putting a block on top. And nobody would say well, you are an idiot, it's not going to stay up there. They just keep going.

"Or when you go to the beach, and you watch the kids digging to get to China. When I was a kid and every time I dug in that dirt, I expected a head to pop up eventually. As a little kid I would always believe that I could dig to China.

"We lose that in companies because it's not rewarded. Just do your job. How many times have you heard, 'That's not your job? Why are you thinking about that? Who cares about how many of our products are returned?'"

Ted talks about a successful company, Origami Owl, started by a 14-year-old that has grown in four years to achieve over $400 million in sales, with many of the products or tools built by those in the warehouse. Origami Owl's problem is that the board is making comparisons with other companies rather than focusing on the success of this one.

"The board is saying that they have too many employees, they have too many customer service people. But this is how they built their company. When people look at them and say, 'How did you do this,' some of the board members are trying to say there is no way that they did that because they are looking at Avon and Amway and this is how they did it. This is the percentage of customer service people versus designers versus customers.

"That's a big mistake – looking at the past instead of looking at your company and intuitively thinking about where we really need to be successful.

"In business, especially if you are selling to consumers, I believe your intuition gets way stronger if you are actually listening. Most companies don't listen. They sit in boardrooms and they make decisions.

"I can't tell you how many marketers and agencies I have seen where some 45 year-old guy is telling me he wouldn't buy something and why are we selling it. Well, I am glad you are not going to buy it because I am trying to sell it to a 26 year-old girl. Why is this guy telling us what he'd buy?

"Consumers are inviting us into their living rooms every single day, and nobody is going. Go to some of these brands and ask how many of you guys, members of your marketing team, go to the Facebook pages of your customers or to the Twitter feed of your followers and see what they are talking about rather than worrying about them coming to your Facebook page.

"To me that is what increases intuition. The more you know about your customer, your family, about your kids, about your friends, about your environment, the more intuitive you are going to be."

GUT!

The fear of failure in corporations has paralyzed their creativity and ability to see beyond the short term results or outdated metrics that are used as benchmarks throughout the company. Ted believes that we need to bring back creativity and allow for mistakes to be made so that we can enhance our intuitive thinking. A corporation that heightens its intuition is poised to leave its competitors behind and excel to heights it may not have imagined.

When ego begins to creep into an organization at whatever level, this begins to not only curtail the intuitive ability of the egotistical employee or management member, but others around this person will not feel comfortable sharing their intuitive thoughts. This dangerous one-to-many relationship will quickly result in an intuitively paralyzed organization. John Sparling's ego caused him to shut down an excellent business model.

12.2 Corporate Ego

Corporate ego can cause problems when a senior management member displays an egotistical attitude in a corporate setting. The decisions and directions made using this ego as a lens become detrimental to the rest of the company and the result could prove disastrous to overall corporate efficiency and negatively affect corporate performance – a situation faced by John Sparling.

GUT!

In the early '80s, John Sparling owned and operated five video stores in several malls in Vancouver. He had no previous experience in the video store market, nor was he a movie buff, but he was encouraged by a friend who had shown him the overall profits from a number of video stores that the friend had owned in Toronto.

"I was successful in running a number of small businesses before, and so had some business acumen. I just happened to be looking for another opportunity when my friend showed me how much he was doing in business every year. When you talk about intuition, it hit me like a ton of bricks. I instantly knew I could do this business, even though I ran (other) businesses before. I was ecstatic."

Seeing these great numbers, John decided to open some video stores of his own. He arranged for financing and signed a 10-year lease agreement with one particular mall. Of course, there was a tremendous amount of competition around the mall, but John decided to employ a strategy to offer paid memberships that allowed customers to get 10% off rental fees, every 10th video rental free, and exclusive reservations for new titles.

"I knew that I had competition. There is a video store everywhere nowadays. I had to think about how I was going to be different. When I want to

do this type of thinking, I actually go sailing. Sunil, when you and I talked about the intuitive medium, mine is sailing.

"So, I went out on the water and thought about trying to ensure my customers kept coming back. I began to think about the other businesses that have me coming back to them for products and services. And I thought about those businesses that I have memberships with. So why not offer memberships with a discount and a freebie every once in a while? My intuition told me that this was exactly what I had to do."

To start the first store, John needed a manager to take over staffing, stocking, and ordering of video titles so that John could concentrate on opening other stores as well as managing the company's finances. Luckily, John was able to source a family friend, Tim, who had previous experience managing several video stores, and brought him on board. Tim advised John that to properly run a video store location, each one required a manager, and one full-time and two part-time employees. John told Tim his plan to expand video locations into other malls, and advised him that when hiring, the employees should be paid minimum wage and the manager a dollar per hour higher.

"I knew that the profit margins in this business were good because I could recoup my initial investment on a movie title through multiple rentals. In my past experience in running small businesses, I always had a focus on saving as much money as I could. I would work 12 or 15 hours a day in the businesses, and continue more work at home, but in the end, the money was mine.

"It's funny that you asked me about the time I ignored my intuition. I will tell you about the time I did with this business, but now that we are talking, I remember that, in my past businesses, when I was putting all of those hours in, my intuition was telling me that I should hire someone else and do other things like open another branch. I had the money to hire someone else, but I just ignored my intuition so I could pocket all of the profits.

"Getting back to this business, I was so focused on keeping all of the profits, like before, that I took offense to someone telling me what to do. I did not want to pay people more than minimum wage. I had experience of running a business. I had to worry about money. I was the one losing sleep at night. I, I, I.

"It was ego. Pure and simple. How could a manager tell me how to run a business? You know what? I knew that he knew what he was doing. My intuition told me to be thankful for hiring a friend who knew more than me about running a business. But my ego did not allow it. And, once again, I ignored my intuition.

"Because of my insistence in keeping my wages low, Tim and I got into an argument right away. He wanted to pay a much higher rate for employees than I wanted to pay, especially for managers. For the regular employees, I thought the position required someone with little to no skill sets, which meant that the position was really worth minimum wage.

"But Tim tried to tell me that by paying slightly more, he would not have to constantly worry about the turnover when managing staff. Someone working for minimum wage would have absolutely no allegiance to the company and I thought that this was ridiculous as we were giving somebody a job."

Then came the discussion about managers.

"What I was paying Tim was an exception because I needed him to start the business, but I suggested that the other managers be paid less. Tim said that this was unfair and that the other managers would find out eventually, putting Tim in a very uncomfortable position. If Tim was going to be running the team, all managers had to be paid equally. If Tim was to hire somebody at a lower rate, then Tim knew that he would be spending more time training this person than having this person actually run a store from the get-go. After seeing that Tim was quite steadfast, I relented, although I was not very happy with the decision. I was actually quite angry that he was trying to tell me how to run the business."

The business opened its doors with a full complement of staff thanks to Tim's help. The customers found out about the membership fees and the value offered, and revenues began to take off. Over the next six months, John opened four other video stores also located in malls and business started to pick up in those locations as well. Despite strong revenues, John was still bothered by three particular line items on the financial statements: lease expenses, inventory costs (the videos themselves), and wage expenses. John also knew that he carried a heavy debt burden, and wanted to pay that off quickly. John could not change the lease agreements, but thought that he could lower his wage expense by trying to lower the dollar per hour rates of the employees. He approached Tim to see if he could convince the employees to take a cut in their wage.

"When I asked Tim about trying to save a dollar per hour for the employees, he gave me a very stunned look. Of course, Tim was not willing to do that and I knew that this would become an issue again and again. So I began losing faith in Tim.

"This was a crucial point in time for me because I was now thinking about letting Tim go. My thought process went like this: He managed employees. Okay. So have I. He orders videos. Okay. He gets a list and makes some tick marks. Not really hard. And there are other duties like balancing cash, and so on. I also saw that Tim seemed to order the more expensive videos from our supplier. Not good. I kept thinking that he is not thinking like a business owner. Why spend that much money?

"But what he was doing, which I realized later, was that he was ensuring that the customer was happy and the employee was happy, which means we make money. And that would make me happy as well. Here is a prime example for you on ignoring intuition."

John kept allowing his miserly thinking to continue and his ego to cloud his intuition's judgment.

John began to calculate that if he could take over Tim's role and somehow get the other employees to increase their responsibilities, then Tim would not be needed and the business would be able to save a significant amount of wages every month.

"I thought to myself, 'I can schedule staff and order the videos, I can also train the other staff to balance the cash,' as it was quite easy. Confident that I could take on this role, I thought I would test it out in one location first."

Once again, John's ego started to tell him, I I I. With his intuition now severely clouded, John took the step of letting Tim go.

"It was not a great feeling. I knew, intuitively, that this was a wrong decision. But two things got me excited. The first was the elimination of someone challenging me and my decisions, and the second the savings I would realize by letting Tim go.

"If I get good at this job, then maybe I can manage two stores at the same time, and I can double my savings. That means more money in my pocket."

The news of Tim being fired travelled fast to the other stores as Tim had gained a significant amount of respect across all the stores. Of course, John was not open about why he let Tim go, stating that things just did not work out. But the business moved forward.

John found that managing the employees was quite easy as the schedules were generally set by the employees themselves, filling all the available shifts.

"Things were really running smoothly for me. I then began to wonder why I felt so bad. I began to really question the value that I placed on Tim's services. At this point, I thought I had overvalued Tim.

"What I didn't understand is that my ego not only affected my decisions with Tim, but it actually affected a lot of the employees because of my management style. These two things were solely responsible, I believe, for the downfall in my video business. And it began with me making a disastrous mistake in picking the right videos for my customers."

At the top of the month, it was time to order videos for that month, and John looked over the video titles. At the top of the form were two featured new releases, Under the Volcano and Rocky III. When looking at the price points, he noticed that Rocky III was considerably more expensive, and he was not impressed with the description of a movie about a boxer. Under the Volcano was much cheaper, and the description seemed more thrilling.

So he ordered only one copy of Rocky III and 10 copies of Under the Volcano. Posters went up notifying the members of the new releases that were soon to hit the video shelves, and many members began reserving Rocky III on a first-come first-serve basis, placing their names on a growing waiting list. There was no waiting list for Under the Volcano.

When the videos actually came in, the employees were shocked that only one copy of Rocky III was ordered, and assumed that because of the popularity of the video, more copies would be coming in the mail at a later date. But they never did come in, and members began to get angry at the staff, and the staff began to get angry at John.

Despite his hesitation at paying a premium price, John was forced to order another nine copies of the Rocky III video. It was clear to the employees that John simply did not know what he was doing when ordering videos.

This lack of product knowledge resulted in an embarrassing situation for John.

One of the complaints that the store often received was that there were not enough videos for children, and John decided to tackle this problem on his own.

"There was a lot of talk in the news about some cartoon movie called Fritz the Cat. I immediately thought that if people were talking about this movie, it must be quite popular. If so, I knew it would then become a hit."

John approached his video supplier, but the supplier told him that they did not carry such videos, which confused John because it was a cartoon. John put up a notice in the store to see if any of his customers were able to find copies of this cartoon.

A week later, a box was left on John's desk with a colour picture of a cartoon cat with the Fritz the Cat title. John immediately put the video out into the children's section, with a note that this children's movie was now available.

That weekend, a parent came in asking John for his suggestion of a good children's video for a birthday party. John proudly pointed to his sign saying that he was able to secure the Fritz the Cat cartoon. The parent had not heard of it, but took John up on his suggestion, paid for it, and went on her way.

The next afternoon, the same parent came back to the store fuming mad. The conversation went like this:

Parent: Where is that damn person that told me to rent this video?

Staff Member: I'll go get him.

John: Hi Ma'am, how can I help you?

Parent: Do you remember me from yesterday? You told me to rent this video.

John: Yes, I did.

Parent: Do you know what type of video this is? Why did you have it in the children's section? Did you not know that it is not appropriate for children?

John: I don't understand. It is supposed to be a popular cartoon is it not? That is why I ordered it.

Parent: It absolutely is a cartoon. But it is a cartoon porn, you idiot!

The parent threw the video at John and stormed out of the store, vowing never to come again, and ensured that she told as many people as possible not to come to the video store ever again.

"I was so embarrassed. I clearly did not know what I was doing. So I appointed one of the other store managers to take over ordering the videos from that point forward."

However, John's obsession with cost-cutting continued, keeping only one or two pens in each store and asking staff to not use much paper. Eventually he made his way back to wages and began asking each employee to take a dollar per hour cut in wage.

"One person had reluctantly taken the cut in wage because he needed to pay off some debt, but it was clear that he was not thrilled with my decision. But then I got excited as the second person looked at me with a big smile on her face and said, 'Absolutely, no problem.' I couldn't believe it. This was very easy to do. She never showed up the next morning for her shift."

News of John's cost-cutting measures travelled fast, and soon, John started losing more staff. He scrambled to rectify the situation by placing ads in the paper and also in the local human resources government office, but at minimum wage, there were no takers.

John began working in the stores as much as possible to make up for the lost staff but this was not sustainable, and he called all the employees that had left, including Tim, to request that they come back to the video store at the same wage, and a small bonus for the inconvenience. But there were no takers.

"My egotistical attitude continued right to the end as I just could not believe that I was being called cheap by the employees who left. And they also told me that they didn't trust me. I tried to justify my thinking at the time as not being cheap but just trying to run a tight ship.

"But what got me thinking was when I called Tim, who still refused to come back, he made me realize what my mistake was. He said that I had everything in hand – happy employees, smooth operations, and returning customers. And for a dollar per hour, all that came crumbling down. For just ONE DOLLAR PER HOUR! When Tim repeated that statement, it hit me really hard. My ego resulted in a lack of trust."

The house of cards came down quickly for John. The employees stopped believing in him as he was wishy-washy and he clearly thought more about being in control, wanting everyone to listen to him, and saving money than the welfare of the individual.

One-by-one, employees started to leave the company and John had no choice but to shut down all but one of the video stores. That store survived for a few more months, but it did not generate enough money to pay down the outstanding debt obtained to open up the five stores. Six months later, John shut the business down for good, and his company filed for bankruptcy soon after that.

"When I do reflect back, given the conversation on intuition that we are having, there were intuitive signposts for me. I just decided not to read the signposts. My ego definitely got in the way. And not just in a small way. With nobody coming back and nobody coming onboard, there was only one way that the business was going."

GUT!

The video business model that John had run was quite successful, with an increasing number of members coming onboard, robust revenues, and both employees and customers happy. When John decided to focus on stroking his ego and penny-pinching, the success he had built up in a short period of time, which had all the signals of being sustained, was wiped out.

In a corporate environment, when ego gets in the way, there is a tendency to not listen to other opinions or there is a tendency to try and be someone that you are not. This stifles creativity, open communication, trust, and ultimately efficiency, performance, and profits. Losing the ego is tough, but if steps are not taken to eliminate it, results such as turnover and substandard performance are to be expected. With all these issues, intuition will never have an opportunity to be expressed.

Despite intuition guiding corporate decisions, some may begin to question the intuitive decision, allowing a flood of emotions to play a heavy role. This is a sure way to cloud corporate intuition as Twee Brown experienced, resulting in a business partner being kept on despite intuition telling her to let this partner go.

12.3 Being Overly Emotional

When emotions begin to swirl around corporate decisions, the intuitive thoughts that should guide these decisions are questioned. This not only leads to self-doubt among some of the employees, but it often takes the company down the wrong path.

This hindrance can apply to any corporate area, including the implementation of a particular process, the realigning of the corporate strategy, or in Twee Brown's case, continuing with a business partner early into a business opportunity when her intuition was telling her that she should cut ties.

GUT!

Twee Brown is the CEO of Adamas Group, proprietor of Ben Thanh and Mein Street restaurants, and President of Empire Home Rentals and Kidscape Indoor Playground. Twee dedicates much of her free time to her family, boards, charitable and advisory committees and management teams.

Twee and her husband, Rob Brown, work closely together to make business decisions in their ventures. Rob is strong in experiential intuition whereas Twee is strong in creative intuition. Together, they are able to make sound intuitive decisions as a team.

However, the one time that intuition was ignored was during the construction stage for Kidscape Indoor Playground, when overly emotional thinking clouded their judgment and prevented them from letting a business partner go, resulting in the partner being involved for a longer period of time than was necessary.

Rob: We come from a restaurant background where a lot of our time has been spent. It wasn't until we had kids when we began to think that there's got to be more to going out with a child rather than being stared at, or stared down at, in a restaurant or circling around the mall for the umpteenth time.

So we had an idea about an indoor playground or a gathering area where people would meet and know that there was a place to go with their kids. We knew that we didn't have the time to put into this. What we were lacking was an operating partner. Our kids started the school year and we met somebody who had almost had an identical idea, the same thought, and was looking to be that operating partner. I introduced her to Twee and later the idea of opening a children's play centre took shape.

Twee: *A friendship naturally developed because of mutual interests and love for our kids, and they went to same school and so on. That was how we started a discussion. Things were going quite well, seemingly, at that time. We were very like-minded and they seemed to have the same goal. When I say they, it is the partner and her husband. Where we differed was that she had time. She was not working. And we did not have time but we had the capital.*

We decided to collaborate in that way. They put in a little bit to have some skin in the game. We were the majority investor and had the business background to run a retail outlet. We would obviously be the background support, but we needed a person to be the face the business and to essentially be that operating partner that we did not want to do, or be, and we did not have time to be. So that's how it started.

As we started down that road in terms of lease negotiations, contract tendering, contractors and the build-out, it was during the time of the build-out that we started seeing a divergence of values and vision. We realized that we were not as like-minded as we thought. It was at that point in time that the friendship was fully developed. We spent a lot of time together, but on the other side we have a real investment that we were making to create this new project, this new business.

Twee's intuition was telling her that something was amiss with her partner's sense of what it takes to open and run a business. Yet she struggled with the possibility of confronting her friend.

Twee: *The struggle for me personally was how do you tell a friend that this is probably not going to be a real fit? Or how do you tell a friend that she* needs to revisit that vision of hers, or to tell her that perhaps her idea in what owning and operating a business entails is not what she's thinking?

There was a big inner struggle that I was trying to repress. 'It's okay. We're experienced enough and well-versed enough. I believe I'm straightforward enough and that I'm forthcoming enough.' Whatever 'we're enough of …' we would be able to groom and develop that person. That was my hope. Of course Rob had a slightly different apprehension.

There were some early signs Rob had experienced which led him to start believing that there might not be a fit with this partner.

Rob: I absolutely knew that there was no way that this person was ever going to get in line with where we wanted to go. It was very obvious that she was very interested in the trappings of being a business owner. We could tell from the build. We would be worried about running the right electrical to different parts of the building and she would be worried about how her office was going to be set up and if she could get a couch in there and how it's going to look and when the business cards were coming so she can hand them out. We just absolutely knew that the ship was not going to right itself and we were just not ever going to get a parallel situation again.

Both Rob and Twee's intuition had been telling them that the business side of the relationship had to come to an end. The reality was that either the business or the relationship was going to survive. Rob and Twee were already financially invested in the playground idea as it had a strong business case. They were going to move forward with the business. So, logically, the partnership had to dissolve. The issue now shifted to the personal relationship and whether that was salvageable. However, overly emotional decision-making had come into play.

Rob: I told Twee that this was not going to happen and we had to pull the ripcord on this and Twee's reaction to this was 'How can we? She's a friend of ours.'

Maybe I should have pushed for it more because I knew going forward, there was no way you were going to maintain the business relationship and the friendship. At least one of them was going to go. And if we ended the business relationship cleanly then we may have been able to save the friendship. If we continue down that road, we're going to lose the business partnership and the friendship.

The business opened with the partner still in the business. Yet another sign of the partner's lack of business acumen complemented with a dose of personal ego was seen when Rob happened to be visiting Costco at the same time as the partner.

Rob: I remember, we were about to open, and we had employees that we were starting to hire and come in and get used to the facility. And we were getting some fruit platters. So, unbeknownst to her, I saw her at Costco dealing with employees there and she was like 'I am a business owner and I'm here to buy some fruit platters'.

Just get the darn platters! Why do you have to do this? But she was making a scene. I was two checkouts away and she was telling another person in line about her business and how she was a business owner. It was odd to me.

That became part of the problem because she had more invested in the business than just the money at this time. She had a lot of herself tied up into it. I think it would've been humiliating for her to not be involved.

Part of the emotional conundrum Twee was facing was her strong sense of commitment to the friendship, a value that she grew up with.

Twee: It was social responsibility. I think it's the obligation that I made a commitment to a friend. It was a commitment to her and I felt that we were taking her hand and leading the way. And I felt that if we cut off that connection, that I did not live up to what I committed to. It's one of those things that you're taught in most households. You are taught to live by the commitment, and you fulfill your commitment, good or bad.

Despite Twee wanting to honour her obligation to a friend, her intuition was giving her strong signals that she needed to let this person go.

Twee: I was hoping, hoping, hoping for the best, but knew it was going to get worse. Obviously, when it comes to business, sometimes, in a situation, you may feel really badly about that social obligation, but you have to do what's best for the business. And where I did not listen to my own intuition, and honestly my husband's strong recommendation and suggestion, I pushed that aside in favour of the social obligation that I felt, which is obviously wrong. Four months after our business was started, the relationship, friendship, everything was severed.

We decided to let her go about one month after the start of the business. There were so many signs that we should have let her go earlier, but the final three straws were her family's interference, her children's behaviour and frequent, unsupervised visits at the business and her inappropriate conduct with the staff. Her children were telling customers to "get out of the playground" because it belonged to them. She was telling the staff about her marital issues and asking them to hide her absences from the centre. At the end, we gave ourselves the permission to set aside the obligation of friendship and commitment and to save the business instead. Thank goodness logic and pragmatism returned.

Ignoring this intuition resulted in a significant number of opportunity costs for them:

- It slowed down the opening of Kidscape
- They lost some staff who were frustrated by this person and her misconduct
- There was a lost opportunity in training another general manager from the start
- She damaged Twee and Rob's personal reputation because she told people that they had forced her out for their own personal gain, despite Rob and Twee offering to sell her their portion of the business because they did not have the time nor the intention to operate Kidscape
- The whole incident increased their frustration levels and caused undue stress
- They lost an unknown and unmeasurable amount of money due to the retraining and rehiring of a staff member to replace her role as the general manager. Because this was the lead position, it took a long time to train and develop that individual fully.
- There were additional financial ramifications as they paid her for a full-time role that was performed on a part-time basis.

GUT!

When we begin to question our intuition with overly emotional thinking, we begin to ask questions or make excuses, delaying, or worse, ignoring the appropriate action that should be taken. In Rob and Twee's case, the commitment to the friendship, although honourable on a personal level, was not the right decision to make for the business. Fortunately for them and the business, although there were significant repercussions, they were able to cut the relationship short. If they decided to continue this relationship, the results could have been significantly worse.

Given this example, companies may want to completely move away from incorporating emotions into corporate decision that are drive by intuition. Unfortunately, some may swing too far and rely too heavily on data.

Data is absolutely valuable when companies need to keep a pulse on how they are doing in the marketplace to discover how successful they may be. Based on certain reports, management can make intuitive decisions on how they would need to proceed to continue to be successful.

However, an over-reliance on data will ignore intuitive decisions that may not be supported by the data, and in fact, tells a company to take a different direction. Unfortunately, if the company takes a completely data-driven path, it may soon find itself in a very inefficient place, soon realizing that it is better off in the other direction. It now needs to rely on intuition to find out how to turn around.

In Mitch Blackwell's case, senior management at his company decided to rally around incorrect data, despite knowing that the data was wrong. In this case, intuitive ignorance meant that two major satisfaction ratings, which were celebrated in every way possible, needed to be changed to truly reflect what they were supposed to be measuring. The company knew that they needed to change, but the consequences were too much to handle.

12.4 Data-Heavy Decision-Making

As companies grow in size and their operations become complex, senior management may not be as close to the front lines as they would wish to be, and may not have a strong sense of company performance. Disconnected managers might then turn to reports, such as market share, return on investment, income statements, departmental profit and loss reports, cost per acquisition, and so on, that provide various data points that reflect how a company is performing in many corporate areas.

These reports are valuable for finding the pulse of a company in the various areas that are being measured, and should be used to support any intuitive decision.

However, one of the major hindrances to corporate intuition is an over-reliance on data to steer the corporate ship. In some case, executives have even tried to find patterns in data that do not exist, a phenomenon called "overfitting" the data[65].

An employee's intuition might indicate that a particular corporate initiative should take a certain direction, for example, yet the data may not support this direction. Data-heavy corporate decision-making ignores this intuition, even when the intuition points to the right decision or action to take.

This intuitive ignorance usually results in substandard performance, missed opportunities, and possible turnover as the company continues to stifle creativity. Not only does this affect the company internally, but it may also begin to affect customers, which was the case for Mitch Blackwell, whose intuition went ignored.

GUT!

Mitch Blackwell had been hired to help a US national trucking company looking to implement efficiencies in their business processes. Mitch had a long career in process improvement while in the transportation industry and was the perfect resource to help this company.

What impressed Mitch about this company was that its marketing touted it as having the highest customer satisfaction and employee satisfaction ratings in the industry. It was also growing as it continued to open offices across North America.

"The first couple of days after joining this firm, I could feel the energy at head office. It seemed like there were statistics and graphs all over the place. And rightfully so given the fact that they led the industry in many areas.

"That weekend, the leadership team flew to a resort to talk about major initiatives and invited me to come along to get my perspective. I was quite honoured to be invited. Once there, although I did not understand much of the industry jargon, I was able to piece things together to get a sense of where some of the issues were.

---

65 Hayashi, A. M. (2001). When to trust your gut. Harvard Business Review, 79(2), 59-65.

"I was asked to give my opinion on what I would be doing, and the first thing I told the executives was that I wanted to make sure that the processes feeding into those key industry-leading areas were as efficient as possible to see if we could increase the numbers ever so slightly. Although many were very happy at my suggestion, I was given a word of caution by one of the vice-presidents. He told me to be careful not to try and change the world. All indicators are showing that the company is better than the competition, and they are going to stay that way.

"My intuition was telling me that something in his comments was quite eerie. The feeling I got was like watching a bad horror movie where you are approaching a closet and everything looks great until you open it and something jumps out at you that scares the crap out of you."

On Mitch's second day on the job, he started trying to understand how the customer satisfaction scores were calculated. His manager told him that a component of these scores were affected by the feedback from customers on the phone with the customer service representatives and also the percentage deliveries that were made on time. Mitch decided to sit down with one of the customer service representatives and ask her a number of questions in addition to listening to the inbound calls.

"I sat down with one of the customer service reps, Brandi, and asked her about the type of calls that she got. Brandi was quite open and began telling me that when a customer phones in, you are not going to expect a customer to give you a verbal pat on the back. Obviously, most of the calls coming in would be due to a late shipment, missing cargo and, in some cases, rude drivers.

"At that time, one of the calls that came in was from one of our larger customers. The manager of the main warehouse phoned in yelling about a shipment being two hours late. Brandi did her best to try and calm her down and began to put notes in the online customer record.

"Brandi changed the on-time status to two-hour delay, which changed the customer satisfaction rating from 98.8% to 98.6%. This slight change somehow triggered my intuition that was telling me that, even though I did not know the formula for this rating, there should have been a lower number that was calculated. My gut was telling me that there was something wrong with this picture."

Once the call was done, Mitch asked the customer service representative if he could see the number of complaints this manager had phoned in for. Mitch was shocked to see that this manager had called 19 times within the last seven months. If this was the case, why would the customer service rating be so high?

Intrigued, Mitch turned his attention to finding out what numbers were used to calculate the customer service rating. He asked Brandi if she knew anything about its calculation. Although she did not know what the underlying formulas were, she explained that a part of this calculation came from the number of hours a shipment was late, which was obvious. What was not so obvious was how late shipments were actually being changed to on-time shipments.

"Brandi started telling me that the sales reps would put in an expected time of delivery once they booked the call. Once the delivery was made, the drivers would phone into the customer service centre and have Brandi or one of her colleagues enter the time of delivery into the customer record. Obviously, if these both match, then there is a 100% customer satisfaction rating based on that one particular event.

"If the driver knows that he is going to be late because he may have gotten delayed at the border or in a traffic jam, he phoned the customer service line to tell the rep to call the customer to say that there was going to be a delay of one hour. The rep would then call the customer and let them know of the delay. When the customer okayed the delay, the rep updated the screen and changed the expected time of delivery so that it reflected the one-hour delay."

"By making this change on the system, a delivery that is expected to be one hour late is now flagged as being on-time once the driver reaches the destination point. Well, no wonder the company was outdoing the industry in on-time shipments. It was masking the late deliveries as being on-time. The only time that the number would go down is if a customer complained.

"I then start to look around the room at all these high customer service percentages, and I had a strong feeling that we were celebrating something that this company should not be celebrating as much."

Every Thursday, the regional representatives in that office would get together to discuss any concerns with the weekly operations and review the on-time deliveries.

"The meeting started with each of the regional reps taping graphs to the walls summarizing their customer satisfaction ratings. Each rep would review the ratings, and then the group was asked if there were any other issues. There was silence.

"At this point, I put my hand up, and when I got a chance to speak, I asked if anyone had known how that percentage was arrived at. After the question, everyone was staring at me with a blank, confused look on their faces. Nobody knew how those numbers were generated, yet not only were they celebrating on a weekly basis, but from what I understand, the bonuses were tied into this rating."

Mitch was obviously not a popular employee at this time, but this did not deter his efforts because the company was making incorrect figures public, and he had to make sure that he was ready to talk about this at the next senior leadership meeting happening in three months.

Mitch requested a meeting with one of the employees responsible for the data that would show up in the reports to try and get a sense of the overall formula that calculated the customer service rating.

"When I finally met with the data analyst who populated the customer service satisfaction rating numbers, he had no clue about the actual formula, and told me that those who established this formula were no longer with the company.

"The data analyst looked at me and said that this formula has been used for years and seems to work because all the customers are happy. I thought that this was a bit of an odd statement because it did not seem like the customers were happy. Of course, the numbers showed that they were happy, but relying on this data was useless."

Mitch then turned his sights to the processes that fed into the high employee satisfaction rating. He hoped that these numbers reflected the true sentiment within the company.

There were two major sets of employees whose scores in the customer satisfaction survey were responsible for the customer satisfaction rating: the customer service representatives and the drivers.

Mitch went back to Brandi to get her thoughts on the survey.

"I took Brandi out for lunch and asked her how happy she was with her job. She was quite happy where she worked, enjoyed the hours, loved dealing with the customers and was quite content with the pay, although everyone wants more money!

"The only issue she brought up was that management had set up unrealistic goals for bonuses. She explained that bonuses were awarded if the customer service reps were to collect money from customers who would be charged extra fees if they made changes to the delivery routes. For example, if a customer changed the routing to go to a different warehouse or changed the cargo size or weight, the customer would be subject to a penalty as this would trigger extra charges and extra work for the transportation company.

"To collect the bonus, which was calculated as a percentage of the extra charges collected, Brandi further explained that she would have to contact the customer and collect cash within 30 hours of the delivery. This was not achievable because the customers could only send a cheque after one week, which was outside the 30-hour window. So why even bother making the call?

"I asked if there was any way for this feedback to be reflected on the employee satisfaction survey, and Brandi told me that the only questions that were asked were if they were paid on time, if the hours were reasonable, and if any training for personal development was completed. There was no room for any feedback or negative commentary.

"No wonder the employees were satisfied. The company was not truly measuring actual satisfaction!"

Mitch now turned to the drivers to see what concerns they had. Mitch was able to touch base with a driver who happened to be in the office.

"He explained that the only complaint he had was that his paycheques were always wrong because there were a lot of transcription errors in the time slips and delivery logs, which the drivers filled out by hand. A lot of the time, the numbers were entered into the pay system incorrectly, which affected their paycheques.

"The drivers had to chase the HR manager to correct this if the drivers were underpaid, and the HR manager had to chase the drivers to correct this if they were overpaid. The drivers and the HR manager were asking for a computer-based system that would eliminate the errors, but the company did not want to spend money on such a system. Once again, the high employee satisfaction rating would not justify such an expense.

"Everyone knew about these problems, yet the driver told me that management would always talk about these nonsensical employee satisfaction ratings at every town hall meeting."

Once again, the driver agreed with Mitch that there was no feedback system. With no feedback system, the company could not tackle issues that the employees had. Despite knowing that problems existed, management seemed to look the other way to maintain a high employee satisfaction rating.

Mitch was in a difficult situation. He wanted to approach management to make changes to the rating schemes, but these changes would uncover the true ratings for both the customers and employees. Mitch was certain that management would know which direction these ratings would be heading.

"I know that I was already unpopular with the regional reps, and so, with me tinkering with these ratings, I better have some good news to tell when I approach management.

"My intuition was telling me that there was a better way for the reps to actually collect the bonuses. When I reviewed our standard delivery contracts, I knew that the customers were contractually obligated to pay for these charges regardless of when they were called. For one of our largest customers, they required a phone call within an eight-hour window, and if not made, the charges were to be waived. But there was no way for the customer service reps to know this."

Mitch proposed that the stipulation required to collect the penalties within 30 hours be dropped. Instead, Mitch suggested that the reps contact the customer within an eight-hour window, which would trigger a payment requirement from the customer, which would surely be made. The bonuses would then be calculated when the actual cheques come in. That way, there was an incentive for the customer service reps to actually make the calls. Mitch received approval to test it with a few of the reps to see if this new incentive would work.

"I tested this new bonus system on Brandi and two of her friends who also worked at the company. In one week, we had a total of 13 customers who were penalized and were subsequently called within the eight-hour period. They all paid within one week. Guess what? The three reps all got bonuses on their next paycheque."

The updated incentive program was extremely well received and expanded to include all of the customer service reps. All of a sudden, a backlogged list that kept track of customers who were to be penalized was empty.

"Within one month, the customer service reps had collected over $187,000 in penalties. This small change would have the potential of bringing in an additional $2 million which the company would have left on the table."

With Mitch now looking to make changes in how the customer and employee satisfaction ratings were calculated, it was no surprise when his intuition told him that any change would end up with lower ratings.

His immediate manager was apprehensive about having Mitch delve deeper into these ratings, knowing that they could be significantly affected, and he suggested that Mitch look to other projects. Mitch quizzed his manager about the confidence he had in the ratings.

"I explained to him about my gut feeling that these ratings were way off. He confided in me that he had the same intuitive feelings. But management was so vested in relying on this data as it affected every aspect of their operations. He had no choice. Embrace the data or find other employment.

"I was quite upset that this company did not care enough to want to make positive changes. They relied on this data too much to make any changes that would reflect badly upon the company.

"I was also disappointed that this large company was essentially lying to its customers and employees. Come to think of it, despite the customer service satisfaction rating being quite high, I would wonder why some of the large customers were constantly asking to meet our senior management on delivery delay times.

"In good conscience, I could not go further ahead without letting the senior executives know. Not knowing what to expect, I asked for a meeting with my manager and the vice-president of the company, and let the VP know what I found out.

"After some idle chit chat, I told them both that I thought that the ratings we constantly celebrated did not truly reflect what they were designed to measure and that I knew how to change them.

"I was told that these numbers were always calculated a certain way, and changing the formulas would be next to impossible. I leaned over towards the vice-president, looked in his eyes and asked him point blank what his gut feeling was. I was so surprised to hear that he had a sense that they were wrong, but he had the audacity to tell me that they were not off by much, so why change a good thing.

"I reminded him that my primary role was to fix these very issues and to maintain integrity in the data and processes that occur. He agreed that this was my role, but suggested that I look to other processes to fix. The meeting then ended, and I looked to find other projects to work on.

"After the president found out that I questioned the numbers, he had asked my manager to terminate me immediately. Not surprisingly, after a couple of days, I was out of a job."

GUT!

Despite Mitch's efforts, the transport company was reluctant to change any of the ratings, being highly reliant on ratings that did not truly represent what they were meant to gauge. Mitch's intuition knew that operational fixes could be made that would result in a true rating that would remain high and would return to high values by fixing the underlying process efficiencies. But management wanted no changes. With Mitch gone, and customers calling the company's management team to talk about delivery problems, the transportation company would have to review these ratings at some point in time, or face a declining customer base.

Had Mitch joined a company that started with an intuitive culture, it would have been much easier to make the changes he needed to make this company even more successful. The easiest time to set an intuitive culture is when the company is in its infancy. Intuitive decision-making should be encouraged at all levels in a company where relevant. Even if a company has not embraced having an intuitive culture, it can certainly make changes to move in that direction. This must mean that every resource should be aware that an intuitive culture is respected and desired. To ensure that this message rings loud and clear, a company needs to understand what its core intuitive values are, a topic David Ciccarelli from Voices.com knows well.

CHAPTER 13

Understand Core Intuitive Values

Core values are operating philosophies or principles that guide an organization's internal conduct and relationships. These relationships include not only those within the company, but they also extend outward to suppliers, customers, and in some cases investors and shareholders.

When a company is in its infancy, its core values are a direct representation of those of the founder. As a company grows in size, it will often revisit its core values and articulate a more formal statement of these values in a corporate mission statement. These core values then begin to shape the intuitive thinking of the business executives.[66]

To ensure that the corporate environment promotes intuitive thinking, the core values should incorporate elements such as open communication, trust, and respect for opinions – elements that encourage everyone to use intuition when appropriate. Not only will this foster creativity to find unique solutions to move the company forward, but the company maintains a culture of creativity that is highly desirable as a work environment. When this is achieved, success is sure to follow, with the employees functioning at a high level, much like Voices.com.

GUT!

David Ciccarelli is Co-Founder and CEO of Voices.com, the industry-leading website that connects businesses with professional voice talent. Its clients include radio and television stations, advertising agencies, and businesses of all sizes, including Fortune 500 companies. The

---

[66] Burke, L. A., & Miller, M. K. (1999). Taking the mystery out of intuitive decision making. The Academy of Management Executive, 13(4), 91-99.

company has over 100,000 voice talents who speak over 100 languages that anybody can hire right through the company website.

David and his wife, Stephanie, started this company with a higher purpose of helping others.

"We are blessed to be a blessing for others. By taking that approach, we view ourselves as merely a channel to helping our voice talent find work. This changes the perception of why we are doing what we are doing. A lot of companies know what they do. 'We sell XYZ.' But why are you doing this? When you build a culture around people understanding why you're doing what you're doing, they come to work with a reason and a purpose. We spent a lot of time on that."

David talks about using intuition in a corporate setting and how he triangulates it with data and collaboration.

"I think that in almost every single decision that you're making, there's a certain degree of, the gut check element, or, 'I have a hunch that this is going to work.' There's a certain element that's going to have to come into play. People don't go through life by only making decisions based upon, you know, if they woke up and the sun was shining that day, am I in a good mood? It's more multifaceted.

"I'm not an analyst by nature; I view myself more creatively. For blue-sky type thinking, I tend to dream up 'How am I going to drive the company forward?' Even more broadly, 'What's next for our company?' In those kind of situations, I'm not staring at spreadsheets or clicking dashboards to come up with that next great idea. Those tend to fall out of the sky, in a lot of ways.

"I then do part of a feasibility study, thinking, is this even possible? Am I going down the right path?

"In that initial ideation, there's going to be some built-in assumptions, and whatever those assumptions are, there's probably some data that I can use to validate those assumptions. Let me pull a few data points. However, in my case, I look at the data after the fact. I will also go about that decision-making process by asking for feedback from others."

One of the first times David used his intuition with Voices.com was during its infancy.

"Intuitively, I felt that changing our company name from Interactive Voices to just Voices.com was going to be one of the best branding moves that we had made and I was willing to risk a lot. We were only two or three people at the time, Stephanie, myself, and one other person. So at a very, very early date, we ended up paying $30,000, which was more money than we had by far, but we broke it up into $5,000 increments every quarter.

"That was just one of those things where we just didn't seem to have the cachet with our customers in terms of brand recognition. We wanted to be proud of the company we were building, and the name was such a big part of that. So that was one that really worked out.

"Frankly, there were no previous case studies, there was no depth to tell us about value. Did we pay too much or too little? Did we know if it was going to generate more traffic to our website? It just sounded like a really solid idea. The price was something I could 'live with,' and if all of these things kind of played out, then we'd be fine, and the company would move ahead."

The name change was a crucial part of the branding strategy, but it came at a huge risk. Thirty thousand dollars, at the time, was all the money they had. Spending that money and not having it work could have led to the company's closure. But David's intuition told him that this investment would pay off in dividends. So he made the investment, and Voices.com grew from there.

Collaboration has always been a core value of Voices.com. If an intuitive decision is made, collaboration can present points that are both positive and negative in nature. This then forms a well-rounded decision that can be moved forward. Voices.com places such emphasis on doing business collaboratively that it has been ingrained in the culture.

"I think you bring up an important point, which is that it starts to form a culture that we want for the long term. Culture forms a basis for those unwritten rules, a guide that helps people, at least our team, to make their own decisions. It picks up where the employee handbook leaves off.

"Culture is basically the way we do things around here. You need people to interact with a small team to have that sure set of decision-making, and to at least appreciate the thought processes of other people.

"I think there are advantages to knowing in a flash what the right decision is to make. The culture tells us what to do and how to handle *those unprecedented customer service requests. In a situation we've never had before, we need to have a certain level of intuition, of how do we do this? What's the right thing? Is there some scenario to draw on from the past that would give me an indicator? Especially if you're on the phone with somebody, or replying to an e-mail, or something high-pressure that needs to happen quickly. You don't have time to confide in all the data and research. In my opinion, I feel like the company's actually getting stronger as we've been able to hone in on some of those, let's call them, personality traits or characteristics that we admire."*

Ingraining collaborative intuitive thinking in the corporate culture and core values of the company gives the employees permission to think about better ways to improve processes and procedures, and not be afraid to share those thoughts.

"It allows us to think a little more creatively. We have this kind of thought: the first assumption is that the reality is that most work in a day is routine-based. It's repetitive in nature. All right, well that means that there must be a way that you are doing the work. And if there's a way that you're doing the work, well then the next line of thought is that there's probably a better way to do what you're doing now. And if there's a better way, then theoretically, there's a 'best way,' and that's what develops our best practices.

"So when I approach somebody at the leadership team level or myself as that department leader, then we're going to dissect a certain process. We're really saying that we feel that this could be improved, it will make life a lot easier, we will highlight the benefits for individuals or groups of people that work in that department, and ask them if we can stick our noses into their work, so to speak, for the next couple of days. And this is all in the name of being more productive and making their life easier, then offering better customer service at the end of the day.

"I think we're gaining that certain level of trust and permission, and it allows people to free up what they want to say. They may say that some stuff is a little cumbersome and so forth, and maybe they have some great ideas on how they could be doing something better."

David ensures that this collaborative culture, ongoing trust, and openness starts when an employee joins the company. He puts emphasis on the hiring process to ensure that he brings in people who really want to be there.

"We've actually changed how we hire people, and we've really seen the results lately. One third of it is a personality assessment, one third is an interview, and the final third would be my one-on-one.

"I look at the assessments and interview responses ahead of time before the final interview with me because it actually helps with some of the questions that come up that I am asking.

"Sometimes people just put the wrong things on the assessments, so you want to understand why. For example, you can put yourself as innovative instead of conventional thinking. Well I want to know some examples. Home or at work, specifically what have you done? Some people might not have the option or might not have had the opportunity at work to express that they're really innovative. Maybe they created something really nice and neat at home, or built something that had never been done. It allows me to dig a bit deeper.

"In some cases, I will ask, 'Tell me about that time when you spotted a better way to do something, and tell me how you presented the idea. Tell me about a time that you presented an idea and it was rejected, or it was tried and it didn't work. How did that make you feel? Do you consider yourself an observer and do you like to people-watch, sit in a small room and watch people go by or sit in a Starbucks?' I just try to understand the personality traits and characteristics.

"Lastly, it's my personal gut check, my intuition, to see if I feel like this is going to be a good candidate based on me grilling them on heart-to-heart non-academic things. I'm trying to put you in real life situations, make you feel somewhat uncomfortable. Do I feel like you're passing that test? Do I get a good feeling of who you are? If he's very relaxed, why is he so relaxed?

"And financially, I've heard studies where it costs $30,000 to $50,000 to replace an employee who doesn't work out after about three months. I can totally believe that. Given that, if it means an hour of two of people's time for the initial interview and an hour of my time, and $50 or $100 for one of these surveys, we may be at $1,000 or less. Even if I have to repeat that three or four times, it's still drastically less. The advantage is that I now know that I am hiring a high performer, instead of someone who could be just mediocre."

GUT!

It is clear that David supports his intuition with both data and collaboration. The data is something that he can get from reports, but the collaborative process must go through a group of people that are open and honest and provide feedback. David selects these people at the interview stage and ensures that this collaboration and intuitive thinking is ingrained in the core values of his company.

Just as David selects those resources that help intuition become the natural decision-making tool in his company, it is also important to remove resources when they no longer fit with where the company is going. Reallocating resources into positions for which they are not suited, or hanging on to resources who have little concern for the success of the company, will have a tremendous dampening effect on corporate intuition.

Brian Scudamore found that his intuitive thinking was being affected and removed all of the resources, giving them the ability to start the company with a clean slate of resources that really cared.

CHAPTER 14

Select Appropriate Resources

Corporate intuition is easy to inculcate in a company at the early stages of its growth. However, through growth and expansion, the firm begins to add structure such as teams, departments, and managerial levels, all of which is tied together with corporate policies and procedures.

A growing employee base creates a larger collective involved in the decision-making process, and the intuitive decisions now depend upon a number of individuals collectively.

Different areas of a firm will require strengths in the different intuitive types. For example, in senior management, marketing, or sales areas, the resources in those areas should have an Intuitive Zone of Influence strong in the creative and possibly relational intuitive areas. Operational areas of a company should have resources that are stronger in experiential areas.

The Intuitive Zones of Influence for the key corporate areas will also differ based on the industry that a company is in and the stage of growth. As examples, companies that are in the hi-tech area or are young will require more creative intuition, whereas companies in the logistics industry or that are mature in the business life cycle will rely more on operational intuition.

To maximize corporate intuition, management must match a resource's Intuitive Zone of Influence with the particular position this resource will fill, assuming that the underlying skill sets are already in place. If there is a mismatch, then the intuition of that resource will not be expressed readily, if at all. This may become the weakest link in the intuitive chain and intuition will be hindered at that particular corporate level.

In Brian Scudamore's case, he realized that the company's intuitive capability was severely strained because the unenthusiastic resources he had in place were only there to get a paycheque every two weeks. If Brian was to be successful, his intuition told him that he only had one choice – wipe the slate clean.

GUT!

Brian Scudamore is Founder and CEO of 1-800-GOT-JUNK?, today a $154 million company. He got the idea of starting this company in 1989 when he saw a beat-up old truck driving through McDonald's advertised 'Mark's Hauling'. Looking to raise tuition money for university, he saw a chance to drastically improve the "junk hauling" business.

In an interview with the Globe and Mail[67], Brian explains,

"I thought, 'I could do better than that.' I decided right then and there to spend my remaining $700 on a pickup truck."

Since then, 1-800-GOT-JUNK? has grown into an international, $154 million junk-hauling enterprise, with more than 800 trucks and 200 franchises located across 8 Canadian provinces and 41 US states, as well as major cities in Australia.

"Business took off, and I set my sights on professionalizing an industry that had never been professionalized on a large scale. We made it a goal to become the FedEx of junk removal."

In the interview for GUT!, Brian mentions that his entrepreneurial endeavours in the home-service based industry has continued with two other brands.

"We have also started a business called 'WOW 1 DAY PAINTING' where we go into someone's home and paint it in its entirety in one day. We have franchised that with over 30 locations in North America and now we have started a new brand, called You Move Me, which is a moving business where we do local moves within one metro and we have 34 franchises there. I'm becoming a bit of a serial entrepreneur in the home service base with three brands and others I am sure."

---

[67] http://www.theglobeandmail.com/report-on-business/small-business/sb-managing/leadership/brian-scudamore-made-his-fortune-in-junk/article4326498

Brian explains his beliefs on intuition.

"I have always been a big believer in using my gut. Intuition is really the brain working quickly to take all of your experiences in your life and trying to get a pulse and go, how does this feel. It's rapid processing, I believe, of the sum total of all of your experiences in your life.

"I often will have a gut feeling and will have trouble articulating why I feel that way. It won't necessarily be one thing that will allow me to say what's going on. In in a blink, you know that this is the right thing to do."

Brian was becoming quite frustrated because he had hired a number of resources that were lackluster in a number of areas. His intuition gave him the only solution that would help propel the company forward – let all the resources go.

"A good example of how intuition played a role in my business life is in 1994 when I had 11 people in my company and decided in a blink to get rid of everybody. My gut just told me that I had the wrong people in place and that I was not going to be able to turn this around and have the right customer experience to build the FedEx of junk removal if I did not start from scratch again. And with nine awful people and two that might not have not been so bad and might have been "save-able", I still thought, you know what, I am still going to start from scratch. I am going to let go of all 11 people.

I let them all go. I let them know that it was my fault not theirs, that I as their leader had let them down. It was time to start fresh again, and the next day I had a business that had no employees and still had customers and had to be creative in turning things around."

There were a number of indicators that informed his intuitive decision.

"I think it was a cultural fit more than anything. These weren't people that I was having fun with, that I was trusting, I felt good about working with. They did not care about the business the way that I did. I don't think they saw what I saw. They didn't see the possibility that we could potentially build with 1-800-GOT-JUNK?. It was just a job. They weren't the right people and my gut told me that I could do better. And I didn't even know what better necessarily looked like at the time but I was committed to finding the right people."

Brian ensured that, from that point, each and every resource was hired using his intuition as a primary filter.

"Moving forward, whenever I brought on new employees, I trusted my gut. After making some wrong decisions, the measure that I would always use is whether this potential hire was someone I would like to spend time with, someone I can invite over for a barbeque or have a beer with. And if I am not going to enjoy their company and don't find them to be an interesting person with passions in their life, then I move on and wait until I find the right people. We can train on skill and hire on attitude. It really is that attitude. It is about hiring interesting people who are interested in our business and doing something in their life and about trusting my gut.

"I know when someone has a personality or a story, and I am thinking, you know, something is just not adding up here. And I feel that I am always right. It could be someone's body language that somehow, when I have seen that type of body language before, subconsciously, it has told me something. It is learning to trust my gut.

"If I have a feeling that something is not right, if I really want to fight with someone in an interview team on it, I'll just say, 'Listen, my gut just says this person is not the right person, and we need to move on,' and we do.

"I don't think you can change people. My gut is that if you have a feeling that someone is the wrong person, and it rings loud enough, you've got to trust that feeling because trying to change someone and hope that they are going to do the right thing just doesn't happen. You have to find that right person from the beginning."

This process has proven time and time again to be successful.

"What I hear from people about our front-line employees is a good example. For 1-800-GOT-JUNK?, I hear from customers, from friends, from family that have used the business. People will say all the time that you've got such great guys. That is literally a quote that I hear all the time. Your guys are great. You have awesome people. I didn't hear that previously. I didn't hear it when we had the wrong people.

"When I hire people that are like-minded, they are passionate, energetic, and enthusiastic, have a sense of humour, people that are taking the job seriously and are enjoying whatever it is they do, that's pretty cool.

That is when the business seems to work with all three brands. We hire people that fit.

"I have got a leadership team that I think are just rock stars. They are very good at finding and knowing my values and vision for where we are going and finding people that support that. My leadership is good at not tolerating the wrong people within the business. If someone does not fit there, we exit them pretty quick. We are slow to hire and we are quick to fire.

"It comes down to they just don't do things the 1-800-GOT-JUNK? way. Our four values are passion, integrity, professionalism, and empathy. So we generally cite someone on a value or two that they don't fit with. Yes, we are using our gut, but we are also using our rigor to say, 'Here's the reason why this isn't working out or it is not going to work out if it doesn't change.'"

However, Brian has ignored his intuition at least once, when he brought in a senior leader of the management team, despite his intuition telling him that he should have stayed in that position himself.

"At one point in time, people were telling me that I was not the one to run my business anymore and I needed to bring someone in more senior, although my gut told me I was the right person to run the business. I hired a number of management personnel to help me take over my role.

"Yet, my gut was saying that I shouldn't move out of the way. I should have stayed and worked closely with this management team to make sure that they were the team for my business.

"They had a different vision, they didn't necessarily believe in me, and together we killed the business and almost bankrupted the business during the financial meltdown. It was a really scary time.

"My gut said I should have believed in myself, I should have been the person to run the business from a vision and culture perspective, and I needed to find a team that would believe in me. And this team didn't believe in me."

Despite this bad experience, Brian knows that his intuitive strength comes from his creative intuition, and he works closely with his current president, who more closely represents the values of 1-800-GOT-JUNK?.

"While I am more a long term, 37,000 foot guy, my president, Eric Church is more short term, near term, 'here is what's going on in front of his face' type of guy. We still communicate quite often and if I say something's not right here he listens to that because he knows that I won't use that term lightly."

Brian's intuitive journey, despite ignoring it the one time, has helped him act on it much quicker.

"Five or 10 years ago I would have a feeling – 'Wow, something's telling me that something's not right and I need to find out what's not right.' Now, I just learn to accept that I don't need to necessarily know why. I know when something isn't right. I tune in. I have learned to trust my gut."

GUT!

Companies that are intuitive will always select the right resources with the right skills, attitude, and intuitive strengths that match the positions needed to be filled. A mismatch will result in inefficient output, a lack of passion, and possible turnover. Not taking the time to select the right resources will not move the company forward as best it can. For Brian, this meant letting everyone go, starting fresh, and making the right selection – and success followed.

Selecting the right resources is an important aspect of fostering an intuitive culture. However, you need to have an organizational culture that embraces intuitive thinking.

When starting a company from scratch, the founder has an opportunity to create that intuitive culture right from the start, much like what Brian had done. However, if an existing culture is not intuitive in nature, then the company's leader needs to transform the culture slowly, with much time and patience starting from the senior management levels and working his or her way throughout the organization.

Of course, this may seem hard to do considering that companies tend to have little time for distractions. But, when transformed, as Vinay Sharma, CEO of London Hydro, had done, the incredible change that happens in all areas of a company will make a leader wonder why he or she did not make the change sooner.

CHAPTER 15

Transform the Culture

Although senior management team members may have agreed upon a core set of values and use intuition themselves to drive their decisions, they must also transform the overall culture of the company to embrace intuition as an accepted way of making key decisions.

This transformation must start at the top level and trickle down because this level sets the cultural tone of the company. If this transformation starts at a middle management level, for example, those at senior management levels could quash the intuitive thinking.

This transformation is not rocket science. Leaders need to ensure that there is open communication, the ability for employees to self-regulate, honest feedback, guided practice, and inherent trust in moving an intuitive decision forward, all of which has shown to be effective in promoting intuitive decision-making[68]. Many companies may state that they practice these aspects of the transformation, but in reality they miss the mark on some of them and fail to remove the resources that stymie this transformation.

These transformative characteristics should not only be a part of the core values of a company, but they should be practiced on a regular basis. With these practices in place, the company is poised to succeed on many levels. This transformation was essential for Vinay Sharma to move the management style from "command and control" to one supportive of corporate intuition.

GUT!

---

68 Salas, E. et al. (2009). Expertise-based intuition and decision making in organizations. Journal of Management.

Vinay Sharma is the CEO of London Hydro, a utility that provides electricity to the residents of London, Ontario. He originally joined London Hydro in 1998 and moved through various departments such as customer service, energy and conservation management, the Smart Meter initiative, retailer management, and business planning.

Vinay relies on his intuition to help guide his decision-making abilities in a corporate environment, setting an excellent example for the rest of the employees. He is quick to point out why intuition is a necessary tool to ensure that a business succeeds.

"Intuition comes from knowledge. Intuition comes from education. Intuition comes from experience. Intuition can lead you to success if you have good self-experience, good self-knowledge, and a very sound thinking pattern. If the intuitive thinking is not supported by intelligence, or draws from good experience, it perhaps will lead to more failures.

"Why do we need intuition, really? Just ask this question. Why do we even make use of it? There's only one reason that it is needed in business. Intuition helps you reduce the time to make a decision, which can add a lot of benefit to a company like ours. Sometimes, you don't have a lot of runway to make decisions or do all the reasoning. You are short of time, and short of dollars all the time. You've got partial information in your head and, at some point, somebody has got to make a decision. At that point, you can have two choices.

"You can say, 'No, I'm going to wait on this decision. I'm going to let the details work out and give myself another year before I make a decision.' Or you can say, 'Okay, I've got enough here to make a decision.' Your path varies: logic-strategy-intuition or intuition-logic-strategy. Either way you look at it, it's a mixture of both."

Vinay talks about the intuitive decision-making process.

"I make intuitive decisions all the time. Intuition creates a story in your head and can give you an idea that produces very good results. Then the story takes place on a piece of paper, and then logic and other details come in to inform the intuition.

"As a leader, you are like the director of a movie. You have a movie in your head and you have a story in your head of what you want to achieve, and then you're going to direct the whole thing. While directing the team, some of the team members may counter and suggest some other ideas, as

they do in making a film. Through their ideas and some of the stories, you get good results. Simply said, edifices are built twice: once in your head, once physically."

Vinay talks about the importance of relying on others in an organization to provide additional expertise and knowledge, which plays an important role in supporting the intuitive decision.

"If you have an accountant in charge of a utility, and that accountant makes an intuitive decision on an engineering project without any trust or advice from the engineering team and executes on that intuitive decision, how can you then say that this decision is correct? If that accountant does not have the wisdom or the collection of knowledge from engineering, he or she cannot make an informed intuitive decision.

"The accountant can absolutely apply intuition to accounting and finance, but not to engineering because he or she does not have wisdom in the engineering area until he or she is smart enough to pick it up on the job over years, which can happen.

"You have to have collective wisdom from the other business areas to make that decision. Intuition only works if you have that basis behind it. Otherwise, the intuition will fail.

"There are three things that you need to ensure that intuition is infused in a work environment: good corporate culture within your corporation, trust, and working very well. Put these together and you make intuitive decisions."

If intuition is to be used throughout the organization, it must be embraced and used at the top management levels.

"After I became CEO, I held many meetings with employees in small groups, and everywhere I went, I was constantly told that 'we are always afraid.' If you're fearful, you can't make a decision. I said, 'Let me find out if that's the case.'

"We did a survey in March of 2011, and, with the exception of one group of five people who were a part of the Continuous Performance Management group that reported to me, the survey showed that the whole corporation was absolutely hierarchal-based. Nobody would make decisions. Everybody would delegate all the decision-making upward. 'You guys make a decision.'

"I had to change it to encourage creativity and innovative thinking by encouraging my employees to do things differently. Do things that nobody else does. Be different from the herd. You'll be better off.

"You don't have to be different 100% of the time. You can be different in small increments. That difference is enough. Looking for that difference wakes you up. It makes you think, is there a better way to do this than the previous way?"

The first order of business when shifting to a more creative and intuitive culture was to ensure that Vinay's leadership team embraced this type of culture.

"I had to form a leadership team that needed to embrace creative thinking, trust, and respect. A difference of opinion never means you disrespect somebody. You can have a disagreement, but still respect each other.

"I knew that the executive team had to change as it shared legacy thinking which created an uncomfortable management environment. Over time, we started training them.

"I hired a CIO and a CFO as two of these senior management members retired. They are very much in the mould that I think one should be. There's a respect for trust and having a more open discussion. The other legacy senior management member had changed. Surprisingly, he said that this new management team is absolutely different, like day and night. We don't fight, we don't scream at each other, we are cooperative and respect each other's viewpoints.

"That same behaviour is now slowly perpetuating throughout the corporation. The directors and managers who have already had 25 to 30 years in service used to stop employees' views from filtering up the chain of command. Now, they have said that the previous way of doing things is nonsense. They now encourage meritorious viewpoints.

"What you notice is that when people have a little freedom, even though they know that approval has to be sought through the proper channels, they begin to take initiatives based on their gut feel – whether they should follow it or not? They are taking initiative, and that is a reflection of the culture. Intuition now plays a role in the corporate culture, especially when you look for intuition at lower levels."

To continue his message of openness and trust that feeds into intuitive thinking, Vinay meets regularly with both the leadership team and the employees.

"I meet with directors every quarter where I share these thoughts of openness with them. The board, the chair, the vice-chair and other board members are welcome. I also meet regularly with a small group of employees in the boardroom. Every month, we have three or four meetings.

"In all of the meetings I have had with the employees, only one employee expressed some negative thoughts, but the rest were expressing very positive feelings for the corporation. The negative feeling came from a gentleman who was retiring and mentioned that he did not really care about the changes. What do you do? You can't change them all.

"With all this communication, what I'm finding is that the employees are engaged, their morale is very high, and they're very enthusiastic about their work. You can actually feel it when you walk around the company and meet with people.

"This respect or this freedom is not given because we want to fail. We want to succeed. Creating fear is not a guarantor of success, but creating respect increases the probability of success.

"For every new employee that comes in the company, it doesn't matter if it is a temporary contractor or permanent employee, a part of their orientation is that they have to meet with me. I inculcate in them the fact that you're respected. Don't be afraid, and if at any time you feel that you're put in an uncomfortable position, tell your supervisor about it. In return, I ask you to also respect them just as much.

"Some of the comments that have been made to supervisors have not been complaints, but rather them expressing the fact that it was a unique experience for them to see the CEO and hear from him how important trust and respect is for the company."

Although Vinay preaches about being empowered to have the freedom to make decisions, there are parameters that need to be adhered to.

"The empowerment of employees is perhaps misunderstood in any corporate culture. It is interpreted as making decisions with ultimate freedom, to do anything that someone wants, but that's not true. Empowerment is to make decisions within the context of the environment that you are in. I have empowerment, but I don't have empowerment to sell London Hydro to some little guy because I feel like doing it, or spending money any way I feel like.

"What is misunderstood is that empowerment is a license to make any type of decision, empowerment seems absolute. But empowerment is not absolute, it has some context and parameters around it.

"I'll give you an example. We had a directors' meeting, and one director said that he did not feel empowered. We began a debate to find out why this was the case. His interpretation of empowerment meant that he wanted absolute freedom to make any decision. I said, 'You are welcome to make a decision, but the board will come down hard on you. There's a budget that defines your plan.'"

Once the organization as a whole embraced using intuition as a decision-tool, employees began making crucial decisions on their own without having to constantly ask permission. Vinay provides an excellent example of how he steps out of the way to make sure his employees have that latitude in making decisions.

"The worst scenario for our corporation is when we have a major outage. That's an emergency for us. There are people who are concerned about safety because there are wires lying on the ground.

"In that emergency, I stand behind because I'm not as well versed with the operational needs as a front-line superintendent of operations. I stay with him, but I stay behind. I don't interfere in the decision-making. I let him go fly with it.

"If I were to impose my intuition in this situation, my intuition only takes me so far. The superintendent knows about the safety issues and the first thing he does is go out to the site and uses his intuitive abilities to assess the situation and use the right tools and resources to mitigate the emergency in a very quick time frame.

"I don't interfere. I don't try and express my logic to his way of doing things because he knows how to do it. I have experienced what they live through in an emergency because I make a point to go out and visit them in the field. I kind of grasp what they're doing.

"When the emergency is over, the superintendent may come to me and ask me to hire an additional resource or buy a tool. That's when I can effectively apply my intuition because I now have the additional experience of what an emergency looks like. So, I will know very quickly whether we need these additional items or not."

Vinay tells of a situation where his intuition helped solve a particular problem with smart meters.

"We had a smart meter deployment throughout the city. Smart meters that are deployed to a commercial customer must be a successful install, working 100% of the time. In September 2013, I received a quality report and noticed that five meters that were installed at St Joseph's Hospital in 2012 needed an update, yet they had not been updated.

"I asked myself, 'Why are we having a failure here?' I went to the supervisor, and he was having difficulties going back to already-installed smart meters because his team was installing other smart meters in the field.

"Vendors would give us a certified meter, the team would go in the field and deploy the smart meter, configure it and then move onto the next one. By the time they come back to some of the earlier smart meters, they won't work because the software or firmware version in that smart meter is different than the version of the rest of the system. So they'll go back and replace it. Even though they do this replacement, in some cases, they'll put in a meter and it will go stale anyway.

"My intuition hit me, and I said, 'Why would you deploy a meter before you have tested it in your own shop?' The supervisor said that he needed an instrument; instantly, my intuition told me that we needed to spend the money to get this instrument.

"Given that little discussion and the resulting decision, we now have a $158,000 lab set up. Within a short two-month period, the board approved the expenditure, and we got the equipment to run a lab so that we don't repeat this behaviour. Normally, to get an approval for a lab from the board, with this type of budget in a corporation like ours, would usually take a long time.

"I took interest, I found out what the problem was, I had my own knowledge base, and I wanted to find out why we could not be speedy enough to look after this part of the business. The board saw my way as well when I reasoned with them. The employees in the field are happy and after a few discussions over the St Joseph's meters, they were replaced."

Vinay provides another example of how he trusted a member of his leadership team despite being uncertain about a particular project.

"My CIO came to me about moving forward on the Green Button initiative. This is an initiative where our energy data is shared with others by converting it into a standard format so that young professionals can create apps. These apps display an individual's energy usage over time, which may allow a person to take action to help reduce energy consumption.

"First, my logic is telling me, who will actually want this Green Button initiative from us? Second, given all the other projects I have on the go, where will this project be slotted? It's not making logical sense to me although I have not looked into this with much detail.

"This is where the gut feeling came in.

"I said, 'You know what? I have to let him go and fly with this.' The basis for that gut feeling came for two reasons. One, I trusted the person that was presenting the case, and second, the long-term view. Let me give him a chance. This may fly.

"Not only did the Green Button initiative successfully deploy over the web, but the government was very interested and gave us money to work with vendors to create apps. It took on a life of its own and the board is embracing this as a significant achievement for London Hydro.

"It has excited everybody that has seen it, including the Ministry of Energy. London Hydro is one of three leading North American utilities at the forefront of this initiative.

"Sometimes intuition can give you a path to great success, but that intuition needs to be based not on only experience, but also on having trust in people that are bringing ideas forward."

GUT!

By being patient and proactive, Vinay inculcated intuition as a decision-making tool into the culture. Not only did this improve results on many different corporate levels, it also significantly increased employee satisfaction.

Although leading an intuitive organization sounds fantastic in theory, moving an organization to become intuitive remains challenging, as Vinay experienced. Maximizing corporate intuition needs to take into account a number of important steps.

CHAPTER 16

Maximizing GUT! Incorporated

Maximizing corporate intuition sounds simple, but it is very complicated. For companies at the early stages of growth, establishing a corporate culture that supports intuition is relatively easy. However, for a growing company that has established organizational structures and rigid policies and procedures, transforming this culture into one that embraces intuition requires significant corporate changes, which will not happen in the near term.

There are a number of steps that need to be taken to ensure that the intuitive strengths for any resource are in alignment with those required by the roles and responsibilities of the position, the corporate area the resource is hired into (sales versus engineering, for example) and the Corporate Intuitive Zone of Influence, which will take into account the industry and lifecycle stage the company is in. These steps include:

- ✔ Reviewing the intuitive capabilities of every resource within a company
- ✔ Enhancing the core corporate values to ensure that intuitive decisions are supported
- ✔ Properly directing the use of power and politics from senior management to ensure that the organization as a whole is better able to tap into corporate intuition[69]
- ✔ Changing the hiring practices to allow for relational intuition to thrive rather than using a standard set of questions in an unfriendly setting

---
[69] Lawrence, T. B., Mauws, M. K., Dyck, B., & Kleysen, R. F. (2005). The politics of organizational learning: integrating power into the 4I framework. Academy of Management Review, 30(1), 180-191.

- ✔ Evaluating resources on their learning style, their current and future aspirations, and discovering their Intuitive Zones of Influence to establish their current and future potential
- ✔ Matching a resource's Intuitive Zone of Influence and associated Intuition Zone Score with the requirements of the position
- ✔ Providing ongoing assessments in intuitive capabilities at both the personal and corporate levels

Performing these steps will take considerable time and effort, but it will be worth the investment. If done in a strategic fashion with the proper assessment tools and techniques, seminars, and expertise[70], a company will be better able to tap into its corporate intuition to be successful in all areas of the company.

With the intuition institutionalized, a company can label itself as being **GUT!** Incorporated.

Trust your GUT!

---

[70] Developed and delivered by Radical Solutions Group Inc. (www.radicalsolutionsgroup.com).